D0204331

WITHDRAWN
LIBRARY
College of St. Scholastica
Duluth, Minnesota 55811

The Shaky Game

Science and Its Conceptual Foundations
David L. Hull, Editor

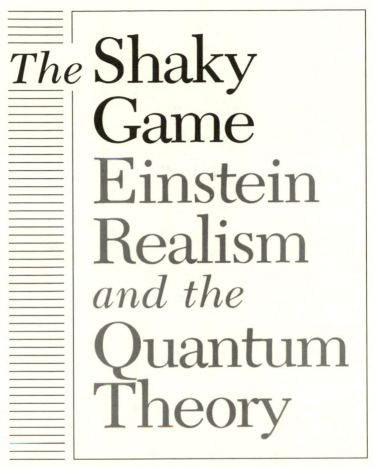

The Shaky Game

Einstein Realism *and the* Quantum Theory

Arthur Fine

The University of Chicago Press

Chicago and London

QC
6
.F54
1986

Arthur Fine is the John Evans Professor of Moral
and Intellectual Philosophy at Northwestern
University. He has written widely in philosophy of
science, physics, and mathematics.

The University of Chicago Press, Chicago 60637
The University of Chicago Press, Ltd., London

© 1986 by The University of Chicago
All rights reserved. Published 1986
Printed in the United States of America

95 94 93 92 91 90 89 88 87 86   54321

Library of Congress Cataloging-in-Publication Data

Fine, Arthur.
  The shaky game.

  (Science and its conceptual foundations)
  Bibliography: p.
  Includes index.
  1. Physics—Philosophy. 2. Einstein, Albert,
1879–1955—Views on realism. 3. Realism. 4. Quantum
theory. I. Title. II. Series.
QC6.F54 1986   530'.01   86-1371
  ISBN 0-226-24946-8

For Rae, and for David too.

Contents

Preface

The essays in this volume that have been previously published represent a body of work developed over a long period of time. There is a strong temptation to use this occasion not only to correct and improve them, but also to unify and regularize their style. I have resisted it, deciding instead to let them show the character of their particular times and places, so far as possible, without cosmetic surgery. On that account, however, a few explanatory words may help guide the reader.

When I began to work with the unpublished Einstein materials, they were available on microfilm housed in the Rare Book Room of Princeton University's Firestone Library, indexed at random, and were the legal property of the trustees of the Estate of Albert Einstein. Since then Princeton has built a new and separate manuscript library, the Seeley G. Mudd Library. Photocopies of the materials have been made, moved there, and uniformly indexed. The materials themselves are now the legal property of Hebrew University of Jerusalem. My varying references and acknowledgments in the essays reflect this history.

Those acknowledgments also reflect a history of support for which I should like to express my appreciation once again. I began the Einstein work under a fellowship grant from the National Endowment for the Humanities, continued that and related projects under grants from the National Science Foundation, and was able to complete the work represented here in the lovely community of Port Townsend, Washington thanks to a fellowship from the John S. Guggenheim Foundation. Those fellowship years were made possible by supplements and time off granted by the University of Illinois at Chicago, when I began the work, and Northwestern University, when I finished it. I want to thank these agencies and institutions for their help and confidence.

Many individuals have supported and assisted this work as well. The various essays already acknowledge some of that help. Some acknowledgments bear repeating. This is especially the case for materials discussed in chapter 5, on the Einstein-Schrödinger correspondence. Linda Wessels gave me access to this correspondence, and Dana Fine organized it and made preliminary translations. I was also helped in that chapter by a translation of Schrödinger's *Naturwissenschaften* article prepared by the (now) late John D. Trimmer (1980), who sent it to me at the suggestion of James McGrath. Lest the footnote reference in chapter 7 go unnoticed, I want to acknowledge the coinventor of NOA, Micky Forbes, whose good philosophical and linguistic sense has guided the development of many of the ideas in the later essays, and their expression. I thank you all.

Chapter 1 opens by referring to one of J. L. Borges's tales. In November 1984, Alberto Coffa gave Micky and me the collection of stories from which that is drawn. He did so mumbling something about how some of the stories reminded him somehow of NOA. We were never able to explore the relevance further, for Alberto died a month later. I believe that Alberto may have meant especially for us to read the story called "On Universal Theater," by way of criticism and caricature of NOA's view of the relationship between philosophy and science. Alberto's form of criticism was always supportive. That critical support was instrumental in building my confidence actually to put this volume together. My different use of a Borges story in chapter 1 is my side of a conversation I never got to have with Alberto; it is here in his memory.

Those without whom this volume would never have been published include my editor, David Hull. By all means, you may hold him responsible.

Finally, between my writing it and its first publication, some small but irritating changes were made in my text of the essay of chapter 7. I have changed them back in this printing—surgery, not cosmetic but merely restorative.

Acknowledgments

The following chapters consist of previously published essays, whose provenance is as stated: chapter 2, "The Young Einstein and the Old Einstein," from R. Cohen et al., eds., *Essays in Memory of Imre Lakatos* (Dordrecht: D. Reidel Publishing Company, 1976), 145–59; chapter 3, "Einstein's Critique of Quantum Theory: The Roots and Significance of EPR," from P. Barker and C. G. Shugart, eds., *After Einstein* (Memphis: Memphis State University Press, 1981), 147–59; chapter 4, "What Is Einstein's Statistical Interpretation, or, Is It Einstein for Whom Bell's Theorem Tolls?" from *Topoi* 3 (1984):23–36; chapter 6, "Einstein's Realism," from J. Cushing et al., eds., *Science and Reality* (Notre Dame, Ind.: University of Notre Dame Press, 1984), 106–33; chapter 7, "The Natural Ontological Attitude," From J. Leplin, ed., *Scientific Realism* (Berkeley: University of California Press, 1984), 83–107; chapter 8, "And Not Antirealism Either," reprinted by permission of the editor from *Noûs* 18 (1984):51–65.

The author wishes to express appreciation to these periodicals and publishers for permission to reprint the above mentioned essays in this volume.

The author is also pleased to acknowledge the cooperation of Hebrew University of Jerusalem, Israel, for permission to quote from the unpublished Einstein papers, and to thank Frau Ruth Braunizer for permission to quote from the unpublished Schrödinger correspondence.

The Shaky Game

"Every absurdity has now a champion." Under this banner J. L. Borges's champion of the awful, H. Bustos Domecq, marches off in defense of modernism. In a hilarious art-critical ramble, Don Bustos recounts the development of Uninhabitables, an architectural movement that began with functionalism and culminated in "Verdussen's" masterly "House of Doors and Windows." The principle that underlies this masterpiece of the absurd is the schizoid idea of utilizing all the basic elements of habitable dwellings—doors, windows, walls, etc.—while abandoning the usual and ordinary connections between them.[1]

The principles and ideas that marked the development of the quantum theory display a curious parallel with those of Borges's tale. As I emphasize in the second chapter, the principle of complementarity that underlies Niels Bohr's influential interpretation of the quantum theory involves precisely "a rational utilization of all possibilities of unambiguous" . . . "use of the classical . . . concepts" (Bohr 1935, pp. 700–701), while also systematically abandoning the usual connections between them. For the policy of complementarity is to segregate the classical concepts into mutually exclusive, complementary pairs. Moreover, where we find Don Bustos describing the Uninhabitables as growing out of functionalism, so we see Bohr, in parallel, describing the quantum theory as a natural generalization of classical physics. Following Borges's example, we would expect the quantum theory to be a monstrous Uninhabitable, which is exactly what Einstein, perhaps its foremost critic, found it to be: "This theory [the present quantum theory] reminds me a little of the system of delusions of an exceedingly intelligent paranoic, concocted of incoherent elements of thoughts."[2]

What bothered Einsten most of all was actually twofold. First, he could not go along with the idea that probability would play an irreducible role in fundamental physics. His famous, "God does

---

1. See "The Flowering of an Art" in Borges (1976), pp. 77–82.
2. Letter (in English) from Einstein to D. Lipkin, July 5, 1952, Einstein Archives.

not play dice" is a succinct version of this idea, which he also expressed by referring to the quantum theory as a "flight into statistics".[3] But, as I explain in chapter 6, usually he expressed this
concern positively, by affirming his interest in pursuing causal (or
determinist) theories. Since Einstein's mode of expression on these
issues was often elliptical, it may not be surprising to discover that
his concerns over the quantum theory had a second focus. It is
featured when he says of the quantum theorists, "Most of them
simply do not see what sort of risky game they are playing with
reality."[4] The risky, or as I like to call it, the *shaky game* puts into
jeopardy what Einstein saw as the traditional program of physics,
the attempt to construct a model of an observer-independent reality, and one that would stand the test of time.

The image of the shaky game, however, which I have adopted
for my title, not only attaches to throwing the dice and toying with
reality, Einstein's concerns over quantum physics, it attaches as well,
I would urge, to all the constructive work of science and of the
philosophical or historical programs that seek to place and understand it. These are games insofar as they involve elements of free
construction and play. These are shaky because, without firm foundations or rigid superstructures, their outcome is uncertain. Indeed
not even the rules of play are fixed. It follows that at every step
we have to be guided by judgment calls. Einstein's use of the risk
factor as a rhetorical weapon represents his own judgment about
the character of the quantum theory. I think he understood that
his dispute over the quantum theory was important precisely because past scientific practice, which he saw as developing a program
for causal and realist theories, did not have built-in rules that would
fix the character of future science. What he saw, I think, was that
just because science *is* a shaky game, the realist program was at
risk.

In chapters 2 through 5 I trace out the development of Einstein's
concerns over the quantum theory. In chapter 6 I isolate Einstein's
realism for separate analysis and evaluation. These reflections on
Einstein's realism form a transition to chapters 7 and 8, which take
up the contemporary philosophical dispute over the realism/anti-
realism issue, especially in the context of science. In these two

3. "I . . . believe . . . that the flight into statistics is to be regarded only as a temporary expedient that bypasses the fundamentals." Letter from Einstein to C. Lanczos, February 14, 1938. Translated in Dukas and Hoffman (1979), p. 68. He repeats
this phrase, and sentiment, in his letter of August 2, 1949, to B. Dessau, Einstein
Archives.
4. Letter from Einstein to E. Schrödinger, December 22, 1950. Translated in
Przibam (1967), p. 39.

chapters I try to show that both houses here are plagued by in-
curable difficulties. The way out, I suggest, is to adopt what I call
the natural ontological attitude (NOA), a stance neither realist nor
antirealist; indeed the very one that moves us to see science as a
shaky game. The last chapter of the book (chapter 9) comes full
circle to reconsider the issue of realism in the quantum theory from
a contemporary perspective, and in light of NOA.

It may help the reader if something is said about the development of these chapters. Some of it will be by way of setting and
highlight, some by way of reflecting on the character of the work
itself. The essays that make up the chapters of this book span a
long period of time, about a decade in all. The essay in chapter 2
was written some ten years ago. Those of chapters 5 and 9 are
brand new. The background to these essays is my own attempt to
come to terms with issues in the interpretation of the quantum
theory, and in particular with the issue of realism there. While
working out the technical defense of both determinate and indeterminate forms of quantum realism (in the face of challenging
"no-go" results concerning a classical setting for probabilities, value
assignments, and quantum statistics), I gradually began to realize
that in some cases Einstein had already pioneered similar ideas and
had been severely criticized for so doing.[5] This fact, together with
the then recent possibility of access to microfilms of the Einstein
Nachlass, set me off to find out just what Einstein's ideas were concerning the interpretation of the quantum theory, and to see how
viable (or not) they appeared some fifty years after the founding
of the theory. The results of that investigation are contained in the
essays that comprise chapters 2 through 5.

In chapter 2 I take on a scientific rumor, insinuated by a variety
of well-known scientists and historians, that by the time of the
development of the quantum theory (1925–27) the old Einstein
(then all of 46) was no longer capable of grasping the radically new
quantum ideas. His dissent from the quantum theory, then, would
appear to be a kind of scientific senility. In the essay I try to put
the lie to this, first by recalling how Einstein's scientific work (right
up to 1926) not only contributed to the new quantum mechanics,
but actually anticipated some of its central features. I then try to
tease out of Einstein's scientific papers a general method of his, *the*

5. I use "determinate/indeterminate" for the technical question of whether the
quantum magnitudes (the "observables") have definite point-values in noneigenstates. This is not the question of determinism, which has to do with the evolution
of things over time. For my involvement with determinate forms of quantum realism
see Fine (1973a, 1974), for indeterminate ones see Fine (1971, 1973b).

method of conceptual refinement, that actually requires significant conceptual change as the vehicle for scientific development.[6] Finally, I argue that it was precisely the conceptually conservative elements of the quantum theory that triggered Einstein's dissent. The nasty rumor, then, emerges as an interesting myth, a tall tale whose function was to protect the fledgling quantum theory from the sharp criticism of this century's most illustrious scientist. Thus Einstein's debate over the quantum theory constitutes a significant episode in which what was at issue was nothing less than the very pattern according to which physics was to grow.

The showpiece of Einstein's dissent from the quantum theory is the paradox of Einstein-Podolsky-Rosen (EPR), published in a little four-page paper in 1935. That tiny paper has been the subject of a voluminous secondary literature, including the mass of material that relates to Bell's theorem.[7] In chapter 3 I report my discovery of Einstein's letter to Erwin Schrödinger of June 19, 1935 (right after the paper was published), where Einstein remarks that, following some discussions, the paper was actually written by Podolsky, and that the central issue got buried in Podolsky's text. In that chapter I work out one version of the EPR argument that Einstein points to in his letter as central. It does not have to do with so-called hidden variables, the concept most readers of Podolsky's text seem to associate with EPR, nor even with the simultaneous assignment of positions and momenta. Rather it has to do with undercutting the Bohr-Heisenberg doctrine according to which puzzling features of quantum mechanics can be traced back to an inevitable and uncontrollable physical disturbance brought about by the act of measurement. Thus, in the version I discuss in chapter 3, Einstein's EPR has to do with the measurement of a single variable (not of two incompatible ones). It introduces a plausible principle governing measurement disturbances (the principle of separation) which is then shown to be incompatible with a particular interpretation of the state function, an interpretation that Einstein associated with Bohr, and that he calls "completeness." Thus what EPR intends to challenge is not quantum theory itself, but rather a particular version of the Copenhagen interpretation. And the way this occurs is by taking the doctrine of measurement disturbance seriously enough to formulate physical principles governing it. The "paradox of EPR" is, therefore, supposed to be a paradox

6. Since writing the essay for chapter 2, I have developed the method of conceptual refinement in an article on Imre Lakatos's philosophy of mathematics, Fine (1981a).

7. Chapters 4 and 9 explain "Bell's theorem."

for the Copenhagen stance toward quantum theory, showing that two of its central components (the doctrine of disturbance and the "complete" interpretation of the state function) are incompatible. I think readers familiar with the usual discussions of EPR will find the version in chapter 3 quite novel. In that version one prominent feature of the EPR text falls by the wayside entirely; namely, the notorious "criterion of reality." In line with this reading, one should note that although Einstein himself later published several versions of EPR, none of them makes any reference to or use of that reality criterion.

Einstein's own published accounts of EPR, however, employ a variation on the argument of chapter 3. I discuss that variant, and some of its problems, in chapters 4 and 5. In chapter 4 I move from EPR, Einstein's showpiece puzzle, to discuss the so-called statistical interpretation, his favored resolution. In that chapter I argue that we do not actually know what Einstein's statistical interpretation was. Einstein's various references to it are altogether too brief and sketchy to pin it down. Hence the widespread idea that Bell's theorem refutes Einstein's statistical interpretation is rather on the order of wishful thinking. There is indeed an interpretation that Bell's theorem does refute, the idea of an ensemble representation, but I argue that Einstein's texts suffer considerable strain if we try to fit them into that particular mold. To drive that argument home I show how much better Einstein's texts fit the pattern of prism models, an interpretative idea that I have developed elsewhere (see chapter 4) as a determinate way of bypassing the Bell theorem. But it is not really my intention to make Einstein into a precursor of my prism models. Rather, I want to challenge the conventional wisdom here, which seems to me altogether too ready to foist onto Einstein some simple (and usually refuted) point of view. The salient fact in the history of Einstein's statistical interpretation is its utter vagueness, and this is coupled with Einstein's almost complete indifference to the "no-go" demonstrations known to him (including at least Schrödinger's version of von Neumann's "no-hidden-variables" theorem).[8] To understand this I think we have to see that the statistical interpretation functioned for Einstein as a temporary expedient, like the quantum theory itself. It provided no more than a setting rhetorically apt for calling attention to the incompleteness of the quantum theory; a way, therefore, of motivating a search for a more complete theory. But Einstein's idea of

8. See note 3 of chapter 4 and my discussion in chapter 5 of the development of section 4 of Schrödinger's *Naturwissenschaften* article.

a completion had nothing to do with adding things to the existing theory; for example, in the manner of hidden variable extensions (not even, as I explain in the appendix to chapter 4, local ones). Rather, Einstein's idea of "completing" the quantum theory was an expression his vision of building an altogether different kind of physics.

In the foundational literature, EPR is the paradox associated with the issues of locality, completeness, hidden variables, and realism. The other great foundational issue, the so-called measurement problem, has a paradox all its own, the one affectionately called "Schrödinger's cat." Its genesis is the subject of chapter 5. There I examine the remarkable correspondence between Einstein and Schrödinger that took place during the summer of 1935. That correspondence was stimulated by the publication of EPR. It began with the correspondents agreeing in their opposition to the quantum theory, but not in their diagnoses of the basic disease nor, therefore, in their remedies. The good-natured joisting over criticisms and cures that ensued challenged each of them to try to undo the pet ideas of the other. Thus Einstein set out a refuting example that prompted Schrödinger to respond by attempting to refute Einstein's statistical interpretation. What Einstein had aimed to refute was what he called the "Schrödinger interpretation" of the state function, exactly the Bohr version of quantum completeness that was the target of EPR. Einstein's refutation involved an intriguing example which Schrödinger identified as being "very similar" to one he had just himself constructed. And then Schrödinger proceeded to tell the plight of the poor cat. Thus the correspondence shows Schrödinger's cat and Einstein's similar example not as pointed to the measurement problem but rather as new versions of EPR. They are indeed arguments for incompleteness that bypass the need for an additional premise having to do with locality (or separation). This places the cat somewhat differently from the way it is generally viewed, but it places it exactly as it is found in Schrödinger's published account of it. Nevertheless, I try to argue on the basis of evidence internal to the correspondence that the cat may well have first occurred to Schrödinger in the context of measurement, and only later been adapted to fit its published place as a demonstration of incompleteness. I confess to having considerable fun in this latter argument, playing historical detective on the basis of very few clues. (I do not know whether draft material or editorial correspondence exists to confirm, or refute, my speculations.) However, the dynamics that relate published scientific writing with concurrent informal reflections of a more private kind is fascinating, even when speculative. In the end I could not resist exploring the possible dynamics and, in a book called *The Shaky Game*, it seemed fair practice to share the material, and the speculations, with my readers.

The issue of completeness, which is at the heart of EPR, Schrödinger's cat, and the statistical interpretation, turns on the idea of realism. As Einstein put it to Schrödinger, "Physics is a kind of metaphysics. . . . All physics is a description of reality; but this description can be either complete or incomplete."[9] The methodological dispute with Bohr, featured in chapter 2, also turns on realism, construed as a program for theory construction. Thus realism links the different subjects of chapters 2 through 5. It is the explicit subject of chapter 6. In this chapter I try to pull together various aspects of Einstein's methodological thinking to construct a detailed account of his realism, which I organize by means of two central concepts: Einstein's "entheorizing" and his holism. Let me just mention two conclusions of that study. The first is that, for Einstein, commitment to realism was commitment to pursuing a specific kind of program for theory contruction, one that already included the idea of causality (or determinism), and one that was to be judged on exactly the same basis as any other scientific program; namely, by judging its empirical success over time. A second conclusion that emerges from examining Einstein's realism is that, for him, realism was not at all a cognitive doctrine, a set of specific beliefs about nature (or the like). Rather, his realism functions as a motivational stance toward one's scientific life, an attitude that makes science seem worth the effort. But it is supposed to do so, somehow, without involving specific cognitive content. At the conclusion of chapter 6 I suggest the psychoanalytic concept of an *imago* as an analogue for this noncognitive, motivational conception of realism.

The work of chapters 2 through 6 represents a sort of hybrid form of scholarship; partly a conceptual (or philosophical) investigation and partly a historical one. Because it traces the conceptual odyssey of a single person, I think of the work as writing conceptual biography. What I have tried to construct is a coherent story line that integrates over time Einstein's various works and thoughts on the conceptual issues that relate to quantum mechanics. In so doing I have pushed hard for Einstein's consistency, some will say too hard. I have not always found it. (See, for example, the discussion

9. Letter from Einstein to Schrodinger, June 19, 1935: "die Physik eine Art Metaphysik ist. . . . Alle Physik ist Beschreibung von Wirklichkeit; aber diese Beschreibung kann "vollständig" oder "unvollständig" sein."

of "bijective completeness" in chapter 5, or, perhaps, the uneasy conception of motivational realism itself in chapter 6.) But I have certainly adopted as a working hypothesis the possibility of basic consistency over time, and I set out to test the hypothesis by making up a basically consistent tale. A kind of historiographical positivism stands opposed even to the effort.[10] It holds that the best one can do, as a historian, is to tell about the various moments in the life-thoughts of an individual. The historian does not, so to speak, have the standing to validate some further integrating scheme. In support of this brand of positivism one might cite, from my very own procedure, the occasions when I have had to select from among the Einstein materials those that go along with my scheme of integration and to demote, or explain away, materials that do not (see, for instance, how I treat the letter to Tanya Ehrenfest over the EPR criterion of reality in chapter 4, note 24; or what I make of Einstein's cognitive-sounding realist language in chapter 6.) This points to the necessity for judgment calls, even on what counts as good data. Moreover, I do not argue that the coherent stories I tell are the only ones that could be told nor, certainly, the best ones. And that shows how loosely the data, even after selection, determine the biographical narrative. But these two elements, the necessity for good judgment and the underdetermination of the theory by the data, are constituents of any creative intellectual endeavor—physics no less than history. I believe that the positivist attempt to use such elements to construct a warrant restricting the character of legitimate intellectual activity rests on a mistake. It is the mistake generally called "epistemology," one of the subjects criticized in chapter 8. In response to the positivist line, I would simply say that in writing conceptual biography I have been trying to tell a true story. Of course, I may have failed to do so satisfactorily, perhaps because some competing story turns out to be better (i.e., truer) or because, as it turns out, there is no true *story* to be told but only discrete historical moments to be catalogued. If so, then that will be a matter of fact and not of divergent historiographical philosophies. Indeed, in coming down strongly on the side of coherence and consistency, I would hope to challenge those skeptical about such accounts to respond and, in this way, to increase our understanding of things.

10. This breed of positivism is by no means restricted to the construction of historical narratives. It flourishes in the area called "critical theory," especially among those who have been influenced by contemporary French thinkers. There it attaches to the entire study of texts. My brief critique below of the historiographical version applies to the whole breed, which is best undone by adopting NOA.

In coming out for the truth of scientific stories (even historical ones) and in rejecting positivist epistemology, I may run the risk of being identified with the opposite philosophical camp, that of the realists. But I have no love for realism, as I hope the charitable reader of chapter 7 will conclude from my opening sentence there, which announces the good news that realism is dead. That chapter develops a "metatheorem" demonstrating how the philosophically fashionable, explanationist strategy for supporting realism simply (and irretrievably) begs the question. It goes on to show how detailed, realist-style, explanation sketches of scientific methods also simply (and irretrievably) fail. This sets the stage for a discussion of the natural ontological attitude (NOA) as a way of saving the concept of truth, while avoiding both the metaphysics of realism and the epistemology of various antirealisms. In its antimetaphysical aspect, NOA is at one with Einstein's motivational realism. But NOA perceives in that realist language and motivational setting a philosophical support system external to science and not actually required for its meaningful pursuit. If we let the scaffolding go, we discover that science stands perfectly well on its own and, indeed, *we* can then see it all the better.

That attitude, to let science stand on its own and to view it without the support of philosophical "isms," is what characterizes NOA. All the *isms* (realism, nominalism, idealism, conventionalism, constructivism, phenomenalism, positivism—and even pragmatism) involve global strategies, approaches to interpreting and providing a setting for science as a whole. Often these strategies derive from an underlying semantics, frequently from a picture or a theory of truth. In chapter 8 I show how the project of an acceptance (or consensus) theory of truth derives from a behaviorist reaction to realism, and how it traps several contemporary antirealisms in a destructive regress. To adopt the realist approach, and construe "truth" as some sort of realist-style correspondence, is not the way out of the trap. The way out is simply not to "construe" *truth* at all. Thus NOA adopts a no-theory attitude toward the concept of truth. It follows that up with an appropriate emphasis on the varieties of local scientific practices, and on the likely nonprojectibility of essentialist reconstructions of these practices. NOA carries this all the way to the practice of science itself, for it opts out of the game of inventing factors whose possession would *make* a practice "scientific" (or "pseudo-scientific", or "nonscientific"). It even opts out of the popular teleological version of this game, the one where you make up aims and goals for science. Here is where good judgment is called for and NOA, if you like, simply judges these games to be altogether *too* shaky!

Various global games, including the game of demarcation, have been the style setters in philosophy of science from Mach through Kuhn. In choosing not to play them, NOA signals its divergence from that whole philosophical tradition. However, NOA should not be counted as preaching an "end-to-philosophy," not even if restricted to philosophy of science. For NOA sees philosophy, like science, as a set of practices with a history. That history constrains our understanding of current practice and structures our evaluation of promising problems and modes of inquiry. Because the practice is varied and self-reflective, it encompasses the possibility of moving on in virtually any direction that can be rationalized in terms of current practice and past history. To adapt a phrase, that means that almost anything *might* go, or go away. NOA would like to see realist metaphysics and empiricist epistemology go away. It promotes as a rule of thumb that we try to connect our concerns about science with scientific life as it is actually lived. This is a vague, wishy-washy rule. It does not comprise a doctrine, nor does it set a philosophical agenda. At most it orients us somewhat on how to pursue problems of interest, promoting some issues relative to others just because they more clearly connect with science itself. Such a redirection is exactly what we want and expect from an attitude, which is all that NOA advertises itself as being. In chapter 7 I refer to NOA as the "core position" sufficient itself to mediate between realism and the various antirealisms. The idea of a self-sufficient core suggests not only that nothing more is required by way of a systematic philosophical framework for approaching science, but also that anything more would actually turn out to be bad for you. Thus the "natural" in NOA is not that of "human nature" or of a "return to nature," essentialisms quite antithetical to NOA.[11] Rather, the "natural" in NOA is the "California natural": no additives, please.

The "no-additives" idea is applied in chapter 9 to the issue of realism and the quantum theory. In that chapter I argue that realism is not to be found in the laboratory life of quantum physics, not even when it arrives at the judgment that certain entities exist. For the scientific practices there rely on a series of in-house judgment calls that do not add up to what realism requires. On the other hand, I adapt an argument over the reference of terms developed by Hilary Putnam to show that, in fact, nothing in the quantum theory excludes the possibility of a realist interpretation. Since Bell's theorem is sometimes thought to stand in the way of

---

11. My colleague Sam Todes pointed to a related danger, that of assimilating NOA to the "natural attitude" associated with Husserl. Please don't. (My thanks to Sam, and to David Levin for a useful discussion on this topic.)

realism, I sketch a minimal realist framework for the quantum theory and show how readily it avoids any problems with Bell. I argue that the perceived problem for realism is actually generated by a reductive attitude toward probabilities. This gets us back to the discussion of ensemble representations and Einstein's statistical interpretation treated in chapter 4. Finally, I use the evident sterility of the minimal realist framework to push home the moral of realism as an idle overlay to science. I try to show up the whole realist program of concocting interpretations of quantum theory as a program lying outside of the life of physics itself. In violating NOA's rule that philosophy of science connect with on-going science, I would judge quantum realism as another instance of a game altogether *too* shaky. To be sure, I recognize that indulging in realist constructions, like building castles in the sky, can address certain felt needs and longings. That is what we saw as the function of Einstein's motivational realism. I suggest, however, that we can succeed in outgrowing the need for that particular game, and that it would represent a sort of growing up in our attitude toward science were we to do so. NOA, I would urge, is a good stance from which to attempt that maturational step. Significantly, I think, Freud would describe this step as substituting the reality principle for the pleasure principle, a move he judged as favoring reason and common sense over the passions. NOA agrees.

The Young Einstein and
The Old Einstein

Fashionable "sociologists of knowledge"—or "psychologists of knowledge"—tend to explain positions in purely social or psychological terms when, as a matter of fact, they are determined by rationality principles. A typical example is the explanation of Einstein's opposition to Bohr's complementarity principle on the ground that "in 1926 Einstein was forty-seven years old. Forty-seven may be the prime of life, but not for physicists."

> I. Lakatos, "Falsification and the Methodology
> of Scientific Research Programmes"

In 1911 Einstein, then thirty-two years old, held the post of Professor of Theoretical Physics in the German University of Prague. He had indicated to his friend and former classmate Marcel Grossmann his interest in returning to Zürich to teach at the Polytechnic (The Federal Institute of Technology). The dossier in support of his appointment there contained a letter from Henri Poincaré who wrote, in part, "What I admire in him in particular is the facility with which he adapts himself to new concepts and knows how to draw from them every conclusion. He has not remained attached to classical principles and when presented with a problem in physics he is prompt to envisage all its possibilities" (Seelig 1956, p. 134). This same liberated quality of Einstein's thought was emphasized in the letter written two years later by Max Planck, Walter Nernst,

Some of the work on this paper was supported by National Science Foundation Grant #GS-37820. The paper was written during the tenure of a Senior Fellowship from the National Endowment for the Humanities. I want to acknowledge the cooperation of the trustees of the Einstein estate in permitting me access to the Einstein microfilms and the pleasant assistance of the staff of the Rare Book Room of Princeton University's Firestone Library, where the microfilms are kept. I want to thank Judith Weinstein and Dr. Theodore Weinstein for their hospitality and kindness while I was gathering materials for this study. I owe Helene Fine credit for leading me to the metaphor describing Bohr's complementarity, and I owe thanks to Sharon Fine and to Dana Fine for help in clarifying the writing. Others have helped too, and I hope that the paper itself will be a sufficient expression of my thanks.

12

Heinrich Rubens, and Emile Warburg in proposing Einstein for membership in the prestigious Royal Prussian Academy of Science. After summarizing Einstein's accomplishments in physics they wrote, "Apart from his own productivity Einstein has a peculiar talent for probing alien, original views and premises and from his experience judging their inter-relationship with uncanny certainty" (Seelig 1956, p. 145). These words were written about the young Einstein, the Einstein who had yet to create the general theory of relativity. The old Einstein, however, was to receive a very different testimonial. From Werner Heisenberg, "Most scientists are willing to accept new empirical data and to recognize new results, provided they fit into their philosophical framework. But in the course of scientific progress it can happen that a new range of empirical data can be completely understood only when the enormous effort is made to enlarge this framework and to change the very structure of the thought process. In the case of quantum mechanics, Einstein was apparently no longer willing to take this step, or perhaps no longer able to do so" (Born 1971, p. x). And from his good friend Max Born, "At first there were quite a number of serious scientists who did not want to know anything about the theory of relativity; conservative individuals, who were unable to free their minds from the prevailing philosophical principles. . . . Einstein himself belonged to this group in later years; he could no longer take in certain new ideas in physics which contradicted his own firmly held philosophical convictions" (Born 1971, p. 72). This is the tale told of the old Einstein.

In one form or another, the biographies have repeated this tale suggesting the contrast between the young man free in his thought whose special talent was to wrest the truth from "alien" points of view and the old man whose mind traveled only in the circle of ideas of his youth, no longer able to cope with the new ideas of the developing quantum physics. To understand the transition between this young Einstein and this old one we might attend to Einstein's own words of 1934, written in memorial to Paul Ehrenfest and about Ehrenfest's struggle with the quantum theory. Einstein wrote, "Added to this was the increasing difficulty of adaptation to new thoughts which always confronts the man past fifty. I do not know how many readers of these lines will be capable of fully grasping that tragedy" (Einstein 1950a, p. 238). These are words from the heart and there is a strong temptation to see them as reflecting Einstein's own struggle with quantum theory for, as he wrote to Born in 1944, "Even the great initial success of the quantum theory does not make me believe in the fundamental dice-game, although

I am well aware that our younger colleagues interpret this as a consequence of senility" (Born 1971, p. 149). In the same vein, reflecting on the permanence (or otherwise) of his work in physics, after an operation in 1949, he wrote to his lifelong friend Maurice Solovine, "The current generation sees in me at the same time a heretic and a reactionary, one who has, so to speak, outlived himself" (Solovine 1956, p. 94). Nevertheless, I think we should resist the temptation of applying Einstein's diagnosis of Ehrenfest's tragedy to himself. For not only did Einstein's thinking about the quantum theory keep pace with the developing physics, his thinking all along was at least as radical in its break with the conceptions of classical physics as were the interpretations promulgated by Niels Bohr and the visitors to the Institute in Copenhagen.

Einstein's own contributions to the development of quantum theory are well-known.[1] The background to the mature theory lies in the work on radiation of Planck and Einstein. It was this work, particularly in the hands of Einstein, that set the problem of the dual nature of light. For despite his interest in a physics based on the continuum, Einstein emphasized the necessity for assuming a grainy structure for light and with it the problem of reconciling the wave and particle aspects. I do not want to rehearse Einstein's other contributions to quantum theory here. I do, however, want to emphasize the way in which Einstein exercised his special talent for probing alien modes of thought during the period of the development of quantum theory, a period ending around 1930 when the current quantum formalism was well in hand. For, as we shall see, Einstein was less bound by classical preconceptions than were most of his contemporaries and, in many instances, it was Einstein who first piloted the flights of fancy that marked the rise of the theory.

The first of these flights was the already mentioned introduction of light quanta in 1905. This move was, of course, a radical break with the continuum physics of the time and was not to become an acceptable option in physics for many years. Equally important, however, is to notice the method of treating physical concepts that Einstein used to find room for the light quantum hypothesis. In the famous 1905 paper "On a Heuristic Viewpoint concerning the Production and Transformation of Light" Einstein wrote, "However, it should be kept in mind that optical observations refer to values averaged over time and not to instantaneous values. Despite

---

1. These contributions have been studied in detail by Klein (1971). Also see the references in the bibliography of the *Dictionary of Scientific Biography* that follows Klein (1971) on pp. 332–33.

the complete experimental verification of the theory of diffraction
. . . it is conceivable that a theory of light operating with continuous
three-dimensional functions will lead to conflicts with experience
if it is applied to the phenomena of light generation and conversion."[2] In an unpublished manuscript written around 1910, Einstein reiterated this theme, saying that Maxwell's electrodynamics
provided only time-averaged values and hence could be viewed as
merely an intermediate stage in the development of a theory that
would deal with discrete but instantaneous values of quantities like
energy. One cannot help noticing the similarity between this line
of thought and the well-known analysis of simultaneity that Einstein
proposed in the 1905 paper on special relativity. In both cases
Einstein examined the way physical concepts are actually applied
in order to show that the full range of application was not completely determined. He then went on to develop new rules that
extended the concepts into this not-determined area. Although
these rules were different from the extrapolations one might make
on the basis of then accepted theories, they were nevertheless constrained by requiring that the refined concepts be coextensive with
the originals inside the already determined area of application, or
at least approximately so. Thus in the background to relativity
Einstein noticed options about distant simultaneity, other than the
use of infinitely fast signals, which yield the same locally simultaneous events. And behind the quantum postulate Einstein found
options about, say, when a particular energy value occurs which
yield, in good approximation, the apparent continuity of energy
in classical electrodynamics. I would characterize this method as
that of examining the limits of application of a concept in order
to make room for a constructive theoretical refinement. No doubt
Einstein learned the first part of this method from the analysis of
concepts in Hume and Mach, but the constructive use of the analysis
is characteristically his own.[3]

In his 1916 obituary for Mach, Einstein described this method
as follows:

concepts which have proved useful for ordering things easily assume so
great an authority over us, that we forget their terrestrial origin and accept them as unalterable facts. They then become labeled as "conceptual
necessities," "*a priori* situations," etc. The road of scientific progress is

2. Quoted in Hermann (1971), p. 52. Also see p. 53 concerning the 1910 manuscript discussed below.
3. See, e.g., Speziali (1972), p. 391, where Einstein acknowledges the influence
of Mach and Hume, especially that of Hume whose *Treatise* he studied during his
early years in Bern.

frequently blocked for long periods by such errors. It is therefore not just an idle game to exercise our ability to analyse familiar concepts, and to demonstrate the conditions on which their justification and usefulness depend, and the way in which these developed, little by little, from the data of experience. In this way they are deprived of their excessive authority. Concepts which cannot be shown valid are removed. Those which had not been coordinated with the accepted order of things with sufficient care are corrected, or they are replaced by new concepts when a new system is produced which, for some reason or other, seems preferable.[4]

The analysis of space, time, and motion represented by the four-dimensional manifold of general relativity is an application of this method. Thus in the shift from special to general relativity, a shift that brought Einstein away from Mach's sensation-based positivism toward Planck's realism, this method of conceptual analysis remained firm.[5] Most of Einstein's later writings on scientific method refer to this process of conceptual refinement as a basic tool in the kit of the theoretical physicist.

Thus from the beginnings of his work on quantum phenomena Einstein employed a method of investigation that was bound not to respect classical theories and presuppositions. His method looked forward to a series of revisions of the classical concepts by first seeking the limits of their application in experimental situations and then by building a theory to refine them. Contrary to the tale of the old man locked into a circle of fixed ideas, it was precisely this open-ended and questioning attitude toward the concepts of classical physics that brought Einstein into conflict over the quantum theory.

This aspect of Einstein's relationship to the quantum theory is brought out in an exchange of letters between Einstein and Erwin Schrödinger. Einstein had been corresponding with Schrödinger in 1926 about problems of gas degeneracy, the so-called Einstein-Bose statistics in the quantum theory of gases. Apparently Planck pointed out Schrödinger's development of the famous "wave equation" to Einstein, who seems to have gotten it garbled. Thus on April 16, 1926, Einstein wrote to Schrödinger arguing that the additivity of energy values necessitated an equation different from the one he (mistakenly) attributed to Schrödinger. Einstein then made the "correction" (deriving, in fact, the time-independent Schrödinger equation!). Within a few days Einstein realized his

4. Quoted in Born (1971), p. 159.
5. See "Mach, Einstein and the Search for Reality" in Holton (1973), pp. 219–59, for Einstein's shift toward realism. Also see chapter 6 below.

mistaken attribution and wrote again to Schrödinger to acknowledge the error. Before receipt of this acknowledgement, however,
Schrödinger had written back to point out Einstein's mistake in
memory. He wrote,

the whole thing would certainly not have originated yet, and perhaps
never would have (I mean not from me), if I had not had the importance of de Broglie's ideas really brought home to me by your second
paper on gas degeneracy. The objection in your last letter makes me
even happier. It is based on an error in memory. The equation [which
Einstein had atributed to Schrödinger] is *not* mine, as a matter of fact,
but my equation really runs *exactly* like the one that you constructed free
hand. . . . I am, moreoever, very grateful for this error in memory because it was through your remark that I first became consciously aware
of an important property of the formal apparatus. [Presumably, it is the
superposition principle to which Schrödinger alludes.] Besides, one's
confidence in a formulation always increases if one—and especially if
you—construct the same thing afresh from a few fundamental requirements. (Przibam 1967, pp. 26–27)

Here then we see Einstein open to the ideas of Schrödinger and
so much on top of the problems of the quanta that he is actually
able to reconstruct the Schrödinger equation from fundamentals,
one of which is a restricted version of the principle of superposition,
a principle that has turned out to be basic to the whole of quantum
theory.

In the next letter (April 26, 1926) Einstein displays his knowledge
of the development of matrix mechanics by Heisenberg and Born.
He thinks this formalism does not satisfy superposition and for this
reason he remarks to Schrödinger that "the Heisenberg-Born route
is off the track" (Przibam 1967, p. 28). Earlier (March 7, 1926) he
had written to Hedi Born, "The Heisenberg-Born concepts leave
us all breathless, and have made a deep impression on all theoretically oriented people. Instead of dull resignation, there is now a
singular tension in us sluggish people" (Born 1971, p. 88). By December 4, however, he wrote to Max Born, "Quantum mechanics
is certainly imposing. But an inner voice tells me that it is not yet
the real thing" (Born 1971, p. 91). If that inner voice included the
conviction that the superposition principle must hold but that, as
he had written to Schrödinger, it actually fails in the matrix mechanics, then Einstein was right in principle but wrong in fact. For,
as Schrödinger was the first to show (in March 1926), the wave and
matrix mechanics are formally equivalent and hence superposition
holds in both representations. Yet here too we see Einstein open-
minded, receptive to new developments and quite properly sub-

jecting them to his keen sense, born of his own work on quantum phenomena, as to what principles might be validly generalizable. How then does Einstein's open-ended method of conceptual refinement bring him into conflict with the developing quantum theory?

The conflict comes out in the letter of May 30, 1928, from Schrödinger to Einstein. Schrödinger enclosed a copy of a letter from Niels Bohr, a letter that Bohr had wanted Einstein to be aware of. Commenting on a recent paper by Bohr, Schrödinger had written him about the limitation on the applicability of the concepts of position and momentum embodied in the Heisenberg indeterminacy relations. Schrödinger expressed the view that these concepts will eventually have to be replaced by new ones that apply not approximately but exactly. He went on to say that these new concepts will be hard to find, so deep is our feeling for the classical concepts of space, time, and causality.[6] Bohr responded in a way that was to become characteristic of his view of quantum theory. He wrote that he strongly disagreed with Schrödinger's emphasis on the necessity for the development of new concepts. He contended that we have only the old concepts with which to organize experience for only these seem to be linked with the human capacity for conceptualization.[7] This theme, that we must stick with the classical concepts and can only attend carefully to their limitations, was a perennial one in Bohr's later discussions of the quantum theory. Later, however, he sometimes shifted his argument for it to considerations involving the necessity for an unambiguous, intersubjective language in which to communicate laboratory experience. Einstein's response to this controversy came in his letter to Schrödinger of May 31, 1928:

> Your claim that the concepts, p, q [momentum, position] will have to be given up, if they can only claim such "shaky" meaning seems to me to be fully justified. The Heisenberg-Bohr tranquilizing philosophy—or religion?—is so delicately contrived that, for the time being, it provides a gentle pillow for the true believer from which he cannot very easily be aroused. So let him lie there. (Przibam 1967, p. 31)

Here, then, is the root of the conflict.[8]

6. See Przibam (1967), p. 29, ed. note 14. The original letter is in the Einstein Archives, microfilm index I B 1, number 22.

7. I paraphrase here from the copy of Bohr's letter in the Einstein Archives, microfilm index I B 1, number 22. For a similar argument see also the 1929 address by Bohr reprinted in Bohr (1961), especially pp. 94–96.

8. In this essay I take Bohr to be Einstein's main protagonist in the debate over the quantum theory. I do this in part for stylistic ease but also because Bohr's discussions of the theory as it developed are the most challenging in the literature, just as historically they were the most influential.

Einstein, with his method of conceptual refinement, was quite ready to scrutinize the concepts of classical dynamics and kinematics with great care, he was prepared to acknowledge their limitations, and he was even willing to take seriously Schrödinger's suggestion that they will eventually have to be replaced. It was Bohr who balked at the idea that one might give up the classical concepts and it was then Bohr who worked out the method of complementary descriptions in order to save these very concepts. This is the method that Einstein castigates as a "tranquilizing philosophy." Thus the tale of Einstein grown conservative in his later years is here seen to embody a truth dramatically reversed. For it is Bohr who emerges the conservative, unwilling (or unable?) to contemplate the overthrow of the system of classical concepts and defending it by recourse to those very conceptual necessities and *a priori* arguments that Einstein had warned about in his memorial to Mach. Whereas, with regard to the use of classical concepts, Einstein's analytical method kept him ever open-minded, always the gadfly who would not be tranquilized.

These considerations should help dispel the myth of the Einstein grown conservative (reactionary, senile, etc.) when faced with quantum theory. But they do not yet display the interesting fine structure of Einstein's dispute. To do that one must draw out the deep methodological similarity between Einstein's approach to the theory and that of the Copenhagen school. Both parties to the dispute shared the methodological heritage of Mach, the method of conceptual analysis that seeks to find the limits of application of a concept (or a system of concepts). Mach (as earlier Hume and Berkeley and others) had used this method only as a critical tool; as a tool, that is, for eliminating or severely limiting the use of a concept (as in Mach's attack on Newton's concept of absolute space). Einstein well understood this aspect of Mach's method. He expressed it graphically to Michele Besso in 1917, "I do not inveigh against Mach's little horse; but you know what I think about it. It cannot give birth to anything living; it can only exterminate harmful vermin."[9] In Einstein's hands the search for the limits of application of a concept became only the preliminary step in the constructive method of conceptual refinement. His way of making Mach's horse fertile was to supplement the analysis of concepts with a good theory that employs new concepts constrained to relate to the old ones in the following two ways. The first constraint is that the new concepts must coincide with (i.e., be coextensional with) the old ones, at least

9. Quoted in Holton (1973), p. 240. See Speziali (1972), p. 114, for the original letter.

approximately, in the central region where the application of the old ones is fully determinate. The second is that the new concepts themselves must apply in a determinate way beyond the region central to the old. The first of these constraints merely expresses the requirement that the new concepts generalize the old ones. The second condition represents the scientist's hope that a good theory will penetrate into nature more deeply than its predecessors; it should advance our understanding by allowing us to put to nature certain questions which were not clearly expressible on the basis of the old concepts, and it should lead us to expect that such questions have determinate answers.

Bohr, too, tried to utilize Mach's method in a constructive way. Like Einstein he recognized that the construction of a good theory calls for a refinement of the old concepts. And the first constraint, pioneered by Einstein's early work on relativity and the light quantum hypothesis, was one that Bohr employed in his 1913 atomic theory. The formal statement of this constraint became known as "the correspondence principle," and this principle was one of the major guidelines in the development of Heisenberg's version of quantum theory. For Bohr the correspondence principle was the means of ensuring that quantum mechanics is a "natural generalization" of the classical theory. He expressed these considerations in 1929 as follows:

A method for making such concepts [mass and charge] useful in other fields than that in which the classical theories are valid has been found, however, in the demand of a direct concurrence of the quantum-mechanical description with the customary description in the border region where the quantum of action may be neglected. The endeavors to utilize in the quantum theory every classical concept in a reinterpretation which fulfills this demand . . . found their expression in the so-called correspondence principle. However, . . . only in recent years has it been possible to formulate a coherent quantum mechanics which may be regarded as a natural generalization of the classical mechanics. (Bohr 1961, p. 110)

So far, then, Einstein and Bohr are in agreement as to what constitutes a constructive use of Machian analyses. They diverge, however, at the next step. For, unlike Einstein, Bohr did not feel that the new concepts must extend the range of application of the old in a uniform way.

Bohr's position over this second stage in the constructive refinement of a system of concepts is not easy to state, for it embodies Bohr's notoriously obscure doctrine of complementarity. The underlying metaphor of complementarity is that we must view the world through the old concepts, that when we attempt to look into the quantum domain in this manner we must select which of these concepts to employ, but that what we see there will depend on our point of view (i.e., on the chosen concepts) in such a way that different perspectives cannot be pieced together into one unitary picture of the quantum world. In terms of the methodology for conceptual refinement that I have been exploring above, one can shift the metaphor this way. According to Bohr the system of classical concepts splits into mutually exclusive packages if one attempts to use this system outside the region of macroscopic physics, the region where all the concepts of the system have a determinate, simultaneous application. To get beyond this central core one must select which package of concepts to use. Different selections will enable one to get beyond the core in different ways. But the results of these different explorations do not combine into some unified picture of a region beyond the core. Bohr thus views the product of conceptual refinement as a wheel-like structure: a central hub from which a number of disjoint spokes extend. Different explorers can move out separately along different spokes but, according to Bohr, the reports they send back will not enable one to piece together an account of some region between the spokes or of a rim that connects them. Thus the new conceptual structure for Bohr looks like the steering wheel of an old-fashioned ship. The beauty of this steering mechanism and the aspect that Einstein saw as a "gentle pillow" is that it enables one to navigate into the quantum domain using only a classical chart in any given direction.

Einstein's dispute with Bohr (and others) is a dispute over this wheel-like structure. Einstein asks whether the spokes must really be disconnected, could there not at least be a rim? This is the question as to whether the quantum theory allows for a realist interpretation, a picture of the world as a single entity with a rich set of simultaneously determinate properties that are observer-independent. And Einstein asks whether the spokes must really be made of the same material as the hub. Must we, that is, stick with just the classical concepts? I do not want to tell here the story of how these questions were asked and what attempts were made to answer them. It is sufficient to recognize these three points about the dispute. First, it was Bohr not Einstein who felt bound by the classical concepts. Second, that both Bohr and Einstein shared Mach's critical method of searching for the limits of application of concepts and that they both wanted to go beyond this purely critical analysis to attempt some sort of constructive extension that would generalize the limited concepts. Third, that the dispute between them was a

dispute about the possibilities and nature of this constructive refinement in the context of quantum theory. This last point is a
crucial one for it shows that the dispute was not over accommo-
dating experimental facts, or understanding the new mathematics
of the quantum formalism, or taking in new physical ideas, or the
like. It was a dispute at the level of methodology over what processes
of concept formation are progressive; i.e., constitute a fundamental
scientific advance.

There is one further aspect of Einstein's approach to quantum
problems that I want to emphasize, for it too represents an early
insight of his that later became part of the accepted outlook of
quantum theory, which point of view was then used to suggest
Einstein's supposed recidivism.[10] What I have in mind is the easy-
going pragmatism of the quantum theory. For the theory is most
often seen as merely a coherent framework for the deduction (or
"prediction") of experimental consequences and a framework whose
principle justification lies in its uncanny success in this enterprise.
Einstein's persistent refusal to accept the quantum framework as
a part of fundamental physics might seem to run counter to this
pragmatic point of view. Because of this, no doubt, many of the
brightest students of physics have been directed by their mentors
away from examining Einstein's actual position. Alfred Landé, for
example, was interested in Einstein's thought, but he writes: "The
more pragmatic Sommerfeld . . . warned his students, one of them
this writer, not to spend too much time on the hopeless task of
"explaining" the quantum but rather to accept it as fundamental
and help work out its consequences" (Landé 1974, p. 460). It is
Einstein, then, who is seen as engaged in the hopeless task of explaining the quantum rather than accepting it and working out its
consequences. Curiously, or at least it ought to seem cruious to
those who see things that way, Einstein's procedure in the development of relativity theory was just the opposite of this. In the case
of relativity, Einstein looked for what he called "generalizable facts"
(such as the constancy of the velocity of light) which could be el-
evated to the status of principles. The theory itself was to be merely
a framework for drawing out the consequences of such principles.[11]
Einstein called a framework of this sort a "principle-theory" and

10. Unfortunately, the criminal overtones of this word, *recidivism*, are not too
strong. In a letter of March 23, 1936, Schrödinger recounted to Einstein a conversation in which Bohr called the attitude toward quantum theory of Schrödinger,
von Laue, and Einstein "appalling" and "high treason." See the Einstein Archives
microfilm index I B 1, number 22.
    11. See Einstein's account in Schilpp (1949), especially pp. 51–53.

contrasted it with a "constructive" theory, one that "attempts to build up a picture of the more complex phenomena out of the materials of a relatively simple formal scheme from which they start out."[12] The charge against Einstein then is that whereas in the case of relativity he was content with the pragmatism of a principle-theory, in the quantum case he made the unpragmatic demand that one build a constructive theory.

But if this were the case, then why was Einstein receptive and so enthusiastic to Bohr's 1913 atomic theory (a principle-theory par excellence), as he was later to be excited by the 1925 matrix mechanics of Heisenberg and Born? The answer is that Einstein's own intensive work on the quantum problems once again led him, quite early, in the direction of the mature quantum theory, in this instance toward the feeling that a pragmatic framework (or principle-theory) was the best hope. After a period of concentrated work on quantum problems, Einstein wrote to Michele Besso on May 13, 1911, "I no longer ask whether the quanta really exist. Also I no longer try to construct them because I now understand that my brain is incapable of proceeding in this way. Rather I look most carefully at the consequences [of this quantum representation]" (Speziali 1972, pp. 19–20). Here, then, we find Einstein expressing in 1911 the attitude that Sommerfeld later tried to impress on Landé and that is characteristic of the pragmatic quantum theory: look for the consequences. That Einstein maintained this attitude constantly is evident from a letter to Born in 1953 where he wrote, "I am quite satisfied if we have the machinery for making predictions, even if we are unable to understand it clearly" (Born 1971, p. 209). It is true that Einstein never felt that merely looking at the empirical consequences was sufficient justification for accepting a physical theory. He always emphasized that one must also look for inner simplicity and perfection among the constellation of theoretical principles. But it is nevertheless clear that from 1911 on he was open to accepting the sort of theory that eventually emerged—a framework or principle-theory—as the fundamental theory of the quantum domain.

I think our story is nearly done. If indeed the thought of the old Einstein was fixed in the circle of ideas of his youth then it traveled among the following stations well-known in the current versions of quantum theory: a firm belief in the existence of quanta, a constant attention to what are the limits of the concepts of classical

12. Quoted in Schaffner (1974), p. 62, which contains an illuminating discussion of the role of Einstein's option for a principle-theory in the genesis of special relativity.

physics, an openness to the revision or replacement of these concepts, and the sense that a theory construed as a framework for drawing empirical consequences is the right sort of theory for the quantum domain. In traveling this route we have seen how Einstein hit upon the notions central to the technical development of quantum theory (the correspondence principle and the principle of superposition) and how quickly, in fact, he was able to assimilate this technical development. Einstein's dispute with the quantum theorists was not a dispute due to hardening of the channels of thought. It was a genuine dispute about the conceptual adequacy of the developed theory. In pressing his side of the story Einstein was no doubt frustrated for the reasons he expressed to Solovine in a different context; namely, "because physicists have little understanding for logical and philosophical arguments" (Solovine 1956, p. 106).

In the end Einstein was more radical in his thinking than were the defenders of the orthodox view of quantum theory, for Einstein was convinced that the concepts of classical physics will have to be replaced and not merely segregated in the manner of Bohr's complementarity. In 1936 he described the quantum theory which results from the decision to retain these concepts as "an incomplete representation of real things, although it is the only one which can be built out of the fundamental concepts of force and material points (quantum corrections to classical mechanics)" (Einstein 1950a, p. 88). He took the advice of the quantum theorists, which was his own to begin with, and attended carefully to the consequences of the theory, especially for macroscopic bodies. He argued that the theory was unable to account for (=predict) even the simplest of these phenomena unless we understand the theory never to treat individual systems but only statistical aggregates of such systems. So understood, he had a deep respect for the theory and for its predictive success, which he expressed in 1936 in this way: "There is no doubt that quantum mechanics has seized hold of a beautiful element of truth and that it will be a test stone for any future theoretical basis, in that it must be deducible as a limiting case from that basis" (Einstein 1950a, p. 92). Because, as he saw it, quantum theory is essentially statistical, he felt that it could not be fundamental in the sense of providing a framework for all of physics. He hoped, instead, that the framework of general relativity—the space/time manifold and the analytical methods appropriate thereto—would enable one to establish the new concepts and the theoretical basis from which the quantum theory would emerge as a statistical approximation. For Einstein this recourse to the space/

time manifold was neither a reversion to classical concepts nor a working out of entrenched philosophical commitments. (For example, in responding sympathetically to a suggestion by Karl Menger that one might be able to develop a probabilistic geometry to replace the space/time manifold, Einstein wrote in 1949, "Adhering to the continuum originates with me not in a prejudice, but arises out of the fact that I have been unable to think up anything organic to take its place" [Schilpp 1949, p. 686]). Einstein hoped that the space/time framework of general relativity would contain possibilities for the systematic treatment of individual quantum systems. He devoted his last years to exploring the possibility for thus finding an account that would penetrate the quantum domain more deeply than does the present theory. He did not succeed. But I think he was genuinely content to have made the effort and that he would be pleased to have this effort seen in the context of his own remark to Besso in 1950, "I have learned on thing in my long life: It is devilishly difficult to get nearer to Him if one is not willing to remain on the surface." (Speziali 1972, p. 439).

Einstein's Critique of Quantum Theory: The Roots and Significance of EPR

The matrix mechanics path to quantum theory was initiated by Heisenberg in the summer of 1925. Dirac received a prepublication copy of Heisenberg's paper and by November he had worked out his own beautiful generalization of the ideas. Independently, and almost at the same time, Schrödinger was developing the wave mechanics route, marked out in his "first communication" at the end of January 1926.[1]

In the early months of 1926 Einstein corrresponded with both Heisenberg and Schrödinger about their work on quantum phenomena. As spring began he summed up his own impressions of the quantum world in letters to Ehrenfest and Lorentz. Heisenberg came to Berlin that spring to talk with Einstein and to the colloquium there, and later, in July, Schrödinger came as well. Thus before the new ideas were a year old, Einstein had acquired first-hand knowledge of them from the originators themselves. Einstein, whose own work on quantum problems played an important role in both lines of development, reacted to the new theory with an uncharacteristic ambivalence.

In a letter to Ehrenfest (February 12, 1926), Einstein criticized the matrix mechanics, focusing on the fact that it is not relativistically invariant and wondering whether the commutation relations for position and linear momentum actually hold in all cases. Yet a few weeks later (March 7, 1926) he wrote to Hedi Born, "The

© 1981 by Memphis State University Press.

Unless a published source is cited, references to the Einstein correspondence and papers are to material on microfilm in the Einstein Archives, housed in the Rare Book Room of the Firestone Library at Princeton University. The correspondence is indexed alphabetically for the correspondents cited. The unpublished manuscripts are on reel number two, IA2–IA7. I am grateful to David Malament and Michael Ferguson for help with the German, and to Micky Forbes for assistance with its English. I am responsible, however, for the translations as given. I want to acknowledge the cooperation of the trustees of the Estate of Albert Einstein with regard to the use of these materials, and to thank them for their permission to reproduce portions here. Part of the research for this study was supported by National Science Foundation Grant # SOC 76-82113.

1. See respectively Heisenberg (1925), Dirac (1925), and Schrödinger (1926).

Heisenberg-Born concepts leave us all breathless, and have made a deep impression on all theoretically oriented people. Instead of dull resignation, there is now a singular tension in us sluggish people" (Born 1971, p. 88). Within the week, however, Einstein wrote to Lorentz (March 13, 1926) that despite a great deal of effort in studying the Heisenberg-Born theory his instincts still resisted their way of conceiving things. He went on, in this letter, to recommend Schrödinger's work as a promising development of de Broglie's ideas. Responding to an earlier request from Lorentz that he address the fifth Solvay Conference (to be held in Brussels in October 1927), Einstein claimed to have nothing new to say and recommended that Schrödinger be invited in his stead. Einstein's endorsement of wave mechanics, however, was short lived. In April he expressed enthusiasm for Schrödinger's work to Ehrenfest, but by January (1927) he remarked to him, "My heart does not warm toward Schrödingerei—it is uncausal and altogether too primitive." ("Mein Herz wird nicht warm bie der Schrödingerei—es ist unkausal and überhaupt zu primitiv.")

I do not think this remark represents some special predilection for causality, rather it is probably Einstein's way of acknowledging to Ehrenfest that wave mechanics is no better, in terms of causality, than is matrix mechanics. In any case, Einstein wrote a critique of wave mechanics early in 1927. (It may be that this critique, which was never published, was made in preparation for the October Solvay Conference. For Einstein had finally yielded to Lorentz's strong personal request and agreed to give a talk on quantum statistics—although, in fact, the talk was never given.) In these notes he criticizes wave mechanics on three grounds: he thinks that because of superposition it will be difficult to recover the classical Hamilton-Jacobi equations even as an approximation; he is worried that the treatment of many-electron systems in configuration space involves correlations between the electrons that violate the principle of action-by-contact; and he thinks that one will have to renounce the treatment of individual systems and will find that the theory offers at best a descriptive completeness only in the sense of statistics.[2]

If we put this critique of Schrödinger's wave mechanics together with the reservations expressed to Ehrenfest over Heisenberg's

2. In note 26 of chapter 6 I point out that what I call here a critique of wave mechanics is actually an unpublished attempt at a hidden variables interpretation (the *Bestimmt* manuscript referred to in that note), together with Einstein's own critique of that attempt. Between the project attempted in the manuscript and his critique of it the three points mentioned in my text do emerge. My thanks to Paul Forman for catching my mistakes here.

matrix mechanics, we find that by the spring of 1927 Einstein had already arrived at the following lines of criticism of the newly emerging quantum theory: (1) the equations of the theory are not relativistically invariant; (2) it does not yield the classical behavior of macroscopic objects to a good approximation; (3) it leads to correlations among spatially separated objects that appear to violate action-by-contact principles; (4) it is an essentially statistical theory that seems incapable even of *describing* the behavior of individual systems; and (5) the scope of the commutation relations may not in fact be so broad as the theory supposes.

Einstein's disagreement with the quantum theory is well known, and it seems to be widely believed that this disagreement is a reaction to the uncertainty formulas of the theory and largely directed at the refutation of them. This is the image, for example, that emerges from Bohr's (1949) retelling of his "debates" with Einstein. It is also the dominant theme of Jammer's detailed story of the Bohr-Einstein dispute up to 1930 (Jammer 1974, pp. 120, 132, 136). It is therefore important to note that Einstein could only have known of the uncertainty formulas in April 1927, for that is when he received a prepublication copy of Heisenberg's (1927) fundamental paper. Thus the five lines of criticism assembled above constitute Einstein's reaction to the quantum theory prior even to the formulation of the uncertainty formulas. Only item (5) on that list is directly relevant to those formulas, and that item is more by way of a question than an objection. It appears, then, that Einstein's initial disagreements with the quantum theory did not have to do with the uncertainty relations but were broader in scope than those relations, and perhaps also more central. Moreover, I believe that these initial disagreements were the ones that lasted, as the subsequent story will show.

Einstein attended the fifth Solvay Conference in October 1927, although he did not give the address on quantum statistics that he had promised Lorentz. He did, however, make a few remarks in discussion on the last day, notes of which he enclosed in a letter to Lorentz on November 21, 1927. His remarks were not addressed to the uncertainty relations, but rather to the question of a statistical versus a complete individual interpretation of the theory. He argued that if the state function were interpreted as expressing probabilities for finding properties of an individual system, then the phenomenon of the collapse of the wave packet would represent a peculiar action-at-a distance. The collapse prevents a particle, whose wave function is continuously distributed over some region of space, from producing an effect at two places in the region at once. It thus represents a peculiar nonlocalized mechanism which,

Einstein suggests, violates relativity. Moreover, he thought that the representation of many-particle systems in configuration space raises two problems: how to obtain the Einstein-Bose statistics, and how to formulate the idea of forces acting only over small spatial distances. These are problems, however, not of the theory itself but of the interpretation according to which the theory gives a complete statistical description of individual systems. The alternative is to interpret the state function as providing information only about the distribution of an ensemble of systems and not about features of the individual systems themselves.

If Bohr's (1949) account of the unrecorded discussions at that meeting is reliable, then these remarks of Einstein's led to an informal discussion over the possibilities for more complete descriptions of individual systems. In this context, according to Bohr, Einstein raised the issue as to whether it might be possible in the case of a double slit experiment to determine both where the particle lands on the detecting screen and through which slit it has passed. In the ensuing discussion Bohr was able to show, apparently, that the possibilities for controlling the transfer of momentum to the diaphragm as the particle passes through are constrained by the uncertainty formulas in such a way as to preclude the required determinations. In effect, Bohr argued that one measurement (at the slits) disturbs the subsequent behavior (i.e., where the particle lands).

There is no record of Einstein's response to these discussions. But Bohr does say that at their conclusion Einstein asked "whether we could really believe that the providential authorities took recourse to dice-playing [ob der liebe Gott würfelt]" (Bohr 1949, p. 218). Within a fortnight Einstein wrote, in a letter to Sommerfeld, "On 'Quantum Mechanics' I think that, with respect to ponderable matter, it contains roughly as much truth as the theory of light without quanta. It may be a correct theory of statistical laws, but an inadequate conception of individual elementary processes."[3] It appears, then, that Einstein left the conference convinced that the only viable interpretation for the quantum theory was the statistical one he had suggested, and not convinced that it was impossible to build conceptions of "individual elementary processes" into a better theory.

Except for the problem of macroscopic approximation, one can see in Einstein's discussions throughout this time expressions of the same concerns that he had accumulated by the spring of 1927. In

3. This is letter 53 of November 9, 1927, in Hermann (1968). I have used the translation by R. and R. Stuewer in a preprint translation of Hermann's collection.

the period between the fifth Solvay Conference and the sixth one (October 1930), I can find nothing in Einstein's published work nor in his correspondence (both published and unpublished) that represents any shift or alteration in these concerns. In correspondence with Schrödinger, however, he does indicate an important conclusion about the quantum theory that he had not acknowledged previously. In the letter of May 31, 1928, Einstein notes his agreement with Schrödinger's conclusion that the limitations on the applicability of the classical concepts that are embedded in the uncertainty formulas indicate the need to replace those concepts by new ones. Einstein wrote, "Your claim that the concepts p, q [momentum, position] will have to be given up, if they can only claim such 'shaky' meaning seems to be fully justified" (Przibam 1967, p. 31). Einstein readily assimilated this conclusion to his concern over the completeness of the theory so that he would later write (in 1936) that quantum theory "is an incomplete representation of real things, although it is the only one which can be built out of the fundamental concepts of force and material points (quantum corrections to classical mechanics)" (Einstein 1954, pp. 315–16).

During the sixth Solvay Conference, Einstein once again made his only contribution by way of the discussion. He continued, here, the informal discussion of the possibility for the description of individual systems, this time explicitly directed to test the limitation imposed by the energy-time uncertainty formula. Einstein proposed a simple thought experiment involving the time at which a photon escapes from a box and which seemed to get around this limitation. Bohr, after a sleepless night, was able to use Einstein's own gravitational redshift formula to show that the determination of the time of the energy change was in fact limited by Heisenberg's relation. Once again Bohr showed how the measurement of one parameter (here weighing the box-plus-clock) directly interfered with the determination of another (here the clockrate). According to Bohr (1949, p. 226), Einstein contributed effectively in helping to work out Bohr's argument against Einstein's own speculation.

That spirit accords well with Einstein's scientific character, and with the fact that nowhere after 1930 do we find Einstein questioning the general validity of the uncertainty formulas.[4] Indeed the following year he published an article, jointly with Tolman and

4. Jammer (1974), p. 136, interprets this as Einstein's turning from a search for the internal inconsistency of the quantum theory to a demonstration of its incompleteness. But this is wrong on both counts for, as we have seen, the issue of completeness was Einstein's concern from the beginning, whereas nowhere do I find him trying to show the inconsistency of the theory.

Podolsky (1931), in which he argued that certain apparent possibilities for determining the history of a particle with an accuracy greater than that allowed by the uncertainty formulas would, in fact, permit violations of those forumlas. Since these possibilities had been allowed by both Bohr and Heisenberg (and simply dismissed with the positivist disclaimer that they would have no predictive value), we find that here Einstein is more orthodox about the uncertainty formulas than are the orthodox themselves.

If Einstein came away from the discussions at the Solvay conferences convinced of the general validity of the uncertainty relations, he must also have seen that the key to Bohr's interpretation of the theory lay in the doctrine of disturbance. For the idea that Bohr had twice used to undermine Einstein's attempts to get at a detailed description of individual systems was the doctrine that certain simultaneous determinations were not possible because any one of them would inevitably disturb the physical situation so as to preclude the others. It was probably clear to Einstein after the 1930 conference that to defend his own statistical interpretation he must somehow neutralize the doctrine of disturbance to be able to demonstrate the existence of real physical attributes that are left unattended by the theory, except insofar as they have statistical significance.

Once he was settled with regard to the uncertainty formulas, Einstein's five original objections to the theory were reduced to four. Of these, two concerned external constraints imposed by other theories: how to reconcile the quantum theory with the requirements of relativity and how to achieve a satisfactory classical approximation from the quantum theory. From his own brilliant work on relativity, Einstein understood that such external constraints are guideposts for the construction of new physical concepts. He knew, therefore, that to develop the new concepts to replace the classical ones it would be necessary to attend to such constraints. He believed, moreover, that working from the relativistic framework was a likely starting point (see chapter 2 for a discussion of Einstein's ideas in this area). But if one were interested in interpreting the new theory, which already relied so heavily on the classical concepts themselves, it may well have seemed reasonable to bracket off the anomalies engendered by these external constraints, at least for a while. If Einstein thought in these ways, then he would have two central problems left. One concerned the question of distant correlations and action-by-contact in the theory, and the other was the central issue of statistics and the description of individual systems. Notice that these very same concerns were the ones expressed by Einstein in the 1927 Solvay

Conference. He was to make one more attempt to combine them so as to neutralize Bohr's doctrine of disturbance and to support his own statistical interpretation.

On March 25, 1935 the editors of *Physical Review* received a short manuscript coauthored by Albert Einstein, Boris Poldolsky, and Nathan Rosen. The paper was published in the May 15, 1935, issue with the awkward title "Can Quantum Mechanical Description of Physical Reality Be Considered Complete?" Most often referred to by slogans incorporating the acronym "EPR," this short (four-page) article is the source of a voluminous published commentary and is the touchstone for several attempts to interpret (or to reinterpret) the formalism of quantum theory.[5]

The argument of the paper is concerned with two assertions:

(INC) *The quantum mechanical description of a system given by the state function is incomplete* (as they say, not "every element of physical reality has a counterpart in the theory").

(NSV) *Observables represented by noncommuting operators cannot have simultaneous reality* (i.e., cannot have simultaneously sharp values).

The argument develops in two parts. The first part demonstrates the validity of the disjunction[6]

(INC) v (NSV).

The second part shows the validity of the conditional

~(INC) → ~(NSV).

The authors then conclude from this that

(INC)

must hold.

We can represent the logical structure of the argument as follows: From PvQ and ~P → ~Q, infer P. And one can show the validity of the argument by reasoning that if ~P then, by the second premise, one can get ~Q; and then, by the first premise, one can get P. So it follows from the premises that if ~P, then P. Since clearly if P, then P, the conclusion P follows by a simple constructive dilemma. Of course this is not the only way to get the conclusion from the premises, but it is perhaps the most straightforward way. (The authors do not give the reasoning, they just draw the conclusion.) The point I want to emphasize is that even from the point

5. See Hooker (1972) and the extended discussion in Jammer (1974).

6. For compactness, below I use standard logical symbols: "PvQ" for "P or Q," "~P" for "it is not the case that P," and "P → Q" for "if P, then Q."

of view of elementary logic, the argument of the paper appears quite complex. The subarguments are even more so.

To establish the disjunction, (INC) v (NSV), the authors show that ~(NSV) → (INC). Thus they suppose that a pair of noncommuting observables of a system have simultaneous values and they note that no state of the system is simultaneously an eigenstate for both observables. Hence they conclude that the description given by the state function for such a system would be incomplete.

To establish the conditional, ~(INC) → ~(NSV), the authors assume the antecedent (i.e., that the theory is complete) and try to establish the existence of simultaneous values for position and linear momentum (in the same direction) in a certain interesting system. This is a system consisting of two particles that interact so as to preserve total linear momentum (in a certain direction) and then fly apart in opposite directions so as to preserve their relative positions (in the same direction). The authors argue from the interaction formalism of the theory that, at least theoretically, there are such correlated two-particle systems. They then introduce the following *criterion of reality:* "If, without in any way disturbing a system, we can predict with certainty (that is, with probability equal to unity) the value of a physical quantity, then there exists an element of physical reality corresponding to this physical quantity" (EPR 1935, p. 777). In the case of the hypothetical correlated system, we can predict, from a measurement of the position of one system, the position of the other, and similarly with regard to linear momentum. If the systems are allowed to separate far enough spatially, there can be no question of the measurement of one system disturbing the other. Hence the authors invoke the criterion of reality to conclude that for such a system at least one particle must have simultaneously definite position and momentum. Since this is the desired conclusion in this part of the argument, the inference is achieved.

I shall reserve comments on the general argument for awhile, but there are several features of this second stage that I should mention. One is to note that the assumption of completeness is never actually used here, the authors simply show (or try to) that a certain system has simultaneous position and momentum. Thus they establish the conditional

~(INC) → ~(NSV)

simply by deriving the consequent, ~(NSV). But if they had just stated this as their objective in this second part, then the conclusion (INC) would follow immediately from the disjunction

(INC) v (NSV)

of part one. So once again the form of argument seems strangely complex. Moreover, the actual text is not as clear as I have made out. For the authors digress (or so it seems) to point out that by choosing to measure either position or momentum on one particle of the pair, one can alter the postmeasurement state function for the other particle at will.[7] And they seem to think that this runs counter to the assumed completeness. Finally it is by no means clear how, even with the stated criterion of reality, the fact that one can assign either a definite position or a definite momentum to the unmeasured particle establishes that the particle has *both* properties at once. Surely, the argument in this second part is both tangled and flawed.

Despite these difficulties of style and logic, I think one can see here just that combination of the ideas of correlated system, action-by-contact, and descriptive incompleteness that Einstein required to provide the background for his statistical interpretation. Moreover, the criterion of reality is clearly aimed at Bohr's doctrine of disturbance. It did not miss its target for, as Rosenfeld recalls, "This onslaught came down on us as a bolt from the blue. Its effect on Bohr was remarkable" (Rozental 1967, p. 128). And Rosenfeld goes on to tell how he worked with Bohr "day after day, week after week" to formulate a response. The response was announced on June 29, 1935, in a letter to the editor of *Nature* and spelled out in a longer paper (six pages to EPR's four) published in *Physical Review* (Bohr 1935). The announcement focused on EPR's criterion of reality which, in a typical phrase, Bohr said "contains an essential ambiguity." It was then precisely the question of disturbance to which Bohr responded. For he argued that the phrase "without in any way disturbing a system" was the ambiguous culprit. There was, he admitted, no question ("of course") of a physical ("mechanical") disturbance of one system brought about by measuring its correlated twin, "but even at this stage there is essentially the question of an *influence on the very conditions which define the possible types of predictions regarding the future behavior of the system.*"

I want to point out two significant features of Bohr's response. The first is that what Bohr himself underlines (the italics are his) is virtually textbook neopositivism. For Bohr simply identifies the attribution of properties with the possible types of predictions of future behavior. (I think this point needs emphasizing, for many commentators seem inclined to suppose that Bohr's tendency to

---

7. The significance of this "digression" is discussed in chapter 4, section 2, and in connection with "bijective completeness" in chapter 5.

obscure language is a token of philosophical depth, whereas I find that, as here, where it really matters Bohr invariably lapses into positivist slogans and dogmas.) The second feature, and one which neither Bohr nor his commentators have acknowledged, is that Bohr's response to EPR marks a definite break from his previously stated view. For in earlier writings and in his response to Einstein at the Solvay conferences, Bohr had always argued that the disturbance created by a measurement of a particular variable caused a real change in the physical situation which altered the preconditions for applying complementary variables. But here Bohr switched from this doctrine of actual physical disturbance to what one might call a doctrine of semantic disturbance. In a way that Bohr does not account for on physical grounds, the arrangement to measure, say, the position of one particle in a pair simply precludes meaningful talk of the linear momentum of the unmeasured (and admittedly undisturbed) other particle. I think it is fair to conclude that the EPR paper did succeed in neutralizing Bohr's doctrine of disturbance. It forced Bohr to retreat to a merely semantic disturbance and thereby it removed an otherwise plausible and intuitive physical basis for Bohr's ideas.

If Bohr's response to EPR is the most famous, it was nevertheless not the first. An equally important response was written a few days earlier, on June 19, 1935, and it was by Einstein himself. On that day Einstein responded to a June 7 letter from Schrödinger. In that letter Schrödinger had reminded Einstein of their discussions in Berlin (presumably in the summer of 1926) about "the dogmatic quantum theory," and responded to the calculations of EPR.[8]

In the June 19 letter Einstein wrote about EPR as follows: "For reasons of language this [paper] was written by Podolsky after much discussion. Still, it did not come out as well as I had originally wanted; rather the essential thing was, so to speak, smothered by the formalism [gelehrsamkeit]."[9]

I think we should take in the message of these few words: Einstein did not write the paper, Podolsky did, and somehow the central point was obscured. No doubt Podolsky (of Russian origin) would have found it natural to leave the definite article out of the title. Moreover the logically opaque structure of the piece is uncharacteristic of Einstein's thought and writing. There are no earlier drafts of this article among Einstein's papers and no corre-

8. See chapter 5 for further details of this letter and of Einstein's reply.
9. "Diese ist aus Sprachgründen von Podolsky geschrieben nach vielen Diskussionen. Es ist aber doch nicht so gut herausgekommen, was ich eigentlich wollte; sondern die Hauptsache ist sozusagen durch Gelehrsamkeit verschüttet."

spondence or other evidence that I have been able to find which would settle the question as to whether Einstein saw a draft of the paper before it was published. Podolsky left Princeton for California at about the time of submission and it could well be that, authorized by Einstein, he actually composed it on his own.

In any case, Einstein goes on in the June 19 letter to sketch the essential features which were obscured. He first tries to convey the sense of the assertion of incompleteness by means of the following illustration. Consider a ball located in one of two closed boxes. An incomplete description of this "reality" might be, for example, "The probability is one-half that the ball is in the first box." A complete description would be, for example, "The ball *is* in the first box." Thus an incomplete description is a probabilistic assertion, with probability less than unity, *made in circumstances in which there is some further truth that could be told.* This seems like an elementary and intuitive idea for incompleteness, but how are we to know whether there is some further truth to be told? That is, of course, the problem of measurement disturbance: does the measured result, so to speak, arise with the measurement or, rather, does the measurement simply reflect what is already there?

Einstein addresses this issue in the letter by continuing with the illustration as follows. He acknowledges that one cannot sort things out without assuming something more, and he then proposes to assume a principle of separation (Trennungsprinzip): "the contents of the second box are independent of what happens to the first box."[10]

If one now assumes an obvious conservation law, that balls are neither created nor destroyed, then I can find out by looking in the first box whether or not the ball is in the second box. (If I find it in the first box, it is not in the second box. If I do not find it in the first box, it is in the second box.) If my theory only allows, in these circumstances, probabilistic assertions (with probability less than unity), then my theory is incomplete. Thus, given the conservation law, the principle of separation would imply the incompleteness of my theory.

Einstein continues in this letter to give a technical reformulation of the EPR argument. It is a little confusing because it introduces

10. Einstein puts it delightfully like this: The separation principle is needed in order to get past the Talmudists. For "the Talmudic philosopher sniffs at 'reality' as at a frightening creature of the naive mind." ("Der Talmudistische Philosoph . . . pfeift auf die 'Wirklichkeit' als auf einen Popanz der Naivität . . .") Although no reference is made, I would guess that Bohr should be counted here as a Talmudist. The obvious ones are the positivists.

a further refinement of the idea of completeness (this time in terms of state functions correlated to real states of affairs). But I think there is enough material contained, as it were, in Einstein's boxes to give at least one formulation of some of the essentials of EPR that were obscured by Podolsky's exposition.

Consider the system of two particles correlated via the conservation law for total linear momentum. Separation is the claim that whether a physical property holds for one of the particles does not depend on measurements (or other interactions) made on the other particle when the pair is widely separated in space. Completeness is the claim that if a certain physical property in fact holds for one particle at a given time, then the state function for the combined system at that time should yield probability one for finding that the property does hold (i.e., the subsystem consisting of the particle should have a state function which is an eigenstate for the property in question).

One can now copy Einstein's box argument as follows. Suppose the two particles (A and B) are far apart and I measure, say, particle A for linear momentum (in a certain direction). Using the conservation law I can infer the linear momentum of particle B from the result of this measurement on A. Thus after the A measurement, the B particle has a certain linear momentum. By separation, this real property of B must have held already at the time when I began my measurement on A (or just before, in the case of an instantaneous measurement). For otherwise I would have created the momentum at B by measuring A, in violation of separation. But at the initial moment of the A measurement, the state of the composite system does not yield probability one for finding *any* momentum value for B, for that state is a nontrivial superposition of products of "momentum eigenstates" for the A and B subsystems. Hence the description provided by the state function given by quantum theory is incomplete. Here, as in the illustration, the argument establishes the incompatibility of separation and completeness.

It is this incompatibility that I take to be the central conclusion, which got obscured in EPR. Many years later, in Schilpp (1949, p. 682) Einstein put it succinctly in these words:

the paradox forces us to relinquish one of the following two assertions:
(1) the description by means of the ψ-function is *complete*
(2) the real states of spatially separated objects are independent of each other.

It is important to notice that the conclusion Einstein draws from EPR is not a categorical claim for the incompleteness of quantum theory. It is rather that the theory poses a dilemma between completeness and separation; both cannot be true. It is also important to notice that the argument I have drawn from Einstein's illustration does not depend in any way on simultaneous measurements or even attributions of position and momentum. The argument depends on the satisfaction of a single conservation law and the inferences drawn from that concerning the measurement of a single variable. This feature of the situation, I believe, is completely buried in the original paper and, because of that, Einstein's ideas concerning completeness and separation have become needlessly entangled with discussions of the uncertainty formulas and hidden variables. In his letter to Schrödinger of June 19, 1935, Einstein says that if the argument he gives applies to pairs of incompatible observables "ist mir *wurst,*" which I would translate loosely as "I couldn't care less." The argument nowhere depends on that, nor do the basic ideas. I think that this feature shows that Einstein has successfully managed to use the correlations to get around Bohr's doctrine of disturbance. For even in the semantic version of that doctrine, measuring the momentum on A does not preclude assigning a somewhat earlier *momentum* to B, which is all the argument requires.

Einstein wanted to use the dilemma posed by EPR to show that if we maintain the ideas of action-by-contact embodied in the separation principle, then we must view quantum theory as providing no more than a statistical account of a realm of objects whose properties outstrip the descriptive apparatus of the theory. As we have seen, he felt that the concepts needed to describe these properties adequately would be other than the dynamical concepts of classical physics. Thus, although Einstein took the incompleteness to be a sign that something better was required, he never showed any interest in the hidden variables program for filling out the theory from within. Rather, he hoped that some unification of quantum theory and relativity would, so to speak, provide a completion from without. This path would address the external constraints of relativity and of classical dynamics together, if it could be successfully followed. Of course, Einstein did not succeed. And now recent arguments by Bell and others suggest that separation alone may be incompatible with the quantum theory, and perhaps even with certain experiments.[11] Should that be correct, then the dilemma of EPR could be resolved by abandoning separation. I do not believe that the Bell arguments are in fact strong enough to

11. See chapters 4 and 9 for discussions of Bell.

force the issue this way, but even if they are, the question of completeness would remain. For it is possible that *both* separation and completeness turn out to be false.

Einstein's reservations about the fundamental character of quantum theory began with reflections about completeness, and these reflections were the home base to which Einstein's thinking about the theory always returned. It seems appropriate, therefore, to close by citing the earliest reference to the completeness issue that I have been able to find. It occurs in a letter of February 18, 1926, which says, "it seems likely to me that quantum mechanics can never make direct statements about the individual system, but rather it always gives only average values."[12]

This comes from a letter written *to* Einstein *by* Heisenberg. Thus, one might say that the original idea and focus on incompleteness came from him.

12. "Denn es scheint mir an sich wahrscheinlich, dass d. Quantenmechanik nie directe Aussagen über d. Einzelprozess machen kann, sondern immer nur Mittelware . . . gibt."

What Is Einstein's Statistical Interpretation, or, Is It Einstein for Whom Bell's Theorem Tolls?

1. Introduction

Einstein regarded the quantum theory as descriptively incomplete. What he meant was that, in typical cases, the probabilistic assertions provided by the theory for an individual quantum system do not exhaust all the relevant and true physical assertions about the system. Put briefly, according to Einstein, the typical statistical story told by quantum theory is not the whole story. Einstein arrived at this doctrine by means of a dialectical strategy that involved several beautiful and simple "in-principle" applications of the theory, elegant thought experiments of a kind characteristic of Einstein's genius for physical insight. His strategy was to show how the alternative idea, the idea of the completeness of quantum theory, was forced into puzzling and unnatural interpretations for these special applications. By switching from completeness to incompleteness everything was supposed to "click" into place: the fly, as it were, was to be let out of the bottle. Certainly Einstein never thought he was offering strict counterexamples to the theory itself. Nor, I believe, did he think he had strictly proved his case for incompleteness, or actually refuted the idea of completeness. Rather, he felt that the dialectical strategy showed his conception to have a powerful intuitive appeal vis-à-vis its competitor.

Research for this paper was supported by the National Science Foundation, and the paper was written during the tenure of a Guggenheim Fellowship. I want to thank both foundations for their support. I am also grateful to Hebrew University of Jerusalem for their kind permission to use material from the Einstein Archives. Those Archives are housed in the Seeley G. Mudd manuscript library at Princeton University, and my references below to unpublished material can be found there, either alphabetically or by using the excellent numerical indexing scheme worked out by John Stachel, and which I refer to when appropriate. I'd like to take this opportunity to commend the friendly assistance of the library staff. Copies of Einstein's 1935 correspondence with Schrödinger were part of a gift package that I received from Linda Wessels. I am in her debt, as will be every reader who finds something of interest in my references to that material. I want to give credit to Dana Fine, who helped enormously with the various manuscripts and their translation, and to Micky Forbes who informed and guided its English. With regard to the residue, however, I do reserve credit (and blame) for myself.

The final stage of that strategy involved showing how the idea of incompleteness could ground a specific understanding of quantum theory, one that would make intelligible the puzzling thought experiments. That understanding comprises what is sometimes called Einstein's "statistical interpretation" of the state functions of quantum theory; in his own words "the ψ-function is to be understood as the description not of a single system but of an ensemble of systems" (Schilpp 1949, p. 671). Using this idea, the seeming paradoxes generated by the alternative conception (that the ψ-function is a complete description of the single system) were supposed to disappear.

From his earliest public comments on the interpretation of quantum mechanics, in the Solvay Conference of 1927, down through his last papers on the subject in the 1940s and early 1950s, Einstein referred to the ensemble interpretation of the state function in language virtually identical to that just cited.[1] So far as I have been able to ascertain, the same is true of his unpublished remarks. This concept of an ensemble interpretation was clearly the cornerstone of his own understanding of the quantum theory. Writing to Born in 1953, he described this concept as "the only one which does justice to the mechanism of the probabilistic quantum theory" (Born 1971, p. 209). It is, therefore, remarkable, although (curiously) scarcely ever remarked upon, that *nowhere at all* does Einstein say in any detail just exactly what this ensemble interpretation amounts to. In particular, he never does so for the very applications that are supposed to be treated by this interpretation "more naturally" than by its competitor. Although it would be intriguing to speculate on the reasons behind Einstein's cryptic brevity here, and even more intriguing to think about the reluctance of his many commentators on the subject to deal with this fact, I shall defer the pleasure of those speculations, just now, in favor of another. For what, after all, was Einstein's ensemble interpretation?

As just noted, there is very little textual material available on which to base on answer. One only finds a couple of vague phrases in one article, and a couple of very similar ones in the others. Despite the scant data, however, the literature seems to have settled on a standard answer.[2] This answer, the so-called statistical interpretation, has been faced with difficulties at least since 1935, dif-

1. See the preceding chapters for an overview of the history of Einstein's ideas on the quantum theory.
2. Ballentine (1972) gives a good formulation of this standard answer.

ficulties known to Einstein and simply ignored by him.[3] Recently
these difficulties have been sharply focused, and have received a
good deal of attention, through the work of John Bell.[4] Bell showed
that, in principle (at least), the statistical interpretation is actually
numerically inconsistent with the quantum theory when applied to
coupled systems, the most favorite of Einstein's provocative examples. If the standard answer is Einstein's, then it appears that
his interpretation of the quantum theory has been refuted. This
conclusion is, I think, the received opinion.

     Given what little Einstein actually had to say on the matter and
given his complete aplomb in the face of earlier difficulties with the
statistical interpretation, it seems to me that we ought at least to be
open to a different opinion. We ought to be open to questioning
whether the standard answer is, really, Einstein's answer. I want to
begin that process of freeing ourselves from the received opinion by
proposing a somewhat different answer. Now, one might have thought
that faced with the prospect of an actual refutation via Bell's theorem,
and given the scant data, probably some ad hoc revision or other of
the standard answer is possible—but so what? The situation with my

     3. I have in mind the difficulties over the quantization of angular momentum
and over the penetration of a potential barrier that are raised by Schrödinger (1935b,
section 4) precisely in order to show that an ensemble interpretation, like Einstein's,
won't work. Schrödinger's objections were developed in correspondence with Einstein during the summer of 1935, as discussed in chapter 5, although Einstein never
responded to them directly. They are, I think, a physical version of the earlier no-
hidden-variables theorem of von Neumann (1932), involving exactly the additivity
over noncommuting observables that Bell (and others) later picked out for criticism.
See Bell's charming review (1982). In his letter of July 13, 1935, Schrödinger does
refer Einstein to von Neumann's book, but not to the section on hidden variables.
I have not been able to find any evidence in the archives suggesting that Einstein
was aware of the mathematical no-hidden-variables literature, although later he
himself offered counterexamples to, and criticism of, several developments of the
de Broglie, pilot-wave version of hidden variables. See, e.g., his (1953b), his letter
of August 9, 1954, to R. Hosemann (along with the September 9, 1954, letter from
von Laue), and his letter to D. Bohm of October 28, 1954. There is a manuscript
in the Einstein Archives entitled "Ist eine deterministische Ergänzung der QM
möglich?" ("Is a Deterministic Completion of QM Possible?") (5–207), from an
unidentified author, that purports to describe an interference experiment in which
the assumption of hidden variables, determined at the source, would contradict
quantum theory. The manuscript is not dated, although it is clear from the footnotes
that it was written after1935. There are marginal markings, and a comment, that
appear to be Einstein's. Thus Einstein probably was familiar with certain attempts
to show a contradiction between some kinds of ensemble representations and quantum theory. Indeed there is correspondence with von Laue (August 29, 1936) in
which Einstein himself attempts to show that a naive representation of quantum
theory, one with instantaneous particle emissions and sharp localization, leads to
false conclusions. Nevertheless, right up to the end, Einstein believed that the conception of the ψ-function as corresponding to an ensemble of systems "was not
logically refuted." (See letter to A. Lamouche, March 20, 1955.)
     4. Bell (1981) is a lovely, recent discussion, with references to the earlier literature.

proposal, however, is not that, as in an ad hoc revision, it fits the data about as well as the original while avoiding a refutation. Rather, as I will show, my proposal actually fits the data considerably better than does the standard answer. It enables us to see what Einstein might have meant by what he actually says. By contrast, the standard answer requires one to read into Einstein's words much that he doesn't say in order to make sense out of what he does say. It also fragments Einstein's thought, as we shall see, for unlike my proposal, the standard answer fails to provide a unified explanatory framework for the variety of Einstein's thought. Thus, relative to my proposal, it is the standard one that appears ad hoc. That the standard answer is also refuted by Bell's theorem is, I hope, not to be counted in its favor.

2. The Standard Answer

Consider the situation of a quantum system S in a given state ψ. Let $A_1, A_2, \ldots$ be measurable quantities of the system (e.g., position, linear momentum, angular momentum, etc.), what quantum theory calls "observables." The standard interpretation of Einstein's remarks about treating the state function as describing an ensemble of systems involves constructing a statistical model for this situation as follows. We make correspond to the state function ψ a (large enough) ensemble E of systems like S. (In quantum mechanical terms we would say that all the systems in E have been "prepared" to be in state ψ.) We make correspond to each observable A_n a function f_n associating with each system in E a real number (always in the spectrum of A_n). One can think of these numbers either as the values of the observables, or as the value that would be obtained if the system were subjected to an ideal measurement for the observable. Then the original system S is treated as though it had been randomly selected from the ensemble E. Thus probabilistic assertions (about the values of observables, or the values found on measurement) are obtained by averaging over the ensemble E. The general rule is

$$P^{\psi}_{A_1, A_2 \ldots}(D_1 \times D_2 \times \ldots) = \langle \chi_{D_1}[f_1(x)] \cdot \chi_{D_2}[f_2(x)] \cdot \ldots \rangle_E$$

(where χ_D is the characteristic function of the set D). A statistical model of this sort for a given family of probability distributions is a well-known probabilistic construct, sometimes called an *ensemble representation*, or a random variables representation. I shall use the former term since it is close to Einstein's own language.[5]

5. Bach (1982) describes a very general version of the concept of an ensemble representation and reviews difficulties more general than Bell's theorem with its use in quantum theory. The rationale for trying an ensemble representation, as well as the implausibility of the idea for quantum theory, is discussed in chapter 9.

The standard construal of Einstein's statistical interpretation, then, is to suppose that for any quantum system in any state the quantum theoretical probabilities are to be obtained from an ensemble representation. But, of course, this immediately raises a consistency question; namely, *can* one make an ensemble representation for the quantum probabilities for any set of observables in any state? The answer is "no," and Bell's theorem yields that negative answer for an especially interesting and simple system, a system of just the sort most frequently used by Einstein to argue for the incompleteness of quantum theory, and hence for the necessity of his statistical interpretation. It is a system with two parts (call them A and B) that have briefly interacted with each other and that later (say, at time t) become spatially separated. Let ψ be the state function for the composite system (at t) (Einstein 1936, p. 317). Bell supposes we have two incompatible observables defined on each partial system; say A_1 and A_2 on subsystem A, and B_1, B_2 on subsystem B. Let these observables have only two possible values; say $+1$ or -1. Then in state ψ quantum theory determines the probabilities for any measurement outcome ($+1$ or -1) for each observable separately (i.e., for A_1 or A_2 or B_1 or B_2), as well as the joint probabilities for any pair of outcomes in a simultaneous measurement of any A_i with any B_j. The question is, can all these single and joint probabilities be given an ensemble representation? The answer, as I have recently shown, is this (Fine 1982a, *Proposition 1*):

Necessary and sufficient for the existence of an ensemble representation for the observables A_1, A_2, B_1, B_2 in state ψ is the existence of a joint distribution function P_{B_1,B_2} arising as the marginal of distributions P_{A_1,B_1,B_2} and P_{A_2,B_1,B_2} whose various marginals P_{A_i,B_j} are themselves precisely those of the quantum theory in state ψ.

Let me put this briefly by saying that there exists an ensemble representation if and only if one can interpolate a well-defined joint distribution for the incompatible observables (the B-pairs) among the given quantum distributions for the compatible ones (the AB-pairs). This equivalence, I might mention, is not only true for the special case considered by Bell, where we have only four observables, each taking only two values, but it holds as well for any number of observables taking any number (even a continuum) of values (Fine 1982b, *Theorem 1*). For the special Bell case there is a further, algebraic equivalence that can be established. Let

$P(S)$ = the quantum probability in state ψ that a measurement of S would yield the value of $+1$, and let

$P(ST)$ = the quantum probability in state ψ that a simultaneous measurement of S and of T would each yield the value $+1$.

In a slightly different setting, Clauser and Horne (1974) focus on the following inequality:

(BCH) $-1 \leqslant P(A_1B_1) + P(A_1B_2) + P(A_2B_1)$
$$-P(A_2B_2) - P(A_1) - P(B_1) \leqslant 0.$$

It turns out that the satisfaction of (BCH) is not only necessary but also sufficient for the existence of an ensemble representation for the quantum probabilities (Fine 1982a). It also turns out that there are well-known composite quantum systems that violate these inequalities for certain physically preparable states ψ. Thus, it follows that one cannot give an ensemble representation for these composite systems in those states. Let me call this conclusion *Bell's theorem*, since John Bell first discovered it (although in a somewhat less general form and with a somewhat different emphasis).

Bell's theorem shows that the statistical interpretation standardly attributed to Einstein (and so attributed, for example, by Bell [1981] himself) is numerically inconsistent with the quantum theory. As an interpretation, therefore, it is ruled out (although not perhaps as a competing theory of the phenomena[6]). But is it Einstein's interpretation after all? My own suspicions here derive from noticing that any ensemble representation must make well-defined joint distributions for incompatible observables (like position and linear momentum, or spin in skew directions), for the functions associated with these observables will be random variables over a common space and these always have well-defined joints. Moreover, in the context of composite systems the possibility of interpolating such joint distributions is fully equivalent, *all by itself*, to the existence of an ensemble representation. The probabilistic framework of quantum theory, however, scrupulously avoids such distributions. This avoidance on the part of the quantum theory is connected with the validity of the Heisenberg uncertainty formulas (which are just special dispersion relations) and, more generally, with the noncommutative structure of the algebra of observables.[7] While not

6. The question is whether it is possible to realize experimental efficiencies high enough (around 90% in the simple case) to discriminate between quantum theory and the predictions of an ensemble representation. See Lo and Shimony (1981) and Fine (1982a, note 5) for some discussion of this issue, and also Garg (1983) for a related investigation of detector efficiency.

7. See Suppes (1961) and Fine (1982b) for some recent results and references. The subject goes back to Wigner (1932), and to even earlier discussions in Berlin (Jammer 1974, p. 422ff.). Thus Einstein might well have been aware of the joint distribution problem.

all of these connections could have been known to Einstein, he certainly knew about the uncertainty formulas and, after 1930 or so, he always avowed his belief in their general validity. I think he took them to be among the lasting contributions of the quantum theory, contributions that subsequent developments in physics would have to reproduce as a limiting constraint. When asked about them in 1931, for example, he replied, "This principle of Heisenberg's is of importance since it makes clear that the quantities which we have hitherto used cannot in their totality be observed."[8] Einstein was, moreover, a master at precisely the sort of statistical calculations involved in checking out questions of dispersion in the format of an ensemble representation.[9] It is hard to believe that with his eyes on the importance of the uncertainty formulas and his hands ready to do the calculations, Einstein would have neglected the issue of the validity of these formulas in an ensemble representation. But if he had addressed the issue, then surely he would have seen problems here, and therefore the necessity for saying something more detailed about the structure of the representations. He did not say anything in detail, and this fact leads me to suspect that it was not an ensemble representation that he had in mind after all.

Let us then look at what he does say in the context of the applications he did have in mind, the ones that were intended to challenge an alternative conception of the state function but to support his own. In particular let us look at what he says about composite systems in the Bell situation. His first publication on the problem of correlated systems is the 1935 paper coauthored with Boris Podolsky and Nathan Rosen (EPR 1935). As I have discussed in the last chapter, Einstein's correspondence in 1935 shows that it was Podolsky who actually wrote the paper (following several group discussions), but that Einstein was not satisfied that the published text really got at the central ideas. Thus one must be careful about what we attribute to Einstein on the basis of that paper. In any case, the EPR paper of 1935 says nothing about the correct reading of the ψ-function formulae, except in the very last sentence where Podolsky wrote, "While we have thus shown that the wave function

---

8. Einstein Archives (4-056), reported in the *Yale News*, February 3, 1931, and in the *New York Times*, February 3, 1931. For a further sense of Einstein's commitment to the uncertainty formulas see Einstein, Tolman, and Podolsky (1931) and, for discussion, Jammer (1974, section 6.2). Einstein understood these formulas as implying a theoretical limit to the simultaneous, empirical determinability of incompatible observables. This fueled his belief that the quantum observables were not the right concepts for physics. This idea goes back to 1928: (Przibam 1967, p. 31), as discussed in the preceding chapters.

9. Pais (1982, part II) reviews Einstein's mastery of statistical physics.

does not provide a complete description of physical reality, we left open the question of whether or not such a description exists. We believe, however, that such a theory is possible."

We are on much safer grounds in getting at Einstein's ideas if we look at his discussion of the EPR situation in the general review article he published the following year (Einstein 1936), the development of which we can also follow in his correspondence with Schrödinger during the summer of 1935.[10]

In the 1936 article, "Physics and Reality," Einstein refers to "the paradox recently demonstrated by myself and two collaborators."[11] The paradoxical feature he focuses his attention on is this: depending on which observable has been measured, say, on the partial system A, quantum mechanics determines different state functions for the other partial system, B. Einstein now supposes that "there can be only *one* physical state of B" after the interaction of the two systems has ("practically") stopped. He also assumes what he describes to Schrödinger as a "Separation Principle",[12] that the real, physical state of B "cannot reasonably be considered to depend on the particular measurement we perform on the system A separated from B." He concludes that "the ψ function is not unambiguously coordinated to the physical state" and that "this coordination of several ψ functions to the same physical state of system B shows again that

10. This correspondence took place during Einstein's stay at Old Lyme, Connecticut, that summer, and it appears from the letter of September 18, 1935, to the Director of The Franklin Institute that Einstein wrote the "Physics and Reality" article in tandem with the letters to Schrödinger. Cross-checks among this material seem, therefore, especially appropriate and useful.

11. Citations from this article, here and below, are from (Einstein 1954, p. 318). Notice that Einstein refers to EPR as a "paradox." This term occurs first in Einstein's letter to Schrödinger on August 8, 1935, and Schrödinger picks it up in his response on August 19 (when Schrödinger refers to "die Antinomie oder das Paradoxen"). Einstein often described EPR as involving a paradox, including his reference to it in his "Reply to Criticisms" (Schilpp 1949, p. 681). In discussing the history of EPR, however, Jammer writes, "The authors never regarded their thesis as a 'paradox'. . . . It was later referred to as a paradox. . .[presumably by others–AF]. . . . Schrödinger called it, probably for the first time, a paradox" (Jammer 1974, p. 186). Jammer then suggests in a footnote that Schrödinger had a predilection for using the word. Perhaps Jammer thinks the same true of Rosenfeld, whose report of a clear precursor to EPR, as Jammer points out, has *Einstein* asking whether it isn't "very paradoxical" (Jammer 1974, p. 173). For some reason, A. Pais in his important study of Einstein follows Jammer in shying away from applying the term "paradox" to EPR (Pais 1982, p. 456), and echoes of the same reluctance can even be found in Bell's discussion (Bell 1981, p. 45). I just want to make it clear that the terminology of "paradox" was Einstein's own, and that he, at any rate, had no scruples about applying it to EPR.

12. The two preceding phrases in quotation marks come from Einstein's letter to Schrödinger of June 19, 1935. The other quotes in this paragraph are from the 1936 article.

the ψ function cannot be interpreted as a (complete) description of a physical state of a single system. Here also the coordination of the ψ function to an ensemble of systems eliminates every difficulty."

In the correspondence with Schrödinger, Einstein gives virtually the same argument for incompleteness. There, Einstein makes it plain that the only essential thing relating to the quantum formalism is that the ψ-functions that can be attributed to subsystem B (depending on the A measurement) are in general different from one another. He remarks that he couldn't care less ("ist mir *wurst*") whether these are eigenfunctions of observables.[13] Thus, and I want to emphasize this on Einstein's behalf, the essential difficulty brought out in the treatment of coupled systems does *not* have to do with a nonlocal influence on the values of observables (the eigenvalues that would correspond to the eigenstates, concerning which Einstein could not care less). It has to do, rather, with a nonlocal determination of alternative state functions. If these state functions were coordinated one-to-one with real physical states, then we should have the sort of puzzling nonlocal causality that Einstein elsewhere mocks as "telepathy," and that he clearly does not believe in.[14]

The puzzle for Einstein, then, is how to understand the state functions in a way that allows for (or better still, accounts for) their nonlocal, alternative determination. The solution, he tells us, is to make the ψ-function correspond to an ensemble of systems (and not just to one). But how is this supposed to do the trick? In his published writings, the only answer given is that in a footnote to the 1936 essay at just the point at which I quoted him earlier. It is the only public data to constrain our understanding of Einstein's ideas in this area, so I will cite it in full. He writes, "A measurement on A, for example, thus involves a transition to a narrower ensemble of systems. The latter (hence also its ψ function) depends upon the point of view according to which this reduction of the ensemble of systems is carried out."[15] Let us ask what sense we can make of this

13. Letter to Schrödinger, June 19, 1935. See chapter 3, and the connection with bijective completeness in chapter 5.

14. In his correspondence Einstein frequently mocks the quantum coupling of distant systems as telepathic. This surfaces in Schilpp (1949, p. 85) and in the biting reference there on p. 683. For a further discussion of the locality issue, and my view that the recent literature has gone off Einstein's track, see the appendix to this chapter.

15. Einstein (1954, p. 317). In a letter to George Breit on August 2, 1935, Einstein is more forthcoming than usual about the correlation of state functions with ensembles. There he compares the ψ-function to the density function in classical statistical mechanics. ("Ihre Bedeutung ist dennoch eine ähnliche wie die der Dichtefunction der klassischen statistischen Mechanik.") He does not spell out the comparison any further, and we know that here he is only speaking loosely and

if we were to take the ensemble representation idea as Einstein's. Suppose we were to measure observable A_1 on subsystem A, in the Bell situation. How do we get "a transition to a narrower ensemble"? Surely just preparing to measure A_1 cannot narrow down the ensemble E associated with the composite state function. For if it did, then our averaging operations would not involve the whole ensemble E, as required. When we do actually measure A_1 we partition E into two disjoint subensembles E^+, consisting of those systems yielding $+1$ as the measured outcome, and those systems, E^-, yielding -1 as the outcome. But the union of these (at least under ideal conditions) is once again E. So the complete measurement by itself does not narrow the ensemble. Thus if we take for "measurement" either "measurement prepared" or "measurement completed" (or both) we fail to get a faithful reading of Einstein from the idea of an ensemble representation. We do get a possible reading, however, if by "measurement" we understand "measurement completed together with a specific result" (either $+1$ or -1). For, on this reading, a "measurement" narrows down E to either E^+ or E^-. Then, when Einstein says that the narrower ensemble depends on the "point of view" according to which the reduction takes place, we must understand by "point of view" a measurement *plus* its result.

Thus the ensemble representation scheme requires us to supplement what Einstein does say by adding to his terminology of "measurements" and "point of view" the idea, which he does not mention, of also taking into account the actual specific result of a measurement. Perhaps, one might say, Einstein just forgot to mention the specific outcome, or was careless about it—or, maybe, took it for granted. But I don't think so, because if we narrow down the ensemble in this way, then what necessarily results is a subensemble that is precisely one corresponding to an eigenstate for some observable in the other system. That is, consider E^+, where A_1 has value $+1$ for each system. Corresponding to A_1 there will be some correlated observable, maybe B_1, on the B subsystem that, in the given composite state, takes a specific value (either $+1$ or -1) if and only if A_1 takes the value $+1$. The corresponding eigenstate for B_1 will be correlated to the ensemble E^+. So, where Einstein couldn't care less whether the state reduction

---

roughly. For, strictly speaking, it is $|\psi|^2$ that represents a probability density, as Einstein (of course) is well aware. Given such a rough analogy, I don't think we can actually tell whether it is precisely the technical construct of an ensemble representation that Einstein had in mind, as opposed to some other (and similar) statistical idea (such as the prism models below). Indeed, it is by no means clear that Einstein had any particular and precise analogue in mind at all. So far as I know, moreover, there is no other context in which his comparison with statistical mechanics is any more precise or detailed than in the sentence just quoted.

on one system produces an eigenstate for some observable of the other system, the ensemble representation reading cares very much—indeed that reading forces it out.

There are further indications, moreover, that the reading based on ensemble representations is too contrived. If we look at Einstein's discussion in his "Autobiographical Notes" (Schilpp 1949, p. 85), he puts in italics that the character of the state of one system depends on *what kind* of a measurement ("was *für eine Art* Messung") we make on the other system. And it is the fact that different *kinds* of measurements (e.g., position or momentum) produce nonlocal state reductions that emerges again as the center of the difficulty. If we refer back to Einstein's unpublished correspondence with Schrödinger, we find the same emphasis on kinds of measurements. In the letter of June 19, 1935, he underlines the "Separation Hypothesis" formulated as *"Now the real state of B cannot depend on what sort of measurement I undertake on A." ("Der wirkliche Zustand von B kann nun nicht devon abhängen, was für eine Messung ich an A vornehme.")* Moreover his elementary calculations in that letter made no use of specific measurement results but show rather that the quantum state reduction that interests him depends only on the observable measured (not on the value observed). A more sophisticated version of these calculations was developed by Schrödinger during the course of the correspondence and published in two articles (Schrödinger 1935a, 1936). The second article begins by describing the first as having shown that, for separated systems with measurements on one part fixing the state of the other, "the state arrived at *depends* quite decidedly on *what* measurements one chooses to take—not only on the results they yield." Thus does Schrödinger state Einstein's case. We know, moreover, from later correspondence, that Einstein regarded Schrödinger's calculations here as authoritative (Jammer 1974, p. 234).

In none of his writings, so far as I am aware, does Einstein describe the situation in terms of measurement results. In the 1935 correspondence with Schrödinger, however, he is a little more explicit about how the ensemble idea is supposed to resolve the difficulty. Let me quote him again in full:

My solution of the paradox presented in our work is this. The ψ function does not describe a state of *one* system, rather (statistically) an ensemble of systems. For a given ψ_1 a linear combination $c_1\psi_1 + c_2\psi_2$ signifies an *expansion* of the *totality* of systems. In our example of the system composed of two parts A, B, the change that the ψ function suffers if I make an observation on A signifies, conversely, the reduction to a subensemble from the whole ensemble; the reduction simply occurs in accord with a variety of points of view, each depending on the *choice* of the quantity that I measure on A. The result is then an ensemble for B, that likewise depends on this choice.[16]

What Einstein plainly says is that the ensemble for B depends on the choice of which quantity I measure on A. This is, plainly, what "point of view" means here and in the 1936 footnote. He does not say that the reduced ensemble depends on the particular value that the measurement subsequently turns up. I think there would be no difficulty in understanding him to mean what he does say if the ensemble representation idea did not require a different interpretation.

3. Prisms

I have been trying to argue that just as the scheme of ensemble representations is inconsistent with the quantum theory for coupled systems, so too it is inconsistent with the text that Einstein provides concerning how to resolve the difficulties that *he* has with coupled systems. What Einstein says he requires is a correspondence between state functions and ensembles of systems that, in the case of coupled systems, makes the reduction to a narrower ensemble depend on the choice of which kind of observable we measure on one subsystem (e.g., position, or spin—along a particular axis.)[17] Moreover, the resultant narrow ensemble should not necessarily be one that corresponds to the eigenstate of some observable. Is there some kind of statistical model that can satisfy these requirements

16. From the letter to Schrödinger of August 8, 1935:

Meine Lösung des in unserer Arbeit gegebenen Paradoxons ist so: Die ψ Funktion beschreibt nicht einen Zustand *eines* Systems sondern (statistisch) ein Ensemble von Systemen. Gegenüber einem ψ_1 bedeutet eine lineare Combination $c_1 \psi_1 + c_2 \psi_2$ eine *Erweiterung* der System*gesamtheit*. Die Aenderung, welche die aus zwei Teilen A, B bestehenden Systems die ψ Funktion erleidet, wenn ich an A eine Beobachtung mache, bedeutet umgekert die Herauslösung einer Teilgesamtheit aus dem ganzen Ensemble. Die Herauslösung findet einfach nach einem verschiedenen Gesichtspunkte statt, je nach der *Wahl* der Grössen, welche ich an A messe. Resultat ist dann ein Ensemble für B, das ebenfalls von dieser Wahl abhängt.

17. Is it correct to take Einstein's reflections on coupled systems as applying to correlated spin systems? L. Ballentine (1974) suggested that maybe not. While the original EPR paper is pointed primarily toward position and linear momentum correlations, the 1936 version is generic, not mentioning any specific observables. This is true of the version discussed in the correspondence with Schrödinger and of later presentations, including those in the Schilpp volume (1949, pp. 85, 681). The adaptation of EPR for spin correlations was worked out in the textbook written by David Bohm (1951). In recommending Bohm to Nathan Rosen, Einstein wrote, "I know Bohm as a scientist from his excellent book about quantum theory . . ." (letter of March 11, 1954). Unfortunately Einstein does not discuss Bohm's version with Rosen, one of the coauthors of EPR. But it seems likely that Einstein knew of it, and he certainly expresses no reservations—e.g., in his longish correspondence with Bohm.

and, if so, is *it* consistent with quantum theory? I think the answer to both questions is "yes."

Let's return to the simple Bell situation where we get an inconsistency with quantum theory for some particular composite state ψ over the statistics of four bivalent observables. Let us make ψ correspond to an ensemble E of systems, just as Einstein suggests. If we now choose to measure A_1 on subsystem A, let us suppose that this choice narrows down E to some subset E_1. How so? Well, one way is to suppose that not all the systems in E are suitable for having an A_1 measurement performed on them, and that this is not an accidental affair but is somehow physically built into the systems. Let's call such systems A_1-*defective*. Similarly, for each of the other three observables there will also be defective systems. Then choosing to measure a particular observable automatically narrows down the whole ensemble E to a subensemble consisting of those systems that are not defective for the chosen observable. With respect to such a subensemble, say E_1, we will suppose that the observable A_1 is treated just as in an ensemble representation, that is, that on systems in E_1 the observable A_1 takes on values (the very ones that measurement would reveal), and that the statistics are derived by averaging over E_1 (and *not* over all of E). If I choose to measure, simultaneously, A_1 on subsystem A and B_2 on subsystem B, then I narrow down the original ensemble E to the intersection $(E_1 \cap E_2)$ of the non-A_1-defectives with the non-B_2-defectives. The statistics for such compound experiments are derived, as in an ensemble representation, from averaging over this intersection.

Elsewhere I have called statistical models built up as above, "prism models," for they derive from the idea that there is a whole spectrum of ensemble representations associated with a given state function, not just one. I have also shown how various different prism models can reproduce the quantum statistics, even in the tangled cases where Bell's theorem holds. There is, therefore, no question of the consistency of prism models, at least in principle, with the quantum theory. (See Fine 1981b, 1982c, and 1982d.) It only recently occurred to me, in rereading the remarks of Einstein concerning coupled systems, that the conceptual workings of a prism model exactly fit Einstein's prescription for what the coordination of state functions with ensembles is supposed to do.

We have seen that to be so already concerning how the preparation of a measurement (without added reference to its outcome) automatically narrows down the ensemble. What of the idea that the reduced ensemble need not be one that corresponds to an eigenstate? For instance if we choose A_1 to measure, then need E_1

(its nondefectives) correspond to some eigenstate of an observable on the B system? This is asking whether the value of some observable defined on B is constant for every system in E_1. There is certainly no reason why this should be so, for there is even no reason why *all* the systems in E_1 must be nondefective for some one B observable. The same flexibility arises for the question of joint distributions for incompatible observables. For, unlike the situation in an ensemble representation, nothing in the concept of a prism model forces incompatible observables to have well-defined joint distributions. The models I have constructed for the puzzling Bell cases do not allow for such joint distributions. But in other cases, where quantum theory is not actually inconsistent with the interpolation of joint distributions, the prism models could readily accommodate them.

It seems to me, therefore, that we have excellent reasons to challenge the received opinion that Bell's theorem rules out Einstein's statistical interpretation. For the interpretation that it rules out, the idea of an ensemble representation, can only be attributed to Einstein on the basis of a contrived interpretive dance. There is, moreover, another interpretation, the idea of a prism model, that does seem to fit Einstein's various remarks snugly, and that is not subject to the Bell theorem.

4. Einstein's Attitude

I mentioned at the outset that Einstein calls our attention to several applications where the incompleteness of the quantum theory is supposed to show itself, and where his idea of the coordination of ensembles of systems to state functions is supposed naturally to fit the application. Apart from correlated composite systems, which we have just treated, there are two other, generic examples. These are both discussed in Einstein's "Reply to Criticism" in Schilpp (1949).[18] The first, and "microscopic" example, concerns the phenomenon of penetration of a potential barrier.

It is fascinating that Einstein chooses just this example, for it was one of the cases urged by Schrödinger (in 1935) against Einstein's ensemble idea (Schrödinger 1935b; see note 3). In 1940 Einstein used this same example to affirm the formulation of the Born interpretation, where the quantum probabilities are read as the probabilities for measurement outcomes. Speaking of the state functions and the Born interpretation, he writes, "They serve only

18. The discussion and citations below are all taken from Schilpp (1949, pp. 667–71) unless otherwise indicated.

to make statistical statements and predictions of the results of all measurements which we can carry out upon the system. . . . The aim of the theory is to determine the probability of the results of measurement upon a system at a given time." (Einstein 1940, p. 491; also in Einstein 1954, pp. 332–33). Notice how carefully Einstein treats the probabilities as those for measurement outcomes, not for premeasurement values. Like most physicists, he was not always so careful in his formulations. He certainly appreciated, however, that this was how the probabilities of the theory were to be understood, an understanding that presumably should be reflected in his ensemble interpretation.

In 1949 he returned to the example of a potential barrier, this time to motivate the ensemble idea. Here the question becomes, "At what instant of time does the emitted particle cross the potential barrier?" The difficulty, it appears, is that the event of crossing the potential barrier corresponds to a sharp change of energy. Hence, according to the time/energy uncertainty relations, if we are in a position to observe the change of energy (here linked to the decay of an atom), then we cannot narrow down the time. Einstein seems perfectly open to accepting that the time of decay is not determinable. But, he asks, can't we postulate it as, nevertheless, real? If we do, "the ψ-function [associated with the emitted particle] is to be taken as the description, not of a single system, but of an ideal ensemble of systems" (Schilpp 1949, p. 688). So here, again, is the same brief phrase and, again, the details are left as an exercise.

Well, if it is prism models that we have in mind, the exercise is easy. The state function corresponds to an ensemble of emitted particles, some defective for observing decay times and some defective for observing decay (i.e., change of energy). If we take the time/energy uncertainty formulas as ruling out the joint determination of decay *and* decay time, then these two subensembles of defectives are complementary and jointly make up the whole ensemble. The statistics for measurement outcomes are obtained by averaging over the subensemble of nondefectives for the particular measurement. And the probability formulas are correctly read as probabilities for measurement outcomes. Moreover, an "underlying reality" of decay times can be postulated for every emitted particle, although not all of these will be—as Einstein concedes to his opponent—"empirically determinable." Prisms, then, seem to provide a perfect fit to Einstein's ideas. Ensemble representations, by contrast, would pinch. For they fail to provide a setting for understanding why, in certain situations, the decay times are not determinable nor why the probabilistic formulas ought to be read as referring to measurement outcomes (rather than premeasurement values). The ensemble representations suggest no basis for the uncertainty formulas, nor the general impossibility of verifying continuous energy/time distributions.

I turn now to the third, and last, of Einstein's generic examples to illustrate the incompleteness of quantum theory. It is, simply, a successor to the previous example, but contrived to eliminate the necessity for postulating something real. Recall, incompleteness is the idea that the quantum story is not the whole story. In the example of radioactive decay, Einstein postulates that something more *could be* true—there could be actual decay times. But, of course, in the realm of the microscopic we can't say for sure. If, however, the "something more" were macroscopic, then indeed we might have no doubt that what quantum theory says is only part of what is actually the case. Einstein's idea, then, is to take the features present in the microscopic example and amplify them up to macroscopic dimensions, for there we already have accepted criteria for judging what is the case.

This is, I think, a beautiful and clever idea. We find it, first, in the correspondence with Schrödinger in 1935. There Einstein develops an example of amplification, very similar to Schrödinger's cat, and uses it to motivate the idea of incompleteness. There too the difficulties involved in taking the ψ-function as giving a complete description (for example, of a smeared out, half alive and half dead cat) are supposed to be resolved "if one views the quantum-mechanical description as the description of ensembles of systems."[19] Since the different particular examples are structurally the same, I will discuss the better-known Schrödinger's cat example, rather than any of Einstein's own. The question once more is, "How do we apply the ensemble idea to resolve the paradox?"

In the final state ψ of the cat-in-the-box system, before we observe whether the cat is alive, the "cat-alive" and "cat-dead" eigenstates are components of a giant tensor product that does not factor in such a way as to enable one to pull out these particular eigenstates. In such a superposition of micro-observables the orthodox rendition of quantum theory is silent concerning the actual values of the observables. Einstein's clever idea is to throw in some macro-

---

19. Schilpp (1949, p. 671). The amplification idea is described by Einstein in his letter of August 8, 1935. There the macroscopic event is an explosion of gunpowder. After receiving this letter Schrödinger responded (August 19, 1935) that he had constructed a "very similar" example, and went on to give a version of the well-known cat example that he later published (Schrödinger 1935b, section 5). See chapter 5.

observables. Whereas the quantum theory likewise remains silent concerning these macro-observables, in real life we do not. Even before we look, either the cat is alive or it is dead. This is, essentially, Einstein's argument here for incompleteness.[20] If we construct a prism model for the cat experiment, we will make the final (preobservation) state ψ correspond to an ensemble of cats-in-boxes. Since the concept of "being alive," like most middle-sized-object concepts, is vague, there will be in our ensemble some borderline cases. Count these as the defectives for the observation of "cat-alive." Then if half of the remaining cats are alive and half are dead, we easily replicate the quantum statistics for the experiment. The act of just looking, then, reduces the ensemble simply by eliminating the borderline cases. Looking and finding a live cat reduces it further, indeed to an ensemble corresponding to a "live cat" eigenstate. A second check on that ensemble would reveal only live cats (well, assuming they don't die off too quickly), just as the "infamous" projection postulate of quantum mechanics demands.

I don't claim here some special virtue for the prism models over an ensemble representation. It is nice that we can build in the realistic ideas of vagueness and borderline cases, but I certainly do not claim that this relates to any expressed ideas of Einstein. Indeed in the realm of macroscopic applications, the idea of an ensemble representation seems quite workable. The devices of prisms, I think, are only required when one treats incompatible observables and, hence, are probably not required for macro-observables. Overall, however, I think that the concept of a prism model fits the whole range of Einstein's ideas much more readily than does the concept of an ensemble representation. It seems to resolve the various difficulties that Einstein calls attention to and in just the way that his brief remarks suggest. Moreover, it avoids the deep difficulties brought out by Bell.

5. Hidden Variables

But wouldn't the prism idea, one might ask, be too cheap, too easy for someone like Einstein? And isn't it, anyway, a bit mysterious and very much pointless? For what good is it? That is, how does it really contribute to our understanding of nature to suppose that quantum systems have built-in properties that predetermine their suitability for measurements, generically conceived?

20. An elegant and brief version of this argument is in the letter to Born of September 15, 1950 (Born 1971, p. 188; see also pp. 214–15.)

These are good questions, and I agree with the negative judgment implicit in them; and so, I believe, would Einstein. For the prism models, just as ensemble representations, are a kind of hidden variables theory. Of course the terminology "hidden variables" is, as Bell (1981, p. 7) says, a piece of "historical silliness" since there need be nothing "hidden" about the added determining factors. But the idea of hidden variables is not silly at all. It is just the idea that, generally, one can try to ground probabilistic assertions by treating them as averages over a domain more complex in structure than is their original home. This is a well-explored scientific program and it has been highly successful in many different domains. The statistician's concept of "latent structure" is one version of it, as is the frequently successful attempt to explain certain correlations as the result of common background causes. The strategy of the program, to use Einstein's terminology, is to treat probabilistic assertions as incomplete descriptions and then to try to supplement the physical variables involved in those assertions by adding further, also physical, factors. This is what Einstein thought of as providing a completion by adding to the theory from within. It is exactly what is suggested by his own various brief remarks about treating the state function as corresponding to an ensemble of systems.

This suggestion, that his remarks about ensembles constitute a kind of hidden variables theory, was actually put to Einstein in a letter from Aron Kupperman (November 10, 1954). In his reply Einstein does not deny the connection but rather downplays its significance by writing as follows, "I think it is not possible to get rid of the statistical character of the present quantum theory by merely adding something to the latter, without changing the fundamental concepts about the whole structure" (letter of November 14, 1954; from the English draft).

If Einstein's remarks about ensembles are brief and unexplored, perhaps that is because his feeling for physics led him to believe that programs for completing quantum theory by adding to it from within were, indeed, too cheap, and were not likely to yield real insight into nature. This is the attitude Einstein expressed to Born concerning the Bohm and the de Broglie hidden variables theories (Born 1971, p. 192). He felt that in fact quantum theory "is the most complete theory consistent with experience as long as one takes as fundamental for the description the concepts of material point and potential energy" (Einstein 1953a, p. 6). In his "Autobiographical Notes" he writes,

It is my opinion that the contemporary quantum theory by means of
certain definitely laid down basic concepts, which on the whole have
been taken over from classical mechanics, constitutes an optimal formulation of the connections. I believe, however, that this theory offers no
useful point of departure for future developments. (Schilpp 1949, p.
87)

Given those beliefs, of course, Einstein was not likely to show very
much detailed interest in the machinery of hidden variables theories, not even when couched in his own languages of states corresponding to ensembles. In his view, quantum theory was dealing
with the wrong concepts (the classical dynamical concepts, plus a
few others, including that of a point-particle), so no program of
adding certain factors on to these would be likely to be any better.
Rather, he felt that one had to try to build a complete theory from
the outside; that is, by formulating new concepts and a new theoretical framework from which the correct statistical predictions of
quantum theory could be derived under special assumptions (or as
a limiting case). That was Einstein's program for how to complete
quantum theory and how to understand why the statistics of quantum theory worked as well as they do. Such understanding was
certainly not supposed to derive from the details of any "statistical
interpretation." As he wrote to Born in 1953, "I do not believe,
however, that this concept ['the interpretation of the ψ-function as
relating to an ensemble'], though consistent in itself, is here to stay"
(Born 1971, p. 209).

I believe that the most important function of the ensemble idea
for Einstein was simply to provide a setting for his doctrine of the
quantum theory's incompleteness. Einstein chose his rhetoric cun-
ningly. For who, learning that a theory is incomplete, could resist
the idea that one ought to try to complete it? Recall the closing
invocation of EPR, their belief that a complete theory is possible.
And listen to Einstein's call to his critics when he says, "For if the
statistical quantum theory does not pretend to describe the individual system . . . completely, it appears unavoidable to look elsewhere for a complete description" (Schilpp 1949, p. 672). Surely
the rhetoric had a bite to it. For part of the passion with which
Bohr and his followers defended the honor of quantum mechanics
as a *complete* theory seems to derive from their own sense of the
temptation to heed Einstein's call.

Einstein's rhetorical call for a complete theory has, however,
suffered an ironic fate. First, contrary to his intentions, it has been
taken as the call to build a completion from within; that is, as a call
for a hidden variables theory. Then, his scant remarks on ensembles

have been fashioned into the technical idea of an ensemble representation, set out as paradigmatic of that sort of completion. Finally, since the silly terminology of "hidden variables" conveys the idea of something physically sterile, Einstein has been criticized for the sterility of his ideas about completing the theory; and then, for good measure, he is supposed to have been refuted! Of course Einstein *wanted* his purely *interpretive* scheme to appear heuristically sterile, for he wanted us to be motivated to move outside the theory in order to explain why the theory (and the scheme) work so well. Perhaps my prism models will satisfy those intentions and perhaps, too, they will stave off refutations, at least for a while. In any case I think Einstein would not be surprised to find himself rather the victim of his own rhetoric. For, as he wrote to Schrödinger, "hardly any of the fellows . . . can get out of the network of already accepted concepts, instead, comically, they only wriggle about inside."[21]

Appendix (Locality)

Since the idea of "locality" is usually associated with the Bell theorem and since I have not featured it in this presentation, I thought I would add some remarks on how the locality discussed in the Bell literature relates to Einstein's ideas on locality, in the context of the EPR example.

I find two formulations of locality that relate to Bell. One is the intuitive physical idea that I shall call *Bell-locality: the outcomes of the measurements of certain quantum-mechanical observables on one system are not immediately influenced by the kinds of measurements directly made on a second system, which is sufficiently spatially separated from the first.* (This intuitive principle also has a statistical rendition, where "outcomes" is replaced by "probabilities for outcomes." What I have to say about the nonstatistical principle, one can readily see, applies to the other as well.) The second formulation is mathematical. It is the condition that I elsewhere refer to as *factorizability* (Fine 1981b). Other terms in use are "locality" and "conditional stochastic independence." Roughly speaking, it is the requirement that for each coupled system (or, for each "hidden variable") in a correlation experiment with separated parts, the probability for a simultaneous pair of outcomes can be expressed as the product of the probability for each outcome separately. Factorizability is built into the construct of an ensemble representation; indeed, these are equivalent notions in the sense that there is a factorizable (stochastic) hidden variables

21. Letter to Schrödinger (August 8, 1935): "Fast alle die Kerle . . . können aus dem einmal angenommenen Begriffsnetz nicht heraus sondern nur possierlich darin herumzappeln."

theory if and only if there is an ensemble representation (Fine 1982a). Factorizability fails for the prism models because not all joint probabilities there would be defined for each coupled system (or, for each hidden variable), so the condition just does not make sense. But Bell-locality holds for the prism models; they involve no outcome-fixing action-at-a-distance, for all the defined outcomes are locally fixed at the source in advance of any measurement arrangements. In general, factorizability has been offered as a mathematical expression of Bell-locality. The prism models demonstrate that is not correct. In particular, the failure of factorizability need not imply the failure of Bell-locality—as the prism models show. The results of the Bell theorem depend on factorizability. It follows that the Bell theorem does not imply the failure of Bell-locality. It is very striking that the literature contains virtually no sustained argument connecting factorizability and Bell-locality. For example, in a presentation of the subject that beautifully motivates all the other apparatus needed for the Bell theorem, John Bell finds only this to say about the mathematical condition on which it all hangs, "It seems reasonable to expect that if sufficiently many causal factors can be identified and held fixed, the *residual* fluctuations will be independent, i.e., . . . [there follows the formula expressing factorizability]" (Bell 1981, p. 55).[22] Thus with no more careful attention than a casual "it seems reasonable to expect" Bell suggests that Einstein's twenty years of reflections on locality in the EPR-type situation would be shaken (Bell 1981, p. 52). But even if factorizability did have something to do with Bell-locality, does the latter principle have to do with Einstein? I think there are good grounds for reservations here.

Einstein's several reworkings of the EPR situation certainly involve a locality principle. It is this:

Einstein-locality. The real, physical state of one system is not immediately influenced by the kinds of measurements directly made on a second system, which is sufficiently spatially separated from the first.

22. I discuss some of the arguments for factorizability in my (1981b). The most sustained version is that by Shimony (1981) in his response. As my text and footnotes indicate there, I do not find Shimony's argument sound. I think it is circular, *using* the very physical interpretation of stochastic independence that it is supposed to be arguing for. Similar problems seem to persist in the more recent version given by Shimony (1984). There Shimony reduces his claim from the truth of factorizability (under the stated conditions) to its merely being "reasonable." But I think the careful reader will find, as I do, that this conclusion scarcely "follows"—and for the same reasons I have already discussed. Other reservations about factorizability are expressed by Hellman (1982). See note 23, chapter 9.

I think my citations in the paper establish this formulation as Einstein's. It differs from Bell's just over what it is that is not supposed to be influenced at a distance. For Bell it is the outcomes of the measurement of certain quantum observables (like spin). For Einstein it is the "real, physical states." In his various writings Einstein says even less about the nature of these postulated real states than he says about his ensemble interpretation, and for good reason. He was urging others, and struggling himself, to build a new theory that would "discover" these states, i.e., invent them. Whatever these states are, they would indeed (in Einstein's conception, at least) determine the real physical variables and, most likely, the outcomes of measurements of *these*. But Einstein is very clear that, in his opinion, the quantum mechanical variables (the "observables") are the wrong ones. They are not the real physical variables, and that is why it is hopeless to try to complete quantum theory from within. Since these quantum variables are not real (i.e., do not correspond to the real properties of the object) there is no special reason to worry over nonlocal influences on measurement outcomes for *them*. (For all we know, Einstein might say, even a "nonlocal influence" on the measurement outcomes of the quantum observables might be merely apparent from the perspective of the fundamental theory. The "real situation" in such a case might well be describable in purely local terms.[23])

Thus I think that we cannot count Bell-locality as a formulation of Einstein's ideas, for Bell-locality might fail and yet Einstein-locality could well be true. After all, Einstein-locality is just the central ingredient in Einstein's idea that we might yet find a theory more fundamental than quantum theory, one where no real things are immediately influenced at a distance, and from which the quantum theory would emerge as some kind of limiting case. Surely no one supposes that a result like Bell's theorem could actually refute such a vision. Indeed, from this perspective, Einstein might have welcomed Bell's theorem and turned it to his own advantage. For Bell's theorem shows that a certain plausible scheme (the scheme of an ensemble representation), when applied to measurement outcomes associated with the quantum observables, cannot actually accommodate all the results of the theory. This goes some way to vindicating Einstein's nose, his intuition that we ought to *give up* the concepts of quantum theory (and that means not take its mea-

---

23. This is just the way that Einstein hedges over whether the quantum phenomena are really (or only "apparently") discontinuous (Schilpp 1949, p. 85).

surement procedures as indicative of "the real stuff") if we want to be successful in completing it.

Inserting a wedge between Bell- and Einstein-locality depends on not taking measured values of the quantum observables as corresponding to real features of the objects. Although there is substantial textual evidence for this position in Einstein's writings, there is also one important bit of material to the contrary. This is the famous "criterion of reality" from the EPR paper: "If, without in any way disturbing a system, we can predict with certainty (i.e., with probability equal to unity) the value of a physical quantity, then there exists an element of physical reality corresponding to this physical quantity" (EPR 1935, p. 777). If we apply this to correlated systems after we have measured an observable on one system and found a certain value, then we can indeed predict the outcome of a measurement of the correlated observable on the second system, and the criterion would lead us to count that outcome as indicative of an "element of reality." While I do not believe that Podolsky simply invented this criterion while drafting the paper, I also do not believe it can have been a principle that Einstein put much stock by. For it never appears in any of his own published expositions of the EPR situation, not those in the same time frame as the article nor those later on. The nearest he comes to an expression of the principle is where he writes, "It follows that every statement about S_2 which we arrive at as a result of a complete measurement of S_1 has to be valid for the system S_2, even if no measurement whatsoever is carried out on S_1" (Einstein 1948, p. 323; as translated in Born 1971, p. 172). If "statement" here were "statement about the value of an observable," then we should nearly have the reality criterion. In context, however, the "it follows" refers back to the preceding sentence where Einstein expresses *his* conception of locality; namely, that distant measurements "can have no direct influence on the physical reality in a remote part R_2 of space." Thus the statements about S_2, mentioned above, are not about values of observables in general but rather are limited to statements about "physical reality," or "real states of affairs." Only this reading makes cogent Einstein's subsequent inference to "different real states of affairs for S_2." Thus the quoted remark is not a version of the EPR criterion, but rather an expression of Einstein-locality.

Perhaps that reality criterion involves some ideas that Einstein toyed with but then thought better of following Bohr's critique of it (Bohr 1935). Certainly in his correspondence with Schrödinger in 1935 Einstein does express his feeling that one cannot get around

Bohr's positivist position with assuming some principle relating to elements of reality. But the principle he articulates there is the "Separation Hypothesis" I quoted above in section 2, a version of what I have called Einstein-locality, and not a principle that tells you when any–old theory has succeeded in referring to something real. It seem clear enough that the reality criterion of EPR need only be valid for "the correct" theory. In any case, Einstein drops the criterion and I think it would be a mistake to take it in support of anything but a temporary position of his. I do not think it provides a sufficient basis for us to swear Einstein's allegiance to Bell's locality.[24]

To sum up. Einstein's locality does not imply Bell's, and Bell-locality does not imply factorizability. But factorizability (or some equivalent) is what is required in order to contradict quantum theory via the Bell theorem. If follows that the difficulties brought out by Bell's theorem are at least two giant steps removed from reaching Einstein's ideas on locality, or *his* vision for a more complete theory.

24. In looking for references to the criterion of reality among Einstein's unpublished material, the one and only place I have found where he makes use of something similar is in the letter to Tanya Ehrenfest on October 12, 1938. There he writes, "Here, however, I can [not (omitted in the text)] reconcile myself to the following, that a manipulation undertaken on A has an influence on B; thus I see myself required to suppose, as actually or physically realized at B, everything relating to measurement outcomes on B that can be predicted with certainty, on the basis of some measurement or other undertaken on A." ("Da ich mich aber dazu entschliessen kann, dass eine an A vorgenommen Manipulation auf B einen Einfluss habe, so sehe ich mich genötigt, alles an B wirklich bezw. physikalisch realisiert anzunehmen was auf Grund irgendwelcher an A vorgenommener Messung mit Sicherheit bezüglich Messungsergebnissen an B vorausgesagt werden kann.") Here, unlike my suggestion in the appendix, Einstein does not derive something like Bell-locality from something like the criterion of reality, but rather the derivation goes the other way around. It is the reality criterion that is derived. The locality principle that Einstein derives it from is rather loosely formulated; it is missing a "not," and the "influence on B" is not qualified by "instantaneous" nor restricted to an influence on "real features" (or the like) of B. If it were made more precise in these ways, as Einstein usually does, then the criterion of reality would no longer follow. Perhaps, then, in a more careful setting, Einstein saw that the reality criterion was not a consequence of the locality over real states of affairs to which he actually subscribed and, perhaps for this reason, he dropped that EPR criterion from his subsequent writings on the topic. In any case, he does seem to drop it.

Schrödinger's Cat and Einstein's: The Genesis of a Paradox

The issue of *Die Naturwissenschaften* for November 29, 1935, contains the first of three installments of a lengthy, semitechnical review article by Erwin Schrödinger (1935b), consisting of fifteen sections in all and entitled "The current situation in quantum mechanics" (*"Die gegenwärtige Situation in der Quantenmechanik"*). The quantum mechanical state function (or ψ-function) is first mentioned in the fifth (and last) section of this initial installment, although it is only discussed and explained (as a "catalogue" of expected measurement results) in the seventh section of the next installment (that of December 6). Schrödinger brings it up in section 5, however, because there he wants to consider the question of how to understand the quantum observables ("variables") in states where they do not have sharp values (i.e., noneigenstates). This fifth section is entitled "Are the variables really fuzzy?" (*"Sind die Variablen wirkliche verwaschen?"*) And Schrödinger wants to answer "No," that although the idea of treating the observables in noneigenstates as referring to a fuzzy or blurred state of affairs is attractive, it is ultimately untenable. He feels it appropriate to raise this issue in terms of the ψ-function since that, he says, is a conceptual device (*Gedankending*) which enables one to portray the fuzziness (*Verwaschenheit*) of all the observables at every moment. So Schrödinger asks whether we should think of the ψ-function as specifying a fuzzy reality for the quantum observables in a way comparable to how a classical state can be thought of as specifying numerically sharp values for all the classical observables. To guard against this idea Schrödinger cites the example of the decay of α-particles from a nucleus. If we confine the domain of fuzziness, so to speak, to the region of the nucleus, then we might, for instance, think of the actual time of decay as well as the direction of emission of the α-particles as somehow blurred. But this picture breaks down if we try locating the emitted particles either by registering them on a surrounding scintillation screen or by "tracking" them using an ionizing gas. The difficulty Schrödinger tries to emphasize is this. By means of ionization or scintillation screens we seem to be able to amplify the presumed microscopic fuzziness into a macroscopic one, and then to make that disappear, as it were, in a flash. To drive home these paradoxical features Schrödinger concludes this section as follows.[1]

One can even make up quite ludicrous examples. A cat is enclosed in a steel chamber, together with the following infernal machine (which one must secure against the cat's direct reach): in the tube of a Geigercounter there is a tiny amount of radioactive material, *so* small that although one of its atoms *might* decay in the course of an hour, it is just as probable that none will. If decay occurs the counter tube fires and, by means of a relay, sets a little hammer into motion that shatters a small bottle of prussic acid. When the entire system has been left alone for an hour one would say that the cat is still alive *provided* no atom has decayed in the meantime. The first atomic decay would have poisoned it. The ψ-function of the total system would yield an expression for all this in which, in equal measure, the living and the dead cat are (*sit venia verbo*[2]) blended or smeared out.

The characteristic of these examples is that an indefiniteness originally limited to atomic dimensions gets transformed into gross macroscopic indefiniteness, which can then be *reduced* by direct observation. This prevents us from continuing naively to give credence to a "fuzzy model" as a picture of reality.

1. Schrödinger (1935b), p. 812:

Man kann auch ganz burleske Fälle konstruieren. Eine Katze wird in eine Stahlkammer gesperrt, zusammen mit folgender Höllenmaschine (die man gegen den direkten Zugriff der Katze sichern muss): in einem GEIGERschen Zählrohr befindet sich eine winzige Menge radioaktiver Substanz, *so* wenig, dass im Lauf einer Stunde *vielleicht* eines von den Atomen zerfällt, ebenso wahrscheinlich aber auch *keines*; geschieht es, so spricht das Zählrohr an und betätigt über ein Relais ein Hämmerchen, das ein Kölbchen mit Blausäure zertrümmert. Hat man dieses ganze System eine Stunde lang sich selbst überlassen, so wird man sich sagen, dass die Katze noch lebt, *wenn* inzwischen kein Atom zerfallen ist. Der erste Atomzerfall würde sie vergiftet haben. Die ψ-Funktion des ganzen Systems würde das so zum Ausdruck bringen, dass in ihr die lebende und die tote Katze (s.v.v.) zu gleichen Teilen gemischt oder verschmiert sind.

Das Typische an diesen Fällen ist, dass eine ursprünglich auf den Atombereich beschränkte Unbestimmtheit sich in grobsinnliche Unbestimmtheit umsetzt, die sich dann durch direkte Beobachtung *entscheiden* lässt. Das hindert uns, in so naiver Weise ein "verwaschenes Modell" als Abbild der Wirklichkeit gelten zu lassen. An sich enthielte es nichts Unklares oder Widerspruchsvolles. Es ist ein Unterschied zwischen einer verwackelten oder unscharf eingestellten Photographie und einer Aufnahme von Wolken und Nebelschwaden.

2. "Pardon the expression."

Schrödinger finishes by observing, "In itself this [fuzzy model] contains nothing unclear or contradictory." For, he notes, "There is a difference between a blurred or out-of-focus picture and a photograph of clouds and patches of fog."

The long passage just quoted, of course, is the original version of Schrödinger's famous cat paradox. This thought experiment is rivaled only by that of EPR in its impact on discussions of the conceptual foundations of quantum mechanics, and, like EPR, it too has recently moved beyond this specialized context to become a subject of popular imagination.[3] Even the structure of the two imagined experiments are similar insofar as they both concern problems over coupled systems, focusing on the situation of one subsystem (respectively, the unmeasured one, or the cat) after its physical interaction with the other subsystem has effectively ceased. In a footnote to section 12 in the third and final installment of his *Naturwissenschaften* article, Schrödinger points to a possible historical connection as well when he writes, "The appearance of this work [EPR] provided the impetus for the present—shall I say report or general confession?"[4] It turns out, in fact, that the historical connection between EPR and "Schrödinger's cat" is both deep and interesting, for the cat has its origins in the correspondence between Einstein and Schrödinger that was generated by the publication of EPR.

During the summer of 1935 Schrödinger was in residence at Oxford, while Einstein was spending the summer at Old Lyme, Connecticut. The Einstein, Rosen, and Podolsky (EPR) paper, as noted in chapter 3, came out in the May 15, 1935, issue of *The Physical Review.* Schrödinger wrote about it to Einstein on June 7, and his part of the correspondence continued with letters to Einstein on July 13, August 19, and October 4. Before receiving the letter of June 7, Einstein had written to Schrödinger on June 17 and then wrote again, responsively, on June 19, August 8, and September 4.

Schrödinger opens the letter of June 7 as follows:

I am very pleased that in the work that just appeared in *Physical Review* you have publicly caught the dogmatic quantum mechanics napping over those things that we used to discuss so much in Berlin. Can I say

---

3. See the three novels by Wilson (1979, 1980, 1981).
4. Schrödinger (1935b), p. 845:

Das Erscheinen dieser Arbeit gab den Anstoss zu dem vorliegenden—soll ich sagen Referat oder Generalbeichte?

something about it? It appears at first as objections, but they are only points that I would like to have formulated yet more clearly.[5]

Schrödinger continues by focusing on certain mathematical aspects of the EPR example. These have to do with the expansion of the state function of a composite system into a bilinear series of functions defined only on the component systems. He points out that the composite EPR case, after the interaction has effectively ceased, is a very exceptional one in this regard, for there all the coefficients of the bilinear expansion are identical. Schrödinger believes that the paradoxical feature of the EPR case (he calls it the "contradiction" [widerspruch]) does not depend on this exceptional identity of coefficients, but is already present in more general expansions, and he tries to outline to Einstein how this goes. In fact the preliminary analysis of the conditions for a contradiction outlined in this June 7 letter finds its way into the Naturwissenschaften article (hereafter NW) in section 11 of the final, December 13 installment. There Schrödinger (1935b, p. 844) calls attention to features of what he refers to as "entanglement" (Verschränkung); i.e., cases where after an interaction between two systems the state function of the composite system no longer factors into the product of component state functions. What is peculiar, according to Schrödinger, is that in these cases, quite generally, one can find two incompatible measurement procedures for one of the systems (corresponding to incompatible quantum observables for that system) each one of which would lead to a resolution of the entanglement by forcing out some definite state for the other system—regardless of what particular measured values actually turn up. Moreover, the states forced out for the unmeasured system would themselves be incompatible (i.e., there is no quantum probability of their joint occurrence). Thus, according to Schrödinger, what is paradoxical about EPR (to which he immediately turns in section 12 of NW) is common to various entangled systems and not just to the special EPR case.

On August 14, 1935, Schrödinger submitted an article "Discussion of Probability Relations between Separated Systems" to The Proceedings of the Cambridge Philosophical Society, where it was later

---

5. Later in the correspondence Schrödinger apologizes for his poor typing. In the interest of responsible scholarship I shall try not to improve on it here:

ich hab mich sehr gefreut, dass Du in der eben erschienenen Arbeit im Phys. Rev. die dogmatische Quantenmechanik auch öffentlich bei dem Schlafittchen erwischt hast, über das wir in Berlin schon so viel discutiert hatten. Darf ich einiges dazu sagen? Es sieht zuerst wie Einwände aus, aber es sind nur Punkte, die ich noch klarer formuliert haben möchte.

published. (I shall refer to this article as *PCPS*.) In this article
Schrödinger rigorously completes the calculations sketched in the
June 7 letter in order to show, as he puts it in *PCPS*, "that the
phenomenon in question is a quite general one; that it is the rule
and not the exception. The representative [i.e., state function] arrived at for *one* system depends on the *programme* of observations
to be taken with the other" (Schrödinger 1935a, p. 556).

The letter of June 7 concludes with Schrödinger remarking that
the difficulties brought out by EPR must have to do with the nonrelativistic character of quantum mechanics, in particular with the
fact that quantum mechanics does not take into account the finiteness of the velocity of light. Similar remarks about quantum mechanics and relativity occur in the concluding paragraphs of *NW*.
As Schrödinger (1935b, p. 848) acknowledges there, these ideas
are rather a hobbyhorse of his.

On June 17 Einstein wrote a short letter to Schrödinger mentioning the possibility of Schrödinger's appointment to the Institute
for Advanced Studies. Einstein follows this with some remarks about
problems relating to the unified field theory program, and then
closes with these characteristic and caustic words on the quantum
theory.

From the point of view of principles, I absolutely do not believe in a
statistical basis for physics in the sense of quantum mechanics, despite
the singular success of the formalism of which I am well aware. I do not
believe that such a theory can be made general relativistic. Aside from
that, I consider the renunciation of a spatio-temporal setting for real
events to be idealistic-spiritualistic. This epistemology-soaked orgy ought
to come to an end. No doubt, however, you smile at me and think that,
after all, many a young heretic turns into an old fanatic, and many a
young revolutionary becomes an old reactionary.[6]

Clearly Einstein was uncertain where Schrödinger stood, at that
point, on the quantum theory, and had not yet received his June
7 letter. Einstein wrote again just two days later, on June 19, ex-

6. Einstein to Schrödinger, June 17, 1935:

Ich glaube von prinzipiellen Standpunkt absolut nicht an eine statistiche Basis
der Physik am Sinne der Quantenmechanik, so fruchtbar sich dieser Formalis-
mus am Einzelnen auch weisst. Ich glaube nicht, dass man eine derartige
Theorie allgemein relativistisch durchführen kann. Abegesehen davon aber
finde ich der Verzicht auf eine raum-zeitliche Erfassbarkeit des Realen ideal-
istisch-spiritistisch. Diese erkenntnistheorie-getränkte Orgie wird sich anstoben
müssen. Gewiss wirst Du aber mich lächeln und denken, dass schon manche
junge Häre eine alte Betschwester und mancher junger Revolutionär ein alter
Reaktionär geworden ist.

pressing his pleasure at Schrödinger's "detailed letter." I have discussed parts of this June 19 letter in the preceding two chapters. It is the one where Einstein identifies Podolsky as the actual author of EPR and expresses his concern that the central point (*"die Hauptsache"*) got buried in Podolsky's text. Recall that Einstein uses the analogy of finding a ball after opening one of two covered boxes in order to explain the idea of completeness and to motivate the intuitive concept of local causality (his "separation principle"). It is in the context of this ball-in-the-box analogy, I believe, that Schrödinger's cat begins. It has to do with the idea of completeness, concerning which Einstein writes this:

Now I describe a state of affairs as follows: *The probability is ¹/₂ that the ball is in the first box.* Is this a complete description?
NO: A complete statement is: the ball *is* (or is not) in the first box. That is how the characterization of the state of affairs must appear in a complete description.
YES: Before I open them, the ball is by no means in *one* of the two boxes. Being in a definite box only comes about when I lift the covers. This is what brings about the statistical character of the world of experience, or its empirical lawfulness. Before lifting the covers the state [of the two boxes] is *completely* characterized by the number ¹/₂, whose significance as statistical findings, to be sure, is only attested to when carrying out observations. Statistics only arise because observation involves insufficiently known factors, foreign to the system being described.

We face similar alternatives when we want to explain the relation of quantum mechanics to reality. With regard to the ball-system, naturally, the second "spiritualist" or Schrödinger interpretation is absurd, and the man on the street would only take the first, "Bornian" interpretation seriously. But the Talmudic philosopher dismisses "reality" as a frightening creature of the naive mind, and declares that the two conceptions differ only in their mode of expression.[7]

7. Einstein to Schrödinger, June 19, 1935:

Nun beschreibe ich einen Zustand so: *Die Wahrscheinlichkeit dafür, dass die Kugel in der ersten Schachtel ist ist 1/2.*– Ist dies eine vollständige Beschreibung?
Nein: Eine vollständige Aussage ist: die Kugel *ist* in der ersten Schachtel (oder ist nicht). So muss also die Charakterisierung des Zustandes bei vollständiger Beschreibung aussehen.
Ja: Bevor ich den Schachteldeckel aufklappe, ist die Kugel gar nicht in *einer* der beiden Schachteln. Dies Sein in einer bestimmten Schachtel kommt erst dadurch zustande, dass ich den Deckel aufklappe. Dadurch erst kommt der statistische Charakter der Erfahrungswelt bezw. ihrer empirischen Gesetzlichkeit zustande. Der Zustand vor dem Aufklappen ist durch die Zahl 1/2 *vollständig* charakterisiert, deren Sinn sich bei Vornahme von Beobachtungen allerdings nur als statistischer Befund manifestiert. Die Statistik kommt nur dadurch zustande, dass durch die Beobachtung ungenügend bekannte, dem beschriebenen System fremde Faktoren eingeführt werden.

To get by the Talmudic philosopher Einstein introduces the separation principle, claiming that if we hold fast to this then the Schrödinger interpretation is excluded, and only the Bornian one remains. This is the argument from separation to incompleteness that I teased out and examined in chapter 3.

In this context it would certainly appear that the point of the incompleteness argument is to show the inadequacy of the following conception: there is "some kind of realization of each variable that exactly corresponds to the quantum mechanical statistics of this variable at the relevant moment." For this seems to be the general version of what would be involved if we were to take the statement, "The probability is ½ that the ball is in the first box," as a complete description of a state of affairs. The quoted general version, however, comes from the introductory paragraph of Schrödinger's *NW*, section 5.[8] Its inadequacy is precisely what the cat is supposed to demonstrate at the end. It thus appears that the cat is just what Einstein would have wanted in order to get past the Talmudic philosophers, to argue against the Schrödinger (or spiritualist) interpretation without recourse to an additional premise like separation. This, then, would be a way of avoiding the idealistic-spiritualistic setting for quantum mechanics, and of putting a stop to the epistemology-soaked orgy.

Unfortunately, the situation is not so clear-cut. To begin with there appear to be two conceptions or "interpretations" of completeness; to use Einstein's mnemonic phrases, the Bornian and the Schrödinger. According to the Bornian conception, a complete description is essentially nonprobabilistic; genuinely probabilistic assertions are necessarily incomplete. In this sense the incompleteness of the essentially statistical quantum mechanics is guaranteed without further argument, and, as discussed in chapter 4, something like Einstein's statistical interpretation might be used to ground it. What is at issue here is how one conceives of probability. The Bornian view is reductive. According to it, probabilities are

---

Vor der analogen Alternative stehen wir, wenn wir die Beziehung der Quantenmechanik zur Wirklichkeit deuten wollen. Bei dem Kugel-System ist natürlich die zweite "spiritistische" oder Schrödinger'sche Interpretation sozusagen abgeschmackt und nur die erste "Born'sche" würde der Bürger ernst nehmen. Der talmudistische Philosoph aber pfeift auf die "Wirklichkeit" als auf einen Popanz der Naivität und erklärt beide Auffassungen als nur der Ausdrucksweise nach verschieden.

8. Schrödinger (1935b), p. 811:

einer jeden Variablen eine solche Art der Verwirklichung, die genau der quantenmechanischen Statistik dieser Variablen in dem betreffenden Augenblick entspricht.

not themselves fundamental but arise as averages, or the like, over a more basic and determinate domain. By contrast, the Schrödinger view is that probabilities can be fundamental, not to be reduced to something else. Thus the Schrödinger conception is that a complete description of a state of affairs can be a probabilistic assertion, with probability less than unity, which (somehow) tells the whole truth about that state of affairs. If there were some further truth to be told, then the probabilistic assertion would be an incomplete description. Drawing on Einstein's ball-in-the-box analogy, in chapter 3, I showed how, on this Schrödinger conception, the separation principle can be used to demonstrate that quantum mechanics is incomplete. It appears from examining section 5 of *NW* that the cat grounds the same conclusion regarding incompleteness in the Schrödinger sense but nicely dispensing with the need for separation.

One way of looking at the cat, then, is to see it as addressing the central issue of Schrödinger completeness that was buried in the published text of EPR. There is, however, a further complication; namely, Einstein goes on in the letter of June 19 to suggest yet a *third* conception of completeness. He does not give it a catchy name, but it occurs at the end of the following passage, right after his discussion of the ball-in-the-box analogy.

The preceding analogy corresponds only very imperfectly to the quantum mechanical example in the paper [EPR]. It is, however, designed to make clear the point of view that is essential to me. In quantum mechanics one describes a real state of affairs of a system by means of a normed function ψ of the coordinates (of configuration space). The temporal evolution is uniquely determined by the Schrödinger equation. One would now very much like to say the following: ψ stands in a one-to-one correspondence with the real state of the real system. The statistical character of measurement outcomes is exclusively due to the measuring apparatus, or the process of measurement. If this works, I talk about a complete description of reality by the theory. However, if such an interpretation doesn't work out, then I call the theoretical description "incomplete." Right away the Talmudist quite properly declares that this stipulation is empty; however, it will soon acquire good sense.[9]

9. Einstein to Schrödinger, June 19, 1935:

Der vorstehende Vergleich entspricht dem quantentheoretischen Beispiel der Abhandlung nur sehr unvollkommen. Er ist aber geeignet, den Gesichtspunkt deutlich zu machen, der mir wesentlich ist.—Man beschreibt in der Quantentheorie einen wirklichen Zustand eines Systems durch eine normierte Funktion ψ der Koordinaten (des Konfigurationsraumes). Die zeitliche Aenderung ist durch die Schrödinger Gl. eindeutig gegeben. Man möchte nun gerne folgendes sagen: ψ ist dem wirklichen Zustand des wirklichen Systems ein-

In the letter, Einstein follows this up with a technical formulation of the argument from separation to incompleteness. This is a version of the incompleteness argument discussed in the preceding chapter (section 2) and drawn there largely from Einstein's 1936 article, "Physics and Reality." The point of the argument is to demonstrate how the state function assigned to an unmeasured system can vary immediately according to the measurement directly performed on its distant partner. If we assume that, after interaction, the unmeasured system *has* some real physical state and if we suppose the separation principle (which prohibits immediate alterations in real states of affairs unless proximately caused), then that real state of the unmeasured system will be the same whatever we do to its distant partner. But this situation conflicts with completeness as stipulated in the passage just quoted, for *that* completeness is simply the requirement of a one-to-one correspondence between real states of affairs and the assignment of quantum mechanical state functions. If we call this more technical conception *bijective completeness,* then one might well say that, just like Schrödinger completeness, the argument concerning it too got buried in the EPR original.[10]

It would be quite unfair, I think, to try to blame too much of this on Podolsky's written text. As the two long passages from the June 19 letter show, even after the publication of EPR, Einstein himself was none too careful about distinguishing the different conceptions. For while he separated off the Bornian from the Schrödinger conception of completeness, there (and elsewhere) he runs together Schödinger incompleteness with the quite different idea of bijective incompleteness, taking arguments for the latter as establishing the former.[11] It is, therefore, interesting to notice

---

eindeutig zugeordnet. Der statistische Charakter der Messergebnisse fällt ausschliesslich auf das Konto der Messapparate bezw. des Prozesses der Messung. Wenn dies geht rede ich von einer vollständigen Beschreibung der Wirklichkeit durch die Theorie. Wenn aber eine solche Interpretation nicht durchführbar ist, nenne ich die theoretische Beschreibung "unvollständig". Diese Festsetzung erklärt der Talmudist zunächst mit vollem Recht für inhaltslos; sie wird aber bald ihren guten Sinn kriegen.

10. See Einstein, Podolsky, Rosen (1935), p. 779, where they conclude (italics in the original), "Thus, *it is possible to assign two different wave functions . . . to the same reality*," but then rush on to some calculations, without drawing the conclusion about (bijective) incompleteness. Cf. note 7, chapter 3.

11. A good example of this is in Einstein (1948), whose interpretations (Ia) and (Ib) correspond, respectively, to the Bornian and Schrödinger alternatives in the June 19 letter. Einstein's argument in this article is also very similar to that of the June 19 letter, arguing from separation ("principle II") to bijective incompleteness, and then taking that conclusion as though it were about (Ib)—Schrödinger completeness.

how Schrödinger's two efforts, in *PCPS* and in *NW*, contribute to the incompleteness argument in each of these two senses. The idea of distant steering into one state or another is precisely the topic generalized in *PCPS* and it is the heart of the bijective incompleteness argument. Whereas the cat from *NW*, as we have noticed, gets us to Schrödinger incompleteness without the need for separation.

In suggesting that cat as an improved version of the EPR argument for incompleteness, I am not trying merely to make the conceptual point that the cat does, in fact, ground Schrödinger incompleteness. Rather, I want to suggest, in addition, that this is exactly what Schrödinger himself was up to in section 5 of *NW*. That is, I believe that the cat was put into *NW* in response to ideas and distinctions generated during the correspondence over EPR. This is certainly not a radical claim, since *NW* was written in tandem with that correspondence (as was PCPS), but it does, nevertheless, require some documentation.

We have seen one important item about section 5 already; namely, that the probabilistic conception which Schrödinger sets up there as problematic is the very same conception as that of Schrödinger incompleteness from Einstein's June 19 letter. Even more striking, however, is the sequence of topics from section 4 to section 5 of *NW*. Section 4 is entitled "Can the theory be based on ideal ensembles?" ("*Kann man der Theorie ideale Gesamtheiten unterlegen?*") The topic is the viability of construing the probabilities of quantum theory as arising by averaging over an ideal ensemble; that is, the viability of what I called an "ensemble representation" in the preceding chapter. As we shall see later in the correspondence, here Schrödinger takes himself to be attacking none other than Einstein's own "statistical interpretation"; i.e., the probabilistic conception that is supposed to ground the Bornian version of completeness. Thus in the June 19 letter, Einstein proceeds first from the Bornian to the Schrödinger interpretation. In sections 4 and 5 of *NW*, Schrödinger follows along in exactly the same sequence. Unlike Einstein, however, he sets out to refute them both.

Einstein's letter of June 19 closes by picking up on the concluding remarks in Schrödinger's letter of June 7, his hobbyhorse of blaming the difficulties in quantum mechanics on its neglect of the finiteness of the velocity of light. Einstein bluntly rejects the idea, and it subsequently drops out of the correspondence. But the critique of the quantum theory continues. Schrödinger wrote back on July 13:

You have made me extremely happy with your two lovely letters of June
17 and 19, and the very detailed discussion of very personal things in
the one and very impersonal things in the other. I am very grateful. But
I am happiest of all about the *Physical Review* piece itself, because it
works as well as pike in a goldfish pond and has stirred everyone
up. . . .

I am now having fun and taking your note to its source to provoke the
most diverse, clever people: London, Teller, Born, Pauli, Szilard, Weyl.
The best response so far is from Pauli who at least admits that the use
of the word "state" ["*Zustand*"] for the psi-function is quite disreputable.
What I have so far seen by way of published reactions is less witty. . . . It
is as if one person said, "It is bitter cold in Chicago"; and another answered, "That is a fallacy, it is very hot in Florida." . . .

My great difficulty in even understanding the orthodoxy over this matter has prompted me, in a lengthy piece, to make the attempt to analyze
the current interpretation situation once and for all from scratch. I do
not know yet what and whether I will publish on it, but this is always
the best way for me to make matters really clear to myself. Besides, a
few things in the present foundation strike me as very strange.[12]

We can see from this the enormously stimulating effect that EPR
had on Schrödinger. The phrase that Schrödinger uses in this July
13 letter to describe his private, lengthy analysis—"the current . . .
situation"—is, of course, the title phrase for *NW*. I think there can
be little doubt that here we see its beginnings. It is interesting,

---

12. Schrödinger to Einstein, July 13, 1935:

Du hast mir mit Deinen zwei lieben Briefen vom 17 und vom 19 Juni und der
sehr ausführlichen Discussion sehr persönlicher Dinge in dem einen und sehr
unpersönlicher Dinge in dem anderen ein grosse Freude gemacht. Hab vielen
Dank. Die allergrösste Freude aber habe ich nach wie vor über die Physical
Review Arbeit selbst, weil sie so richtig als Hecht im Karfenteich wirkt und
alle Leute aufwirbelt. . . .

Ich mache mir jetzt den Spass und nehme Deine Note zum Anlass um die
verschiedensten gescheiten Leute daraufhin zu reizen, London, Teller, Born,
Pauli, Szilard, Weyl. Am meisten ist noch bei Pauli herausgekommen, der
wenigstens zugibt, dass die Verwendung des Wortes "Zustand" für psi-function sehr anrüchig ist. Was mir bisher angedruckten Reaktionen vor Augen
gekommen, ist wenig geistreich. . . . Es ist so, wie wenn einer sagt: in Chicago
ist es bitter kalt, und ein anderer antwortet: das ist ein Trugschluss, es ist sehr
heiss in Florida. . . .

Die grosse Schwierigkeit, mich mit den Orthodoxen in der Sache auch nur zu
verständigen, hat mich den Versuch machen lassen, in einem längeren Scrip-
tum, die gegenwärtige Interpretationssituation einmal ab ovo zu analysieren.
Ob und was ich davon publiziere weiss ich noch nicht, aber es is für mich
immer der beste Weg, mir die Sachen wirklich klar zu machen. Dabei haben
sich mir ein paar Dinge in den derzeitigen Grundlagen als sehr merkwürdig
herausgehoben.

therefore, to try to track the development of the ideas of *NW* in Schrödinger's letters.

The July 13 letter from Schrödinger goes on to raise three general points about the quantum theory. The first of these concerns the retention of the classical dynamical concepts in the theory. For Schrödinger notes that even though probability is introduced, one is always constrained to speak only about the probability for the measurement of some classical quantity. Concerning this he writes: "But in doing so one gets the feeling that only with difficulty can precisely the most important statements of the new theory be forced into this Spanish boot".[13] Schrödinger illustrates this by citing as examples the probability for the various energy levels of an oscillator and, "even worse," (*noch schlimmer*) the probability of finding the angular momentum of a point-mass with respect to an arbitrary coordinate origin.

In section 3 of *NW*, "Examples of probability predictions" ("*Beispiele für Wahrscheinlichkeitsvoraussagen*"), these very same examples are used to make exactly the same point. Even the unusual "Spanish boot" metaphor recurs when Schrödinger follows his presentation of the oscillator and angular momentum examples with the comment:

Now doesn't one get the feeling in both examples that only with some difficulty can the essential content of what is being said be forced into the Spanish boot of a prediction of the probability for finding this or that measured value for a variable of the classical model?[14]

It would appear, therefore, that the material for section 3 of *NW* was already worked out by July 13.

Schrödinger's second critical point in the July 13 letter concerns the curious fact that the entire state function can be fixed in a moment by a single measurement. Schrödinger does not pursue this issue in any detail. It may have to do with the idea of an exact temporal instant, and so relate to his relativistic hobbyhorse, or

13. Schrödinger to Einstein, July 13, 1935:

Dabei hat man aber das Gefühl, dass gerade die wichtigsten Aussagen der neuen Theorie sich wirklich nur mit Mühe in diese spanischen Stiefel zwängen lassen.

14. Schrödinger (1935b), p. 810:

Hat man nun nicht in beiden Fällen das Gefühl dass der wesentliche Inhalt dessen, was gesagt werden soll, sich nur mit einiger Mühe zwängen lässt in die spanischen Stiefel einer Voraussage über die Wahrscheinlichkeit, für eine Variable des klassischen Modells diesen oder jenen Messwert anzutreffen?

maybe it concerns the notorious collapse of the wave packet. These topics are discussed together in section 14 of *NW*.

The third issue raised in the July 13 letter expresses reservations concerning the exact measurability, according to quantum mechanics, of observables (like position and linear momentum) that have a continuous spectrum. Schrödinger summarizes von Neumann's (1932, chap. 3, section 3) treatment of this issue (via course graining) and remarks, "I believe that here, due to our Jonny, the chisel has been set at just the place where reform is necessary."[15] Schrödinger then proceeds to set out briefly what he thinks is going on; namely, that the classical physical model has in fact been abandoned but that instead of replacing it with another, one has simply declared all of its determinables to be exactly measurable in principle and "in addition prescribed with wise, philosophical expressions that these *measurements* are the only real things, which is, of course, metaphysics. Then in fact it does not trouble us at all that our claims about the *model* are monstrous."[16]

The themes of this third part of Schrödinger's critique in the July 13 letter are repeated in section 6 of *NW*, "The conscious shift in the epistemological point of view" (*"Der bewusste Wechsel des erkenntnistheoretischen Standpunktes"*). The vulgar positivism that Schrödinger identifies as metaphysics in the letter becomes "epistemology" in section 6, but the central point about exact measurability is the same. In *NW* Schrödinger prepares the way for his discussion of this in terms of "models" by devoting the first two sections there to explaining his understanding of the concept of a classical model, and how quantum theory turns this into predictions for what can be measured. Thus by July 13 we can see that the essential content of sections 1, 2, 3, and 6 of *NW* is already well formed. Although we know that the order of sections 4 and 5 follows that of "Bornian" to "Schrödinger" in Einstein's June 19 letter, no sign of how Schrödinger intends to refute these interpretations, nor even of his interest in that project, has yet appeared.

Einstein wrote back on August 8, expressing his agreement with Schrödinger that we really need new concepts but that instead of

15. Schrödinger to Einstein, July 13, 1935:

Ich glaube, dass hier von unserem Jonny schon der Meissel angesetzt ist an der Stelle, wo Reform nottut.

16. Schrödinger to Einstein, July 13, 1935:

. . . erklären alle seine Bestimmungsstücke als prinzipiell messbar und setzen mit philosophisch weiser Miene hinzu, dass diese *Messungen* das einzig Wirkliche sind, was darüber hinaus ist, ist Metaphysik. Dann stört es nämlich gar nicht, dass unsere Behauptungen *am Modell* monströs sind.

trying to get outside of the network of the classical ones, most investigators, "comically, only wriggle about inside" (see the end of section 5 of the last chapter). The letter continues (in a passage discussed in section 2 of the preceding chapter) by giving Einstein's "solution" of the EPR paradox in terms of his statistical interpretation. This is the Bornian alternative mentioned in the June 19 letter, and here Einstein moves once again from it to the Schrödinger interpretation.

> But you seen something entirely different as the origin of the intrinsic difficulties. You see ψ as a representation of the real and would like to alter or altogether to abolish its connection with the concepts of ordinary mechanics. Only in this way could the theory really and truly stand on its own feet. This point of view is certainly coherent, but I do not believe that it is capable of avoiding the felt difficulties. I would like to show this by means of a crude macroscopic example.[17]

In this passage Einstein reminds Schrödinger, who introduced the ψ-function into quantum physics, that he himself originally tried to understand it in terms of some kinds of wavelike models, models that might validate his original derivations of the "Schrödinger equation." In fact Schrödinger quickly saw that the particular models he tried out were too limited to accommodate the various applications of the theory, and he abandoned them and gave up the active pursuit of a program for treating the ψ- function as a directly referential device.[18] Nevertheless, Schrödinger probably continued to find the idea of some sort of direct interpretation tempting, as his later publications show.[19] It is not clear from the correspondence whether Einstein has forgotten Schrödinger's move away from a direct interpretation program, or whether he knows well enough that Schrödinger is still somewhat attracted to the idea and is, in effect, chiding Schrödinger for it. Either way, the history here explains Einstein's choice of the terminology of "Schrödinger" incompleteness, and Einstein's target now in the

---

17. Einstein to Schrödinger, August 8, 1935:

Du aber siehst als Ursache der inneren Schwierigkeiten etwas ganz anderes. Du siehst in ψ die Darstellung des Wirklichen und möchtest die Verknüpfung mit den Begriffen der ordinären Mechanik verändern oder überhaupt abschaffen. Nur so könnte ja die Theorie wirklich auf ihre eigenen Beine gestellt werden.
Dieser Standpunkt ist gewiss folgerichtig; ich glaube aber nicht dass er geeignet ist, die von uns empfundenen Uebelstände zu beseitigen. Ich möchte das durch ein grob makroskopisches Beispiel begründen.

18. See Wessels (1979) for some of the details here and for further references.
19. See the late essays in Schrödinger (1956).

August 8 letter is just that.[20] For what Einstein lays the groundwork for is a "crude macroscopic example" that will exhibit the same "difficulties" as the two-particle microscopic system of EPR. What we learned from the June 19 letter is that these concern incompleteness, in the conflated Schrödinger and bijective senses. Since Einstein's focus here is Schrödinger, what he ought to try to show, by means of his macroscopic example, is that there is a state of affairs whose best description in quantum mechanical terms (i.e., via the ψ-function) involves probabilities less than unity when, in fact, there is some further and actual truth to be told. Of course Einstein had already set the stage for this with his ball in the box whose "best" description was supposed to be that the probability for being found in the box was ½. What Einstein is claiming to do now is to sketch a quantum mechanical example structurally the same. Here is the example:

The system is a substance in chemically unstable equilibrium, perhaps a charge of gunpowder that, by means of intrinsic forces, can spontaneously combust, and where the average life span of the whole setup is a year. In principle this can quite easily be represented quantum-mechanically. In the beginning the ψ-function characterizes a reasonably well-defined macroscopic state. But, according to your equation, after the course of a year this is no longer the case at all. Rather, the ψ-function then desribes a sort of blend of not-yet and of already-exploded systems. Through no art of interpretation can this ψ-function be turned into an adequate description of a real state of affairs; [for] in reality there is just no intermediary between exploded and not-exploded.[21]

20. As for why the other alternative is called "Bornian," see Einstein's use of the same terminology in his contribution to the *Born Festschrift* (Einstein 1953b), especially on pp. 37–38. In his correspondence with Born, Einstein refers to this article as "a little nursery song about physics" that "is meant to demonstrate the indispensability of your statistical interpretation of quantum mechanics, which Schrödinger, too, has recently tried to avoid." (Born 1971, p. 199). Of course Einstein means *his* "statistical interpretation," via ensembles, not just the use of the so-called Born rule. But Born does not pick up on this.

21. Einstein to Schrödinger, August 8, 1935:

Das System sei eine Substanz in einem chemisch labilen Gleichgewicht, etwa ein Haufen Schiesspulver, der sich durch innere Kräfte entzünden kann, wobei die mittlere Lebensdauer von der Grössenordnung eines Jahres sei. Dies lässt sich im Prinzip ganz leicht quantenmechanisch darstellen. Im Anfang charakterisiert die ψ-Funktion einen hinreichend genau definierten makroskopischen Zustand. Deine Gleichung sorgt aber dafür, dass dies nach Verlauf eines Jahres gar nicht mehr der Fall ist. Die ψ-Funktion beschreibt dann vielmehr eine Art Gemisch von noch nicht und von von bereits explodiertem System. Durch keine Interpretationskunst kann diese ψ-Funktion zu einer adäquaten Beschreibung eines wirklichen Sachverhaltes gemacht werden; in Wahrheit gibt es eben zwischen explodiert und nicht-explodiert kein Zwischending.

There is certainly a striking similarity between this exploding gunpowder example of Einstein's and Schrödinger's cat. They are aimed at the same target and use the very same conceptual idea of amplification up to the macroscopic, which they implement by means of the same technical idea of letting the ψ-function for a micro-macro system evolve over time. Moreover they even use the same description of the final quantum mechanical state as a "blend" (*Gemisch*) between, respectively, exploded and not-exploded, or, living and dead.

Einstein follows this example up by suggesting that although what we know from crude macroscpoic experience, therefore, is already sufficient to show the breakdown of the "Schrödinger" interpretation, Einstein's own statistical interpretation is as viable here as in the original EPR example. Einstein's language throughout the correspondence is warm and friendly. Nevertheless, almost inevitably one would think, his attack on Schrödinger's old ideas along with his reiteration of his own had somewhat the character of a challenge. And that is how Schrödinger responded, only eleven days later, on August 19:

Many thanks for your lovely letter of 8 August. I believe it doesn't work [*das geht nicht*] that one relates the ψ-function to an ensemble of systems and thereby solves the antinomy or paradox. To be sure I do not like the idiom "*das geht nicht*" at all, for it expresses the prejudice of the people with blinders who take certain computational devices as permanently established because otherwise they could not advance their own [ideas].[22]

Schrödinger proceeds to sketch a rather complex example of a series of operators whose measured values, he thinks it clear, could not be derived from the preexisting values of an ensemble of systems without "altering the connection with the concepts of ordinary mechanics" ("*dass man die Vernüpfung mit den Begriffen der ordinären Mechanik ändert*"). Recall that in his August 8 letter Einstein uses this very same phrase to characterize Schrödinger's original idea for a direct interpretation of the ψ-function. So, in his response of August 19, Schrödinger—in effect—strikes back by trying to make

---

22. Schrödinger to Einstein, August 19, 1935:

Vielem Dank für Deinen lieben Brief vom 8. August. Ich glaube, das geht nicht; dass man die ψ-Funktion auf eine Systemgesamtheit bezieht und dadurch die Antinomie oder das Paradoxon löst. Ich habe zwar die Redeweise "das geht nicht" gar nicht gern, denn sie wird mit Vorliebe von den Scheuklappenleuten gebraucht, die gewisse rechnerische Dinge als unabänderlich feststehend ansehen, weil sie sich's ohne das nicht vorstellen können.

exactly the same charge stick to Einstein's idea of a statistical interpretation.

The dialectical exchange here, involving the refutation of the statistical interpretation and of the old Schrödinger interpretation, corresponds exactly to the topics of sections 4 and 5, respectively, of *NW*. And here, most likely, we are witness to Schrödinger's motivation for including them in *NW*. The time frame for this suggestion, as we learn later in Schrödinger's August 19 letter, is just right; for there Schrödinger informs Einstein that Arnold Berliner, then editor of *Naturwissenschaften* has "from one day to the next" (*vom einen Tag auf den anderen*) been removed from that position. Concerning Berliner, Schrödinger writes,

> I had exchanged several letters with him in connection with the previously mentioned article, and about a week ago I sent him the MS. I received a moving letter a couple of days later: indeed, he expected that the MS. would be turned over to him for handling, for he was still allowed to continue on as a consultant, but as of twenty-four hours ago he was no longer editor.[23]

(Schrödinger, I might mention, considered withdrawing the manuscript from *Naturwissenschaften* but he decided not to, specifically in response to a request from Berliner. Moreover, at Schrödinger's suggestion, Einstein subsequently arranged to bring Berliner to Princeton.)

From the Berliner episode we learn that Schrödinger submitted the manuscript of *NW* sometime after Einstein's exploding gunpowder letter of August 8 and before this letter of August 19. Thus we could reasonably expect that the complex example used in that letter to attack Einstein's statistical interpretation is to be found in the section of *NW* devoted to the same purpose, section 4. But, surprisingly, no trace of that example appears there. Instead, in that section, Schrödinger uses the two examples mentioned in connection with the "Spanish boot" metaphor in his July 13 letter and that occur in a similar context in *NW*, section 3: angular momentum with respect to an arbitrary origin, and the energy levels of a harmonic oscillator. In section 4 of *NW*, Schrödinger suggests that it is just not possible to endow an ensemble of systems with values for angular

23. Schrödinger to Einstein, August 19, 1935:

> ich hatte wegen des oben erwähnten Aufsatzes einige Briefe mit ihm gewechselt und als ich ihm vor etwa einer Woche das MS. eingesandt hatte, erhielt ich ein paar Tage darauf einen rührenden Brief: er erwarte zwar, dass das MS. ihm zur Erledigung übergeben werde, da er noch weiterhin als Berater mitwirken dürfe, aber Redakteur sei er seit 24 Stunden nicht mehr.

momentum which will duplicate the given discrete quantum spectrum for that observable when calculated classically with respect to *any* coordinate origin *whatsoever*. Similarly he suggests, in effect, that it is not possible to account for quantum tunneling (the penetration of a potential barrier) by assignments of energy values and of distances separating the two particles in an ensemble of harmonic oscillators. Although on August 19 Schrödinger claimed not to care for the "no-go" idiom (*"das geht nicht"*) since it was associated with the prejudices of the other camp, these are exactly the terms in which the angular momentum case is introduced in section 4 (Schrödinger 1935b, p. 811). The conclusion seems inescapable that section 4 was put together only after the August 19 letter and was not part of the original maunscript sent to Berliner. Moreover, it is quite unlikely that the difficult example that Schrödinger does use on August 19 to attack the ensemble idea would itself have constituted the original content of section 4. For the exposition in *NW* builds up slowly, and the reader would by no means have been prepared to understand this example at that stage of the development of the quantum mechanical language. Indeed, Einstein himself did not understand it, as he wrote on September 4: "If I claimed to understand your last letter, it would be a big lie."[24]

Einstein goes on in his September 4 letter to raise some questions of clarification concerning Schrödinger's attempt to refute the statistical interpretation, and he then writes: "If I now gloss over all that is not understood I do not see why it is contradictory to take the ψ-function as referring to a statistical ensemble."[25]

Thus Einstein remains unconvinced, and so Schrödinger tries again in a letter dated October 4: "I am terribly embarrassed to have expressed myself the other day so unintelligibly. So, first off, with regard to the statistical interpretation of the ψ-function. I made it all unnecessarily complicated. I will take the simplest example."[26]

24. Einstein to Schrödinger, September 4, 1935:

Wenn ich behauptete, ich hätte Deinem letzten Brief verstanden, so wäre es eine dicke Lüge.

25. Einstein to Schrödinger, September 4, 1935:

Wenn ich nun über alles Unverstandene hinweggleite, so begreife ich nicht, warum es widerspruchsvoll ist, anzunehmen, dass sich die ψ-Funktion auf eines statistische Gesamtheit beziehe.

26. Schrödinger to Einstein, October 4, 1935:

Ich hab mich sehr geniert, dass ich mich neulich so unverständlich ausgedrückt habe. Also erst einmal das mit der statistischen Deutung der ψ-Funktion. Ich habe das ganz unnötig kompliziert. Ich will das einfachste Beispiel nehmen.

The example that Schrödinger now finally takes up, on October 4, is the angular momentum case, presented substantially as it occurs in section 4 of *NW*. There is one small difference; namely, in the October 4 letter Schrödinger says that the angular momentum spectrum consists of all integral multiples of h, which is not how it comes out in *NW*. With regard to the complex ("unintelligible") example suggested in the August 19 letter, Schrödinger refers Einstein to section 3 of *PCPS* and, although he thinks that Einstein might find it trivial, he also says that it took him two days to work it out and, even now, he is not quite sure that it is entirely correct. If we recall that *PCPS* was submitted on August 14, then it makes sense that when Schrödinger wrote to Einstein only a few days later he might well have tried to make use of some calculations with which he had lately been struggling. (Indeed scrutiny of *NW* reveals that section 13 contains a simplification of the example of section 3 of *PCPS*, and of the August 19 letter, although not there directed against the statistical interpretation.)

It appears that Einstein's exploding gunpowder attack (August 8) on Schrödinger's old idea of a direct interpretation for the ψ-function stimulated Schrödinger to try to find a comparable difficulty for Einstein's own pet idea for a statistical interpretation. This dialogue set the topics and content for sections 4 and 5 of *NW*. But Schrödinger did not find a satisfactory counter to Einstein's ensemble idea until sometime after his letter to Einstein of August 19. This strongly suggests that section 4 of *NW* was a late insertion in the text, not included in the original manuscript sent to Berliner before August 19. But if section 4 was only written in after August 19, then most likely section 5 was a later addition as well; since, in both the exposition of *NW* and the prehistory examined here, the two sections form an integrated whole. Moreover, we have seen that the contents of sections 1, 2, 3, and 6 of *NW* were already fairly well shaped by July 13, and indeed that their content too forms a natural unit. Perhaps, then, section 5 and its cat were only conceived after Schödinger saw Einstein's similar, exploding gunpowder example. But writing on August 19 Schrödinger says otherwise:

I am long past the stage where I thought that one can consider the ψ-function as somehow a direct description of reality. In a lengthy essay that I have just written I give an example that is very similar to your exploding powder keg. . . .

Confined in a steel chamber is a Geigercounter prepared with a tiny amount of uranium, so small that in the next hour it is just as probable to expect one atomic decay as none. An amplified relay provides that the first atomic decay shatters a small bottle of prussic acid. This and—

in a more gruesome way—a cat is also trapped in the steel chamber. According to the ψ-function for the total system, after an hour, *sit venia verbo,* the living and dead cat are smeared out in equal measure.[27]

There are only minor discrepancies between this cat and that of *NW.* Here the "radioactive material" of *NW* is identified as uranium. But this version does not contain the picturesque mechanism of the hammer breaking the glass, nor the acute metaphor of a blend (*Gemisch*), which is in *NW* and also in Einstein's gunpowder example. Perhaps this image of a blend was indeed a later addition. Overall, however, this is certainly a cat we would recognize from section 5. But is that its original context?

Schrödinger does not say; that is, in the letters he does not explain the purpose of the cat example in the original version of *NW.* If my speculation is correct, that sections 4 and 5 were later additions to the manuscript, then we might guess that the cat originally occurred further along, somewhere after the reader had been introduced to the ψ-function. For, recall, that in *NW* the ψ-function is only explained in section 7, although its interpretation is the subject of section 5. Recall too that the cat of section 5 is only a "ludicrous example" of the other cases discussed there. These involve the detection of α-particles and are all cases of quantum measurement. The quantum theory of measurement occupies three sections of *NW,* sections 8, 9, and 10. And, indeed, in section 10 (p. 827) there is a (parenthetical) reference to the cat. The context is that of the so-called problem of measurement; i.e., the problem of reconciling the definite state of the macroscopic instrument at the conclusion of a measurement interaction with the description of that situation by means of the evolved ψ-function. This is, of course, exactly the puzzle raised by the cat, and, moreover, it is the context in which the cat is usually discussed. My conjecture, there-

---

27. Schrödinger to Einstein, August 19, 1935:

Ich bin längst über das Stadium hinaus, wo ich mir dachte, dass man die ψ-Funktion irgendwie direkt als Beschreibung der Wirklichkeit ansehen kann. In einem längeren Aufsatz, den ich eben geschrieben, bringe ich ein Beispiel, dass Deinem explodierenden Pulverfass sehr ähnlich ist. . . .

In einer Stahlkammer ist ein Geigerzähler eingeschlossen, der mit einer winzigen Menge Uran beschickt ist, so wenig, dass in der nächsten Stunde ebenso wahrscheinlich *ein* Atomzerfall zu erwarten ist wie keiner. Ein verstärkendes Relais sorgt dafür, dass der este Atomzerfall ein Kölbchen mit Blausäure zertrümmert. Dieses und—grausamer Weise—eine Katze befinden sich auch in der Stahlkammer. Nach einer Stunde sind dann in der ψ-Funktion des Gesammtsystems, sit venia verbo, die lebende und die tote Katze zu gleichen Teilen verschmiert.

fore, is that the cat was originally used to illustrate the problem of measurement, but that the dynamics of the dialogue with Einstein moved Schrödinger to reemploy it, just as Einstein had used the exploding gunpowder example, to provide a new argument for incompleteness, a counter to the old Schrödinger program aimed at giving the ψ-function a direct interpretation.

In his letter of September 4, Einstein welcomed Schrödinger's cat.

As for the rest, your cat shows that we are in complete agreement concerning our assessment of the character of the current theory. A ψ-function that contains the living as well as the dead cat just cannot be taken as a description of a real state of affairs. To the contrary, this example shows exactly that it is reasonable to let the ψ-function correspond to a statistical ensemble that contains both systems with live cats and those with dead cats.[28]

Einstein never responded to Schrödinger's October 4 letter, the one with the simplified angular momentum counter to his statistical ensemble idea. Nor, as we discussed in the last chapter, did he later respond explicitly in his publications or in his correspondence to the various other "no-go" results that have been taken as challenging his statistical interpretation. He seems to have felt that they somehow missed their mark.

Some fifteen years later, however, in one of his last letters to Schrödinger, Einstein pays inadvertent tribute to their remarkable correspondence during the summer of 1935. In one delightful slip (which I capitalize below) Einstein puts together the exploding gunpowder example and the cat, emphasizing as well the EPR context of an argument against (Schrödinger) completeness. Writing to Schrödinger about "contemporary physicists" on December 22, 1950, Einstein says,

They somehow believe that the quantum theory provides a description of reality, and even a *complete* description; this interpretation is, however, refuted most elegantly by your system of radioactive atom + Geiger

28. Einstein to Schrödinger, September 4, 1935:

Uebringens zeigt Dein Katzenbeispiel, dass wir bezüglich der Beurteilung des Charakters der gegenwärtigen Theorie völlig übereinstimmen. Eine ψ-Funktion, in welche sowohl die lebende wie die tote Katze eingeht, kann eben nicht als Beschreibung eines wirklichen Zustandes aufgefasst werden. Dagegen weist gerade dies Beispiel darauf hin, dass es vernünftig ist, die ψ-Funktion einer statistischen Gesamtheit zuzuordnen, welche sowohl Systeme mit lebendiger Katze wie solche mit toter Katze in sich begreift.

counter + amplifier + CHARGE OF GUNPOWDER + cat in a box, in which the ψ-function of the system contains the cat both alive and blown to bits.[29]

Perhaps it would be appropriate to refer to his blended version as *Einstein's cat.*

29. Translated in Przibam (1967), p. 39.

Einstein's Realism

The success of this mode of appraisal, in which one of the criteria is model-fertility tested over the appropriate time-span, is the best argument for taking the theoretical models of the scientist realistically. Not, of course, as description, but as metaphor, which is the only way that complex things forever somewhat out of reach *can* be known.

Ernan McMullin (1976)

1. Introduction

Recent scholarship has begun to document Einstein's philosophical development away from the empiricist and positivist influences that marked his early scientific thinking, and toward the realism that played an increasingly central role in his conception of science, following the articulation of general relativity.[1] In correspondence in 1948, Einstein reflects on his development in a way that nicely confirms the scholarship. Referring to the period around 1905, and the origins of special relativity, he writes, "At that time my mode of thinking was much nearer positivism than it was later on. . . . my departure from positivism came only when I worked out the general theory of relativity."[2] Recent discussion of Einstein's position on the quantum theory has also begun to recognize the importance of his realism (and not just his interest in a causal or

Research for this essay was supported by the National Science Foundation and by the Guggenheim Foundation. The paper was written during tenure of a Guggenheim Fellowship. I want to thank both foundations for their support. I am also grateful to Hebrew University of Jerusalem for their kind permission to use material from the Einstein Archives. A copy of the archives is housed in the Seeley G. Mudd manuscript library at Princeton University, and if I give no published source for a reference it can be found there. (Where I translate from archival material in German, I also give the German text; otherwise there is an English original for my citation.) My thanks to Dana Fine for his help with the archival manuscripts, to Don Moyer for copies of the *Nature* references (nn. 15 and 29), and to Micky Forbes for considerable "fine-tuning". I hope the essay itself will express sufficient "thanks" to various correspondents whose interest has also helped.

1. See, e.g., "Mach, Einstein and the Search for Reality" in Holton (1973), pp. 219–59, and Barker (1981).

2. Letters to D. S. Mackey, April 26 and May 28, 1948.

determinist base) as a focal point of his attitude.[3] Here too Einstein's late correspondence supports the story. In 1950 he wrote, "In the center of the problematic situation I see not so much the question of causality but the question of reality (in a physical sense)."[4]

While there can be no doubt that Einstein turned away from positivism to realism, or that realism was important in his thinking about the quantum theory, there is considerable room for speculation concerning exactly what Einstein's realism involves.[5] For, despite the many brief and casual references to realism in his writings, Einstein was not disposed to discuss the various elements of his realism in a systematic fashion. To understand Einstein's realism we must, I think, first construct it from his own scattered remarks. That task of construction is the primary task of this essay.

2. *Theorizing*

To facilitate that task it will be useful to begin by focusing on some central features of Einstein's epistemological thinking, for these will help us organize his remarks on realism. There are two features that will prove especially useful for our purpose, Einstein's "entheorizing" and his holism. I coin the word "entheorize" to describe the following move (one well known in analytic philosophy): when asked whether such-and-so is the case, one responds by shifting the question to asking instead whether a theory in which such-and-so is the case is a viable theory. This is a move entirely characteristic of Einstein's post-positivist thinking, and one that comes out clearly, for instance, in his treatment of causality. For example in 1952, commenting on a manuscript concerning the principle of sufficient reason, Einstein wrote to E. Zeisler recommending Hume's conclusion that we have no direct knowledge of causality. He says of causality, "We speak of it when we have accepted a theory in which connections are represented as rational. . . . For us causal connections only exist as features of the theoretical constructs."[6] Frequently, Einstein would cite Heisenberg's uncertainty formulas to ground the necessity for entheorizing the issue of causality. The

3. See Pauli's sorting out of the misunderstanding between Einstein and Born (Born 1971, pp. 221ff.), and see John Bell's comments on this (Bell 1981, pp. 46–47). This is one of the themes in Brush (1980), and in Jammer (1982). Jammer draws on my essay in chapter 2.

4. Letter to J. Rothstein, May 22, 1950.

5. See, e.g., Howard (1983).

6. Letter to E. Zeisler, December 10, 1952: "Wir sprechen von ihm, wenn wir eine Theorie akzeptiert haben, in welcher sich der Zusammenhang als rational darstellt. . . . Kausal-Zusammenhang für uns nur als Eigenschaft des theoretischen Constructs existiert."

following sequence of quotations shows some of the details of this path.

Heisenberg has shown that the alternative as to whether causality (or determinism) holds, or fails to hold, is not *empirically determinable*.[7]

On this account it can never be said with certainty whether the objective world "is causal." Instead one must ask whether a causal theory proves to be better than an acausal one.[8]

Still it is really not clear when one should call a theory "causal." Instead of "causal" I would prefer to say: a theory whose fundamental laws make no use of probabilistic concepts.[9]

The upshot is to move the entire issue of causality out of the empirical realm, where it would be conceived of as more or less separately and directly subject to experimental test. Instead, one gets at the issue of causality by specifying what counts as a causal theory (namely, one with nonprobabilistic laws), and one replaces questions about whether causality holds in nature by questions about which theory is better. These questions, as Einstein tells us in his "Autobiographical Notes," have two aspects, external verification and inner perfection (Schilpp 1949, pp. 21–23). We need not further pursue the "weighing of incommensurables" (Schilpp 1949, p. 23) that constitutes Einstein's ideas on theory choice. But we ought to notice that the device of entheorizing links up with the holism that, I think, is also crucial for understanding Einstein's brand of realism.

In the first instance, holism applies to the testing of hypotheses in a way that is usually associated with Duhem and Poincaré (and later with Quine). Here the idea is that the natural unit for experimental confrontation is an organic theory and not some separable hypothesis. This trend in Einstein's thinking is clear already in 1921, where his essay "Geometry and Experience" concedes to Poincaré that indeed only the total system of geometry-plus-physics is testable, at least *"sub specie aeterni"* (Einstein 1921, p. 236). In his 1938 book with Infeld the idea is expressed this way: "It is really

7. Letter to A. Lamouche, March 20, 1955: "Heisenberg hat gezeigt, dass das Gelten oder Nicht-Gelten der Kausalität (bezw. Determinismus) Keine *empirisch entscheidbar* Alternativ ist."

8. Letter to H. Titze, January 16, 1954: "Ob die objektiv Welt 'kausal ist', kann deshalb nie mit Sicherheit gesagt werden. Wohl aber muss man fragen, ob eine kausale Theorie sich besser bewährt wie eine akausale."

9. Letter to J. J. Fehr, March 25, 1952: "Dabei ist es gar nicht klar, wann man eine Theorie 'kausal' nennen soll. Ich würde statt 'kausal' lieber sagen: eine Theorie deren Fundamentalgesetze nicht vom dem Wahrscheinlichkeitsbegriffe Gebrauch machen."

our whole system of guesses which is to be either proved or dis-
proved by experiment. No one of the assumptions can be isolated
for separate testing" (Einstein and Infeld 1938, pp. 30–31)[10] When
Einstein returns to the discussion of geometry in his "Reply to
Criticisms" (Schilpp 1949, pp. 676–79), he tries to turn the table
on Poincaré's conventionalism by suggesting that not only testability
but also the internal criterion of simplicity must apply to the *whole*
system of physics-plus-geometry. And then Einstein goes on as the
"nonpositivist" to extend his holism from theory choice and simplicity to questions of meaning, for he suggests that the natural
unit for issues relating to the meaning of individual concepts is also
the whole theory. Perhaps this holistic idea has its roots in his earlier
agreement with Schlick that the axioms of a system provide implicit
definitions of its concepts (Einstein 1921, p. 234), a doctrine that
Einstein retains in his later discussion of the conventionality of the
analytic/synthetic distinction (Einstein 1936, p. 293). In any case,
his "Reply" reiterates this holism over meanings in its curt dismissal
of Bridgman's demand that each concept, separately, be given an
operational definition (Schilpp 1949, p. 679).[11] The sharp way that
Einstein takes with operationalism may well reflect a harsh judgment that he makes on his earlier self. For instance in 1920 (or
1921) he wrote to Solovine espousing the orthodox operationalist
line: "Every physical concept must be given a definition such that
one can in principle decide, in virtue of this definition, whether or
not it applies in each particular case" (Solovine 1956, p. 20). By
contrast in 1951, in the context of some of his reading of Mai-
monides, Einstein shows his holistic shift in attitude: "The strangest
thing in all this medieval literature is the conviction that if there is

10. In correspondence with Solovine concerning the French translation of this
book, Einstein points out that, apart from providing a needed source of income for
Infeld, there was a special purpose to writing it; namely, to emphasize the role of
a realist epistemology in the history of physics, as an antidote to the rising tide of
positivism. Einstein also makes it plain that the epistemological aspects were worked
on with special care ("*recht sorgfältig*"). See the letter to Solovine, April 24, 1938
(Solovine 1956, p. 70). Pais (1982, p. 495) suggests that Einstein was not enthusiastic
about the book, citing a remark from a letter to Infeld in 1941. ("One should not
undertake anything which endangers the tenuous bridge of confidence between
people.") But while that remark may throw some light on the interpersonal aspects
of their collaboration, Einstein's only reservation that I know of concerning the
actual content of the book is contained in a letter to Solovine on June 27, 1938,
where he urges Solovine (in the French translation) to fix up a passage that refers
misleadingly to the time at which the sun sets. Einstein also says that he prefers the
German title (*Die Physik als Abenteuer der Erkenntnis* [*Physics as an Adventure in Knowledge*]) to the English, since it gives a certain psychological emphasis (Solovine 1956,
pp. 72, 74). I think we are, in fact, on solid ground in taking the epistemological
point of view in this book as authentically Einstein's.
    11. See Howard (1983) for further discussion of Einstein's holism.

a word there must also be a clear meaning behind it, and the only problem is to find out that meaning."[12] What emerged from this shift was a holism that entheorizes questions of meaning along with questions of testability.

To see how this treatment of meanings operates, and to see just how serious Einstein is about it, I want to display and then discuss Einstein's explicit remarks about the concept of truth. For a realist, of course, we would expect truth to be understood as some sort of "correspondence with reality." But, as we shall see, Einstein's remarks suggest no such idea, and this will be an important sign that his realism may be quite different from the standard metaphysical view that bears that label.

There is, first of all, a set of four responses given by Einstein in 1929 and gathered together under the title "On Scientific Truth." Only the first response has to do with truth, and it is this:

It is difficult even to attach a precise meaning to the term "scientific truth." Thus the meaning of the word "truth" varies according to whether we deal with a fact of experience, a mathematical proposition, or a scientific theory. "Religious truth" conveys nothing clear to me at all. (Einstein 1929, p. 261)

Twenty years later in his "Autobiographical Notes" Einstein interrupts the historical narrative to state what he calls his "epistemological credo." It contains the following paragraph relating to the concept of truth.

A proposition is correct if, within a logical system, it is deduced according to the accepted logical rules. A system has truth-value [*Wahrheitsgehalt*] according to the certainty and completeness of its coordination-possibility to the totality of experience. A correct proposition borrows its "truth" from the truth-value of a system to which it belongs. (Schilpp 1949, p. 13)

In 1951, Einstein wrote a brief letter (in English) on the same theme, and which I give here in full:

Truth is a quality we attribute to propositions. When we attribute this label to a proposition we accept it for deduction. Deduction and generally the process of reasoning is our tool to bring cohesion to a world of perceptions. The label "true" is used in such a way that this purpose is served best.[13]

12. Letter to Rabbi P. D. Bookstaber, August 24, 1951.
13. Letter to S. Candido, November 4, 1951.

These remarks on truth defy the traditional philosophical categories of correspondence or coherence theories. Indeed, I don't think the remarks point to any genuine "theory" of truth at all. Rather they call our attention to structural features in the use of the concept, primarily the role of truth in logical inference. In the 1929 remarks, which appear to respond to questions about religion, Einstein catches hold of a certain indexical quality to truth judgments; i.e., the way those judgments depend on the larger context of inquiry. In the later remarks, this insight shifts in the direction of his entheorizing holism. That shift makes the truth of individual propositions subsidiary to their being an essential ingredient of a "true theory." But there is no special concept of a true theory apart from the ordinary scientific idea of a theory being observationally well confirmed, or verified—ideally, by all possible observations ("its coordination-possibility to the totality of experience"). This idea is expressed by Einstein in a cryptic footnote to his article in the 1953 Born *Festschrift*, where he writes, "The linguistic connection between the concepts 'true' ['*wahr*'] and 'verified' ['*sich bewähren*'] is based on an intrinsic relationship" (Einstein 1953b, p. 34). I understand this as an expression of the idea that the truth of a proposition signifies nothing more than its role in an observationally verified system. In particular, there is nothing in Einstein's remarks to suggest the realist idea that the truth of a statement marks a special relationship that the statement bears to "reality," such as "correspondence" or "picturing," or the like.

I believe that Einstein's treatment of truth is entirely characteristic of his attitude toward the meaning of concepts in general. I would summarize it this way. When asked for the meaning of a concept (or statement) in science Einstein responds, first, by referring us to its role in systematic inquiry, and then (where appropriate), by pointing out the observational dividends that accrue to the theory that employs the concept and organizes the inquiry: "our concepts . . . and systems of concepts are human creations, self-sharpening tools whose warrant and value in the end rests on this, that they permit the coordination of experience 'with dividends' ['*mit Vorteil*'] " (Einstein 1953b, p. 34). In general, no specific dividends are tied to any particular concept (or statement). Benefits, when they accrue, are credited to the theory as a whole. I think we might well adapt Russell's famous remark about mathematics to paraphase Einstein's conception of science: according to Einstein, in science we can never know exactly what we mean, nor whether what we are saying is true.

3. Realism

We are now in a position to put together a picture of Einstein's realism. I shall begin right in the middle of one of his discussions of the quantum theory, for there we can observe him using the machinery laid out in the preceding section, and we can see very concretely how it shapes his realism.

The context is a preliminary skirmish in Einstein's battle to have the quantum theory seen as an incomplete description of individual systems.[14] In this particular discussion Einstein focuses attention on the decay of a radioactive atom. The uncertainty formulas for energy and time rule out the possibility of determining the exact time of a specific decay, since the decay is a change of energy state. The quantum theory only gives probabilities for what we will find if we look for the decay. Einstein points out, therefore, that *if* the atom does have a definite decay time, then the probabilistic quantum description must be counted as incomplete. But, one might well ask whether there actually *is* a definite time of decay. Such a thing is unobservable, but could it nevertheless be "real" (the scare quotes are Einstein's)? Einstein then continues:

The justification of the constructs which represent "reality" for us, lies alone in their quality of making intelligible what is given by the senses. . . . Applied to the specifically chosen example this consideration tells us the following.

One cannot simply ask: "Does a definite moment for the decay of a single atom exist?" but rather instead "Within the framework of our total theoretical construction, is it reasonable to assume the existence of a definite moment for the decay of a single atom?" One cannot even ask what this supposition *means.* One can only ask whether or not such a supposition is reasonable in the context of the chosen conceptual system, with a view to its ability theoretically to grasp what is empirically given. (Schilpp 1949, p. 669)

Here then we see how Einstein takes the concept of a "real" event, entheorizes it, and then refuses the question of its meaning (or significance), shifting instead to the question of the empirical adequacy of the relevant theory. He might have put it this way. We don't know what it means to say that the atom "really" had a definite decay time, nor do we know whether that is "true." We can only ask whether a theory that incorporates such decay times is a good theory, from an empirical point of view. If so, then we do say that

---

14. By an "incomplete description" here Einstein means that the probabilistic assertions provided by the theory do not exhaust all the relevant assertions about the actual, physical state of the system.

the atom has a decay time, and we do count that as a description of reality (whatever that means). *These two moves, to entheorize concepts relating to "reality" and to refuse further inquiry into their significance (deflecting inquiry to the empirical adequacy of the whole theory) constitute the foundation of Einstein's realism.*

Before proceeding to fill in some more of the details of that realism, I want to cite two further passages to illustrate these dual themes of entheorizing and meaning-avoidance. The first passage begins with a wonderful sentence that Einstein uses to summarize his debt to Kant. "The real is not given to us, but put to us (by way of a riddle) [*Das Wirkliche ist uns nicht gegeben, sondern aufgegeben (nach Art eines Rätsels)*]." Einstein comments:

This obviously means: There is a conceptual model [*Konstruktion*] for the comprehension of the interpersonal, whose authority lies solely in its verification [*Bewährung*]. This conceptual model refers precisely to the "real" (by definition), and every further question concerning the "nature of the real" appears empty. (Schilpp 1949, p. 680)

The second passage is from his 1938 book with Infeld, and occurs just after the remarks cited in section 2 about experiment confronting the theory as a whole. The authors recite the tale, familiar to readers of Descartes, of how building an explanatory theory is like trying to figure out the workings of a closed watch:

If he is ingenious he may form some picture of a mechanism which could be responsible for all the things he observes, but he may never be quite sure his picture is the only one which could explain his observations. *He will never be able to compare his picture with the real mechanism, and he cannot even imagine the possibility or the meaning of such a comparison.* (Einstein and Infeld 1938, p. 31)

The emphasis on this last sentence is mine, for I want to draw attention again to the vehemence with which the idea of a "correspondence with reality" is rejected, as both pointless and meaningless.

We have seen that Einstein's realism is arrived at by entheorizing "the real." To say more about this realism, then, we must say something more about what sort of theories are open to carry the idea of realism. That is, I propose to treat the issue of realism the way Einstein treats the issue of causality. In that context Einstein entheorizes by specifying what counts as a causal theory, and then agrees to let causality stand or fall according to whether causal theories turn out to be better than noncausal ones. For realism, then, I will try to begin by specifying what counts as a "realist theory." If we look at Einstein's remarks on realism, I think the basic idea surfaces right away. Its clearest and most succinct statement is this: "Physics is an attempt conceptually to grasp reality as it is thought independently of its being observed. In this sense one speaks of 'physical reality' " (Schilpp 1949, p. 81).

The key realist idea here is that the conceptual model (or theory) is to be understood as an attempt to treat things as we imagine they would be were they not being observed. Of course such a theory must pass the test of empirical adequacy before one can be satisfied with it; that is, it must succeed in encompassing the outcomes of all possible experiments (or observations). Moreover, one could imagine a theory that is empirically adequate, in this sense, but not realist. This sort of theory seems to be what Einstein had in mind in 1922, in one of his earliest criticisms of Mach. "Mach's system studies the existing relations between data of experience; for Mach science is the totality of these relations. That point of view is wrong, and, in fact, what Mach has done is to make a catalogue, not a system."[15] Mach's catalogue leaves out the realist idea that one seeks to connect up the experimental data by treating them as data *about* an "observer-independent realm." It is interesting to note that Einstein's critique of Mach on this score antedates the development of the quantum theory. For the quantum theory that developed in 1925 to 1927 was quickly interpreted in a "sterile positivist" (Einstein 1953b, p. 33) manner; i.e., as providing *no more than* a device for coordinating the outcomes of all conceivable experimental procedures. Some of Einstein's earliest concerns over the quantum theory were on just these realist grounds,[16] and his continuing criticism of what he graphically referred to as the quantum theorists' "epistemology-soaked orgy"[17] was that they were playing a "risky game . . . with reality".[18]

Thus Einstein seems to have had a reasonably clear picture of a particular sort of nonrealist theory—some version of Mach's "catalogue"—by contrast with which we can get at this idea of a realist theory. Roughly speaking, a realist theory binds together the observable data by means of a particular sort of conceptual model; namely one whose basic concepts bear a standard interpretation

15. Reported in *Nature* 112, no. 2807 (August 18, 1923):253.
16. See, for example, his letters to Sommerfeld of August 21 and November 28, 1926, in Hermann (1968). Almost certainly Einstein's realism here had to do with the possibility of a causal space/time representation, as I discuss in section 4. For some other early concerns of Eintein's see chapter 2.
17. "*erkenntnistheorie—getränkte Orgie,*" in letter to Schrödinger on June 17, 1935.
18. Letter to Schrödinger, December 22, 1950, (Przibam 1967, p. 39).

that does not refer to observers, acts of observation, or the like. (I use the locution of "standard interpretation" as a way of emphasizing what realism actually requires, but which no model can, by itself, guarantee. See chapter 9 for a discussion of this issue.) Despite the roughness of this characterization, I think it will do well enough for our purposes. We can test it, as Einstein's, by seeing that it makes a Machian "catalogue," which *only* coordinates the data (even with predictive success), nonrealist. And this nonrealism extends to the quantum theory if we read the probabilistic formulas of that theory in the orthodox manner; that is, as merely probabilities for the results of observations (not for what is there independent of observations).

We can now proceed to entheorize various realist expressions. Thus "real" objects (e.g., events, properties, etc.) are objects described by the basic concepts of a realist theory. The "real external world" is itself just the structure posited by the conceptual model. What of "realism" as a doctrine? Here Einstein enters a caveat, for realism is not to stand or fall with any one realist theory. Rather, Einstein understands realism as a *program*; namely, as the program of trying to construct realist theories that, ideally, would be empirically adequate for all possible experimental data. He expresses this idea in his "Reply to Criticism" as follows, "After what has been said, the 'real' in physics is to be taken as a type of program, to which we are, however, not forced to cling *a priori*" (Schilpp 1949, p. 674). In 1955 he reiterates this idea:

It is basic for physics that one assumes a real world existing independently from any act of perception. But this we do not *know*. We take it only as a programme in our scientific endeavors. This programme is, of course, prescientific and our ordinary language is already based on it.[19]

It was clearly this conception of realism as a program that enabled Einstein to retain his realist orientation in the face of the mounting success of the nonrealist quantum theory. Thus in 1949 Einstein's response to some questions raised by Adolf Grünbaum includes the remark, "In my opinion the positivistic tendency of physics to try to avoid the concept of reality is futile, even if it will take some years to realize this."[20] For Einstein, then, the success or failure of realism is a question of whether the program of doing physics by constructing realist theories is a progressive or a degen-

19. Letter to M. Laserna, January 8, 1955.
20. Letter to A. Grünbaum, December 2, 1949.

erative one.[21] But the progress (or not) of a program is a matter of integrating historical judgment over time and, logically speaking, the question cannot be settled by attending to the fate of the current theory in the field—no matter how successful (or unsuccessful) that theory is by itself.

It accords well with this construal of "realist theory," and of realism as a program for constructing such theories, that Einstein bases his continued adherence to realism on an appropriately historical argument. He treats the history of physics (from Newton to Maxwell to his own general relativity) as a triumph of the realist creed.[22] He refers to realism as "a program that was absolutely standard in the development of physical thought until the arrival of quantum theory" (Einstein 1953b, p. 34). Thus Einstein suggests that the program of realism, although not a conceptual necessity, has stood the test of time so far, and this grounds his belief that it will continue to do so. It is important to see that Einstein's realism is subject to the usual canons of scientific judgment, in the manner of any research program. Although it may well express a prejudice of Einstein's, his realism is not at all the silly metaphysics of "whether something one cannot know anything about exists all the same," a description supplied by Otto Stern and one that Pauli and Born were rather too eager to accept (Born 1971, pp. 223, 227).[23]

It is also important to see that Einstein counts the program of realism a successful one, at least up to the advent of the quantum theory, despite his own understanding (and emphasis) that the ontologies of the various theories within the realist program have made radical shifts over time. Roughly speaking, the "real objects" have changed from the point particles of Newton to the continuous fields of Maxwell-Lorentz, and later of Einstein. Such a radical shift of ontology, then, is quite compatible with Einstein's realism. For Einstein, realism does not involve any idea like that of the "successive approximation to reality." The conceptual objects of successive, successful realist theories can be as radically unlike one another as point particles are unlike continuous fields. There is,

21. This is the terminology of Imré Lakatos's "methodology of scientific research programmes." I think that Lakatos's methodology provides a good framework for the issue of "testability" raised by Einstein's realism. See Worrall and Currie (1978). Hacking (1979) is an excellent review of Lakatos's ideas.

22. See his essays on Newton (Einstein 1927) and Maxwell (Einstein 1931), and his "College of Surgeons" lecture (Einstein 1950b). As I pointed out in note 10, the triumph of realism is the main underlying theme of the book with Infeld (Einstein and Infeld 1938).

23. Von Laue, in a letter to Einstein on August 8, 1934, quotes Otto Stern as saying, "You are just as reactionary as Einstein" [*"Sie sind ja noch reaktionärer als Einstein"*].

moreover, no entity (e.g., "the real, external world") that stands "outside" the theories and to which the sequence of conceptual objects could be compared (to see how well they "fit"). I should point out here that just as the "realist" idea of science making successively better approximations to reality is not part of Einstein's realism, neither is the pragmatist (especially Peircean) idea of defining reality (and truth) by reference to the ideal limit in which continued inquiry would (supposedly) finally result. Einstein is properly skeptical about the idea of such an ideal limit. He holds that "our notions of physical reality can never be final" (Einstein 1931, p. 266), that any system of concepts "will have validity only for a special field of application (i.e., there are no final categories in the sense of Kant)" (Einstein 1936, p. 292). As to whether scientific theorizing "will ever result in a definitive system, if one is asked for his opinion, he is inclined to answer no"[24] (Einstein 1936, p. 294).

4. Realist Theories

There are, however, other features of realism that *are* built into Einstein's concept. So far we have merely required that a realist theory be organized around a conceptual model of an observer-independent realm. I believe this is the core of Einstein's concept of a realist theory. But in most presentations of this concept Einstein links it with two others that must also be counted as central to his realist program. These are the ideas (1) that the conceptual model be a space/time representation and (2) that this representation be a causal one (i.e., one with strict = nonprobabilistic laws). Here are some typical ways these ideas get linked:

1930. Physics is the attempt at the conceptual construction of a model of the *real world*, as well as [*sowie*] its lawful structure.[25]

1940. Some physicists, among them myself, cannot believe that we must abandon, actually and forever, the idea of direct representation of physical reality in space and time; or that we must accept the view that events in nature are analogous to a game of chance. (Einstein 1940, p. 334)

1950. Summing up we may characterize the framework of physical thinking . . . as follows: There exists a physical reality independent of substantiation and perception. It can be completely comprehended by a theoretical construction which describes phenomena in space and

24. Howard (1983) gives further references for this attitude of Einstein's.
25. Letter to M. Schlick, November 28, 1930. Translated by Holton (1973), p. 243. (For "*sowie*" I have put "as well as," where Holton used "and.")

time. . . . The laws of nature . . . imply complete causality. . . . Will this credo survive forever? It seems to me a smile is the best answer. (Einstein 1950b, pp. 756, 758).

The more complete version of the realist program, then, is to build theories in which "everything should lead back to conceptual objects in the realm of space and time and to lawlike relations that obtain for these objects" (Einstein 1953b, p. 34). Thus for Einstein the concept of a realist theory generally includes both the idea of a space/time representation and the idea of causality, along with that of observer-independence. These three components of realism are not logically connected. That is, a theory could incorporate any one (or any two) of them and not incorporate the other(s). In particular, one can have a theory that does not involve a space/time representation, but whose laws are nonprobabilistic and whose basic concepts are understood as referring to observer-independent entities; i.e., a causal and observer-independent, but non-spatio-temporal theory. The difficulties presented by the quantum theory actually led Einstein to consider such a possibility.

In 1927 Einstein attempted to construct a space/time extension of Schrödinger's wave mechanics. In the unpublished draft for a presentation to the Prussian Academy (for May 5, 1927) he introduced his project as follows:

As is well known, the opinion currently prevails that, in the sense of quantum mechanics, there does not exist a complete space/time description of the motion of a mechanical system. . . . Contrary to this, it will be shown in what follows that Schrödinger's wave mechanics suggests how every solution of the wave-equation corresponds unambiguously to the motion of a system.[26]

26. This is from the fragment of a manuscript entitled "*Bestimmt* Schrödingers Wellenmechanik die Bewegung eines Systems vollständig oder nur im Sinne der Statistik?" ["Does Schrödinger's Wave Mechanics Determine the Motion of a System Completely, or Only in the Sense of Statistics?"] in Kirsten and Treder (1979), p. 134. I want to thank Paul Forman for sending me a copy of the fragment. There is a typescript of the whole manuscript in the Einstein Archives (#2-100-1), which includes a postscript stating the difficulty over coupled systems, discovered by Bothe, that I point out below. At the very end Einstein alludes to a suggestion (by Grommer) for modifying the scheme to deal with this objection, and remarks that the modification should be tried out, first, on some examples. But Einstein never allowed this manuscript to be published, and so most likely Grommer's idea did not work. In Born (1971), p. 96, the undated letter (#57) from Einstein refers to this manuscript. (It was written on the bottom of a letter from Ehrenfest that Einstein passed along to Born. Born does not give the date of Ehrenfest's letter, but it is the letter of April 16, 1927.) In a letter from Heisenberg to Einstein on May 19, 1927, Heisenberg says that he has heard about this idea of Einstein's from Born and Jordan, and then Heisenberg wonders whether it could be investigated experimentally. Einstein's remarks at the Solvay Conference in October 1927 contain no

But Einstein abandoned this project, apparently because of difficulties in applying his scheme to coupled systems. In particular, Bothe seems to have called Einstein's attention to a consequence that, as Einstein puts it, must "from a physical standpoint" be rejected; namely, the scheme violated the requirement that the interpolated motion for a total system be a combination of the possible motions of its component subsystems. This difficulty over coupled systems may well have sparked the interest in the issue of "locality" in quantum mechanics that later surfaced in Einstein, Podolsky, and Rosen (1935), the famous EPR paper. I think the failure of this space/time project did lead Einstein to take seriously the idea that the physics of the future may not be spatio-temporal at all.

In his review article of 1936, Einstein calls such a non-space/time physics "purely algebraical" and, because the mathematical concepts for such a theory had yet to be invented, in 1936 he rejects the idea as "an attempt to breathe in empty space" (Einstein 1936, p. 319). Nearly twenty years later he is no more enthusiastic, and for exactly the same reason. "My opinion is that if the objective description through the field as an elementary concept is not possible, then one has to find a possibility to avoid the continuum (together with space and time) altogether. But I have not the slightest idea what kind of elementary concepts could be used in such a theory."[27] If we read these remarks in conjunction with his reply to Karl Menger in 1949 ("Adhering to the continuum originates with me not in a prejudice but arises out of the fact that I have been unable to think up anything organic to take its place" [Schilpp 1949, p. 686]), then I think it clear that a non-spatio-temporal kind of realism (a "purely algebraical" realism) would be an acceptable alternative for Einstein to his own pet idea for a continuous field theory, even if one not so highly prized.

---

reference to this "Bestimmt" scheme. But they do suggest "locality" problems reminiscent of Bothe's objection. See my discussion of Einstein's remarks at that conference in chapter 3, and my argument for why we must distinguish Einstein's ideas on locality from those current in the Bell literature in chapter 4 above, especially the Appendix. I should like to use this note on the "Bestimmt" manuscript to point out an error in the narrative of chapter 3. The manuscript I refer to on p. 27 is this same 1927 one, and it does *not* contain the critique of quantum mechanics that I say it does. That critique, I am afraid, was an artifact of my own rather garbled notes. Nonetheless the "worries" that I there attribute to Einstein (over completeness, locality, and the classical limit) were certainly his, at that time as well as later, and they could even be read *between the lines* of "Bestimmt".

27. Letter to D. Bohm, October 25, 1954. Quoted in Stachel (1983), who discusses and gives further references to Einstein's ideas about a "purely algebraical" physics. See Jammer (1982) on this point too.

With regard to the acceptability of a realism that was not causal, however, I do not think that Einstein showed the same degree of tolerance. His commitment to causality comes out in one of his earliest public reactions to the quantum facts, the concluding passage of his 1927 essay on the occasion of the two hundreth anniversary of Newton's death, where he wrote:

Many physicists maintain—and there are weighty arguments in their favor—that in the face of these facts not merely the differential law [i.e., "how the state of motion of a system gives rise to that which immediately follows it in time"] but the law of causation itself—hitherto the ultimate basic postulate of all natural science—has collapsed. Even the possibility of a spatio-temporal construction, which can be unambiguously coordinated with physical events, is denied. . . . Who would presume today to decide the question whether the law of causation and the differential law, these ultimate premises of the Newtonian view of nature, must definitely be abandoned? (Einstein 1927, p. 261)

Notice here that although Einstein identifies both causality and a space/time representation as thrown into doubt by the quantum theory, it is only on causality that he focuses (for safeguarding, of course) in the final, rhetorical question. His letter to the British Royal Society, on the same occasion, also targets causality rather than the space/time representation, when Einstein closes his letter with, "May the spirit of Newton's method give us the power to restore unison between physical reality and the profoundest characteristic of Newton's teaching—strict causality."[28] Of course Einstein clearly recognized the possibility for an indeterministic physics, just as he recognized the possibility for a purely algebraic physics. But whereas he could (reluctantly) accept the idea of abandoning a space/time representation, he seems never to have reconciled himself to the idea of abandoning causality. In the early years of the quantum theory he expressed his recognition of the possibility of an indeterministic physics, and his rejection of it, this way:

In itself it is already sufficiently interesting that a reasonable science can exist at all after dispensing with rigorous causality. It is furthermore not to be denied that this surrender has really led to important achievements in theoretical physics, but nevertheless I must confess that my scientific instinct reacts against foregoing the demand for strict causality. (Einstein 1928, col. 4)

In his later correspondence the sticking point comes out as clear as could be. In 1945 he writes, "I don't believe that the fundamental

28. A translation of this letter is given in *Nature* 119 (March 26, 1927):467.

physical laws may consist in relations between *probabilities* for the real things, but for relations concerning the things themselves."[29] What Einstein expresses here is an adherence to a causal realism, and he seems never to have seriously entertained a realism divorced from causality (in *his* sense of nonprobabilistic laws).

In this regard we should be careful not to overemphasize the role of realism (i.e., observer-independence), as opposed to causality, in assessing Einstein's attitude toward the quantum theory. For if one examines the grounds that led Einstein to reject the acceptance of quantum mechanics *as a fundamental theory*, then these turn out to involve the statistical aspects of quantum theory every bit as much as the issue of observer-independence. That is, Einstein's concerns had *two* foci. The idea that realism *rather than* causality is at issue owes some currency, I think, to the publication of Pauli's remarks in the Born-Einstein correspondence, where Pauli says, "In particular, Einstein does not consider the concept of 'determinism' to be as fundamental as it is frequently held to be (as he told me emphatically many times). . . . Einstein's point of departure is 'realistic' rather than 'deterministic,' which means that his philosophical prejudice is a different one" (Born 1971, p. 221). Pauli then goes on to summarize one line of argument of Einstein's. The crucial point, and the one that Pauli does not accept, is Einstein's contention that

a macro-body must *always* have a quasi-sharply-defined position in the "objective description of reality.". . . . If one wants to assert that the description of a physical system by a ψ-function is *complete*, one has to rely on the fact that *in principle* the natural laws only refer to the ensemble-description, which Einstein does not believe. . . . What *I* do not agree with is Einstein's reasoning [above] . . . (please note that the concept of "determinism" does not occur in it at all!). (Pauli, in Born 1971, p. 223)

If Pauli sees in this line of reasoning only realism and not determinism (i.e., "causality," in Einstein's sense), that can only be because he has fallen into the trap that Einstein warned about in 1933, "If you want to find out anything from the theoretical physicists about the methods they use, I advise you to stick closely to one principle: don't listen to their words, fix your attention on their deeds" (Einstein 1933, p. 270). No doubt Pauli correctly reports Einstein's insistence on realism as the central issue. But even in Pauli's reconstruction we can see that Einstein's line of thought

---

29. Letter to M. C. Coodall, September 10, 1945. This is virtually the same expression that occurs near the end of his Herbert Spencer lecture (Einstein, 1933), p. 276.

involves causality as well. For the remark that Einstein does not believe that "in principle the natural laws only refer to the ensemble-description" is exactly an expression of Einstein's rejection of the idea that the probabilistic framework of quantum theory (the "ensemble-description") is to be accepted "in principle"; i.e., as a permanent part of fundamental physics. This is, of course, Einstein's adherence to causal (i.e., nonprobabilistic) theories. The full idea that Pauli sketches in this passage is none other than Einstein's idea for natural laws (nonprobabilistic) relating "real things," i.e., Einstein's idea of causal realism. Einstein's own expressions of the line of thought that Pauli tries to summarize are quite clear on this point.[30] In 1952 he put it to Besso this way:

If one regards the method of the current quantum theory as in principle definitive, that means that one has to forego all claim to a complete description of real states of affairs. One can justify this renunciation if one accepts that there simply are no laws for real states of affairs, so that their complete description would be pointless. . . . Now, I can't reconcile myself to that. (Speziali 1972, pp. 487–88)

Once again it is the conjunction of realism *and* causality ("laws" = nonprobabilistic laws) that is characteristic of Einstein's thought. And, even in the same breath in which Einstein tells us that realism is more central than causality, he actually conjoins the two of them— almost as though he didn't notice that they are linked together.

The question of "causality" is not actually central, rather the question of real existents [*realen Existierens*], and the question of whether there are some sort of strictly valid laws (not statistical) for a theoretically represented reality. (Letter to Besso, April 15, 1950; Speziali 1972, p. 439)[31]

Similarly, in correspondence with Solovine where Einstein explains his entheorizing attitude toward *determinism*, he writes (on June 12, 1950):

The question is whether or not the theoretical description of nature should be deterministic. Especially in that regard, in particular, there is the question of whether there is in general a conceptual picture of reality (for the single case) that is in principle complete and free of statistics. Only concerning this do opinions differ. (Solovine 1956, p. 99)

30. See Schilpp (1949), p. 672, and Born (1971), pp. 188, 209, and recall (see note 14 above) that Einstein's distinction between complete and incomplete descriptions involves precisely the question of whether statistics are fundamental (i.e., the question of causality).

31. The letter to Rothstein (see note 4, above) that also begins by emphasizing realism over causality proceeds, similarly, to bring the issue of causality right into the discussion.

I do not think that in these various passages Einstein is conflating causality and realism. Rather I take their constant conjunction in Einstein's remarks as a sign that *for him* the only sort of realism worth taking seriously, as a program for theory construction, was a realism built up by using strict, nonprobabilistic laws. Thus, unlike his attitude toward a space/time representation (which he clearly desired but could imagine doing science without) I believe that for Einstein causality was a *sine qua non* for a worthwhile program of realism. I should like to express this by saying that causality and observer-independence were *primary* features of Einstein's realism, whereas a space/time representation was an important but *secondary* feature.

5. Secondary Features

For a rounded picture of Einstein's realism I must mention two other secondary features. The first is connected, essentially, with a space/time representation. For Einstein makes it plain, in discussing his reservations about the quantum theory, that when real objects are represented in space and time they must satisfy a *principle of separation*.[32] In discussing the space/time framework, Einstein expresses the idea this way:

It is . . . characteristic of these physical objects that they are thought of as arranged in a space-time continuum. An essential aspect of this arrangement of things . . . is that they lay claim, at a certain time, to an existence independent of one another, provided these objects "are situated in different parts of space." (Einstein 1948; as translated in Born 1971, p. 172)

In his "Autobiographical Notes," Einstein puts it like this:

But on one supposition we should, in my opinion, absolutely hold fast: the real factual situation (or state) of the system S_1 is independent of what is done to the system S_2, which is spatially separated from the former. (Schilpp 1949, p. 85)

In chapters 3 and 5 I discussed the role of this separation principle in Einstein's critique of the quantum theory and, in chapter 4, the important distinction between Einstein's principle and the "locality" principles employed in the Bell no-hidden-variables literature. Here, I just want to point out how this principle depends on a prior commitment to a realist description (the "real factual situation [or state]") and to the causal nexus, which must *not* allow distant *real things* to have any immediate causal influences on one another. A realist space/time framework that would fail to satisfy

32. Einstein's term is *"Trennungsprinzip"*. See chapter 3.

the separation principle is one that Einstein ridicules as "telepathic" (Schilpp 1949, p. 85) and "spooky" (Schilpp 1949, p. 83).[33] It seems clear, then, that if we are to pursue realism in a space/time setting, Einstein requires that setting to respect his principle of separation. Separation is a necessary part of Einstein's conception of a space/time theory, although both the space/time representation and separation are secondary within the program of realism itself.

A further secondary feature of Einstein's realism is that, ideally, he would prefer the ontology of realist theories to be essentially monistic. That is, he considers it not really satisfactory for there to be more than one kind (or category) of real object; for instance, point-particles *and* continuous fields. His whole program for building a unified field theory is centered on the realization of this ideal.[34] His reductionist attitude toward psychology, and the mind-body problem, also seems to derive from this monism.[35] One might speculate that, perhaps, the deep source of this monistic attitude lies in Einstein's reading of (and "reverence" for) Spinoza.[36]

The "round" picture that we now have of Einstein's realism, then, is this. In the center are the linked, primary requirements of observer-independence and causality. Important, but not indispensable, are the secondary requirements of a spatio-temporal representation, which includes separation, and of monism. This whole circle of requirements, moreover, is not to be interpreted directly as a set of beliefs about nature, but rather it is to be entheorized; i.e., to be taken as a family of constraints on theories. Realism itself is to be understood as a program for constructing realist theories,

33. In a letter to E. Cassirer on March 16, 1937, Einstein uses the phrase "a sort of 'telepathic' coupling" ["*eine Art 'telepathischer' Wechselwirkung*"] to show his rejection of interpreting quantum mechanics in a nonseparable framework. This is the earliest use I have noticed of the particular language of telepathy, although the insistence on separability in quantum mechanics certainly goes back at least to the difficulty with his "Bestimmt" manuscript (see note 26, above). The letter of March 21, 1942, to C. Lanczos also uses the term "telepathic" in this context (Dukas and Hoffman 1979, p. 68). See Earman (forthcoming) for the varieties, and difficulties, of separability.

34. See Pais (1982), chapter 26, for a discussion of that program, and also Stachel (1983).

35. The opening passages of Einstein (1928) and the closing passages of Einstein (1950b) give one a good feel for Einstein's monistic reductionism.

36. The connection with Spinoza's monism fairly jumps out from a 1937 "aphorism" of Einstein's recorded by Dukas and Hoffman (1979), p. 38. "Body and soul are not two different things, but only two different ways of perceiving the same thing. Similarly, physics and psychology are only different attempts to link our experience together by way of systematic thought." See Hoffman (1972), pp. 94–95, for Einstein's "reverence" for Spinoza, and his view of himself as a "disciple." The Spinoza connection, of course, involves determinism as well as monism.

so conceived. And realism is to be judged on exactly the same basis as any other program for theory construction in science. Whatever are the nuances and "incommensurable" elements that enter into such judgments, "in the end" they are understood by Einstein to be based on the instrumental success of the scientific endeavor— the "dividends" that it yields, in its "coordination of experience," in terms of novel, successful predictions. The particular tenets of realism that are built into a realist theory are themselves to be judged "true" just to the extent that we hold the theory to be well confirmed observationally. But what the "truth" of these realist tenets amounts to ("concerning nature") is not a question that can be answered. It is, rather, to be deflected by turning instead to inquire about the instrumental success (or failure) of the program of realist theory construction that employs these tenets.

If this summary of Einstein's realism seems to trail off evasively, that is because, as I have emphasized, Einstein was deliberately evasive concerning the significance of his realism. And if this evasive sidestepping seems to make his realism a little paler and more shadowy than one might have expected, I'm afraid that too is because, in point of fact, Einstein's realism is not the robust metaphysical doctrine that one often associates with that label. What then are we to make of this frail creature, and is it a realism worthy of the name at all?

6. Was Einstein a Realist?

After this rather lengthy and detailed account of Einstein's realism, it may seem frivolous to be asking, at this point, whether Einstein was indeed a realist. Perhaps so, but then, as we have seen, Einstein's realism is a very peculiar kind of object, and one certainly ought to inquire how that object fits in with realism as it is more commonly understood. In the recent philosophical literature there are several positions that have been singled out as characteristically realist. One that Hilary Putnam has persuasively labeled "metaphysical realism" is centered on the belief in an external world, a world with a determinate observer-independent structure to which, increasingly, our scientific theories approximate by means of correspondence relations linking theories and the world.[37] I think this is close to the conception of realism that Gerald Holton ascribes to Einstein when he writes:

37. This "metaphysical realism" is labeled and attacked in Putnam (1981a). For a different line of attack and for reservations about Putnam's positive view see the next two chapters.

In the end, Einstein came to embrace the view which many, and perhaps he himself, thought earlier he had eliminated from physics in his basic 1905 paper on relativity theory: that there exists an external objective physical reality which we may hope to grasp—not directly, empirically, or logically, or with fullest certainty, but at least by an intuitive leap, one that is guided by experience of the totality of sensible "facts." (Holton 1973, p. 245)

There are, to be sure, many passages of Einstein's that express ideas close to that of such a metaphysical realism. But I think we ought to take Einstein seriously when he instructs us on how to read those passages; namely, that we are to entheorize the "realist" language and deflect questions of meaning (and "correspondence") onto questions of empirical support for the theory as a whole. I have certainly emphasized these themes already, but perhaps one more quote would not be amiss. In a typical metaphysically realist passage, in an address at Columbia University, Einstein raises the question as to the purpose and meaning of science, rejects the ideal of a merely positivist catalogue, and then says:

I do not believe, however, that so elementary an ideal could do much to kindle the investigator's passion from which really great achievements have arisen. Behind the tireless efforts of the investigator their lurks a stronger, more mysterious drive: it is existence and reality that one wishes to comprehend. (Einstein 1934, p. 112)[38]

Here, indeed, we have Holton's Einstein, the metaphysical realist. The address continues, however:

But one shrinks from the use of such words, for one soon gets into difficulties when one has to explain what is really meant by "reality" and by "comprehend" in such a general statement.

Thus Einstein deflects questions of meaning and, just as we would expect, goes on to entheorize and to focus on empirical adequacy instead:

When we strip the statement of its mystical elements we mean that we are seeking for the simplest possible system of thought which will bind together the observed facts. (Einstein 1934, p. 113)

These strategies of entheorizing and deflecting enable Einstein to use the vocabulary of metaphysical realism but to pull its metaphysical sting. For when we come to understand what Einstein means by his realist language it turns out to involve a program of

38. Stachel (1983) cites this as a lecture given at UCLA in 1932 and gives his own translation.

theory construction that is to be judged on the same physical basis as any other scientific program, and hence not a "metaphysical" program at all. Similarly, I would argue, the sting of Einstein's "realism" is also pulled by these strategies. For realism is not a matter of words ("external world," "real state of affairs," etc.) but rather a matter of what beliefs and commitments we have in uttering those words. Einstein is very clear in telling us that his commitments extend no more than to the pursuit of "realist" theories, and that his beliefs do not go beyond believing in the potential such theories have for organizing the observable data "with dividends." The metaphysical realist, however, has commitments and beliefs that go much further than these. Metaphysical realism involves precisely those elements that Einstein refers to (above) as "mystical," and that he is at great pains to strip off.

It is very tempting to call Einstein's realism a "nominal realism," for although Einstein uses a realist nomenclature he carefully instructs us not to understand it in the usual realist way. I shall point out below, however, that there is a feature of Einstein's realism that we have yet to come to terms with, and that will suggest a better label. To continue, then, exploring the "realism" of Einstein we might attend to another current candidate for what is characteristic of realism. I have in mind Bas van Fraassen's characterization of "scientific realism": "Science aims to give us, in its theories, a literally true story of what the world is like; and acceptance of a scientific theory involves the belief that it is true" (van Fraassen 1980, p. 8).

Since this account is already framed in terms of scientific theories, it holds out some immediate promise of touching Einstein's way of thinking. The key ideas here have to do with the *aims* of science (a literally true story about the world) and the nature of belief engendered by the *acceptance* of a theory (namely, belief that the theory is true). These concepts, having to do with the aims of science and the nature of theory-acceptance, also seem congenial to Einstein's conceptual framework. Moreover, in the passage just quoted from his Columbia address, for instance, Einstein does describe the aim of science as the comprehension of reality. This is much like the passage cited earlier from his "Autobiographical Notes," "Physics is an attempt conceptually to grasp reality . . ." (see section 3, above). On the surface, I don't think there is much distance between this conception of Einstein's and van Fraassen's formulation in terms of a "true story about what the world is like." However, if we push a little deeper and inquire about what such a true story (or, rather, true theory) is for Einstein, then, I think, we come to a parting of the ways. For, as I discussed in section 2, when

Einstein attaches the concept of truth to a theory, what he means is just that what the theory says about all the *observable* features of the world will be confirmed ("the coordination of experience 'with dividends' "). But this explication of "true theory" is almost exactly what van Fraassen means when he says that a theory is "empirically adequate" (van Fraassen 1980, p. 14). The difference between the literal truth of a theory and its empirical adequacy comes out if we attend to unobservable features described by a theory. Literal truth is just that (whatever "that" is). Empirical adequacy is something less. It allows us to accept statements about unobservables for logical processing and the like, but to hold as belief only that the theory as a whole will be confirmed by all possible observations. Einstein's way with the concept of truth is just the same. He would say, perhaps, that some statement involving unobservables "is true." But what he *means* is just that incorporating that statement in the relevant theory, and processing it logically there, leads to an empirically adequate story. (Recall his discussion of the decay time of an atom in section 3.) Once again it is easy to be misled by Einstein's words, his insistence (e.g., concerning the decay time) that statements about unobservables can indeed be true. But if we follow his own directions to get at what he means, then the realist tone of his words gets damped by the empiricist constraints that he places on that meaning. Indeed it would not be too far off if we summarized Einstein's views this way: "Science aims to give us theories which are empirically adequate; and acceptance of a theory involves as belief only that it is empirically adequate."

Of course students of van Fraassen will recognize those words as his, and that passage in particular as van Fraassen's informal characterization of his own empiricist and nonrealist position, which he calls "constructive empiricism" (van Fraassen 1980, p. 12). My argument, then, is that if we understand Einstein in the way that he asks us to, his own realist-sounding language maps out a position closer to constructive empiricism than to either "metaphysical realism" or "scientific realism."

I think there is no backing away from the fact that Einstein's socalled realism has a deeply empiricist core that makes it a "realism" more nominal than real. This is, perhaps, not so surprising if we recall the intellectual debt to Hume and Mach that Einstein often acknowledged explicitly,[39] and that is implicit in much of his scientific writings. But then, too, we should not back away from the

---

39. See, e.g., Schilpp (1949), p. 13 and p. 21ff. The letter to D. S. Mackey of April 26, 1948 (see note 2, above), is informative on this score, emphasizing especially the influence of Hume.

fact that Einstein did insist on using the nomenclature of realism, and that he explicitly opposed the positivism and empiricism that was mobilized, especially, in support of certain interpretations of the quantum theory.

His characteristic expressions of opposition were terms like "sterile positivism" or "senseless empiricism." We could understand the adjectives here ("sterile," "senseless") as expressing Einstein's negative attitude toward the probable long-term success of an empiricist or positivist program for doing science. But we could also take his expression as applying to the feeling-tone involved in pursuing a positivist (or empiricist) program. It would, he might say, feel pointless to *do* "positive" science; there would be no underlying motivation or drive; it would not make science seem really worthwhile or meaningful.[40] I invent, on Einstein's behalf, but not much. For if we look again at his Columbia address, then we see that whereas he quickly backs off the *cognitive* force of his realist remarks, he fully embraces the *motivational* force of that realism—especially by contrast with the program of positivism. I believe that here is the clue to Einstein's realist language, and that here we find what makes Einstein's realism more than nominal. To anticipate the answer, let me suggest the term "motivational realism" for Einstein's view.

7. Motivational Realism

As early as 1918, Einstein's expressions of realism are presented in terms of motivations for the pursuit of science. In his moving and oft-quoted address in honor of Max Planck's sixtieth birthday, Einstein identifies both a "negative motive" (to "escape from everyday life") and a "positive" one (to "substitute" the (realist) "picture of the world" for "the world of experience, and thus to overcome it").[41] There too Einstein compares the realist attitude to a kind of "religious feeling" that drives the scientific effort with "no deliberate intention or program, but straight from the heart" (Einstein 1918, pp. 225, 227). Einstein uses similar expressions in his "Autobiographical Notes" to describe the period of his childhood (before the age of twelve), when he was immersed in "the religious

40. A similar feeling comes through in Einstein's castigation of the quantum theory in a letter to D. Lipkin on July 5, 1952: "This theory (the present quantum theory) reminds me a little of the system of delusions of an exceedingly intelligent paranoic, concocted of incoherent elements of thought."

41. Translated as "Principles of Research" (Einstein 1918), the original title of this address was "*Motiv des Forschens*" or, loosely, "Motives for Research." Holton (1973), pp. 376–78, retranslates some passages from this talk, as does Howard (1983). I have used the "official" translation.

paradise of youth," as a "first attempt to free myself from the chains of the 'merely-personal' " (Schilpp 1949, p. 5). His second attempt (around the age of twelve) was in fact his turning to science, when he began to feel that "out yonder there was this huge world, which exists independently of us human beings and which stands before us like a great, eternal riddle, at least partially accessible to our inspection and thinking" (Schilpp 1949, p. 5). Note the realist language *and* the motivational context.

The idea of pursuing science as a replacement for the "religious paradise of youth" is not suggested, of course, in terms of cognitive appeal, but rather in terms of what motivates, enlivens, and gives meaning to one's activities. In their late correspondence, Einstein's old friend Solovine chides him for using the word "religious" in this context, to which Einstein replies (January 1, 1951):

I have no better expression than the term "religious" for this trust [*Vertrauen*] in the rational character of reality and in its being accessible, at least to some extent, to human reason. Where this feeling is absent, science degenerates into senseless [*geistlose*] empiricism. Too bad [*Es schert mich einen Teufel*] if the priests make capital out of it. Anyway, there is no cure for that [*ist kein Kraut gewachsen*]. (Solovine 1956, p. 102)

In these various ways, from 1918 on, Einstein tells us that realism is the main motive that lies behind creative scientific work and makes it worth doing. But he clearly suggests that realism does not motivate scientific work in the manner of a deliberate intention or plan or duty (e.g., "to seek realist theories"). It is not as though we were first persuaded that realist theories are somehow best and then, on that account, rationally enjoined to pursue them. The operation of realism as a motive is, rather, like that of a "drive." It produces behavior that accords with and instantiates an inner "trust," both behavior and trust coming "straight from the heart." I think that in this way Einstein is placing realism among the prerational springs of human behavior (not, of course, among the irrational ones), those springs that we often conceive of not just as the source of creativity, but also as the source of deep satisfaction in creative endeavors.

These ways of characterizing the motivational aspects of realism suggest to me the ideas of depth psychology, the unconscious mechanisms that cause certain actions and lend them a certain feeling-tone. This association is, perhaps, not so removed from what would be acceptable to Einstein himself. In 1953 he wrote:

Even if we think that much of Freud's theory may be mythology produced by a mighty imagination, nevertheless I believe that there seems to be much truth in the idea of suppression and inhibition, and in the fact that most of the causation in our mental life is not accessible to our consciousness.[42]

The particular psychoanalytic concept that seems to me most apt for Einstein's realism is the concept of an *imago*—the complex ideal of the parent, rooted in the unconscious, elaborated by means of childhood fantasies, and bound with the strong affect of that childhood period. The parental imago lies behind and drives certain of our behavior just as Einstein tells us that realism "lurks behind" and drives our work as scientists. Properly integrated, the imago can be the source of deep commitment and of deep satisfaction, just like realism. The fantasy elements associated with the imago will, however, find some outward expression. In Einstein, I would suggest, the fantasy elements associated with his realist imago were expressed precisely by his realist vocabulary. Their fantasy nature, I believe, is marked clearly by Einstein's instant retreat from them just as soon as they are let out into the open. I think Einstein knew perfectly well that spinning the tales of "reality" was just letting childhood fantasies have their head. But he also knew that the affect bound to these fantasies was a factor in scientific life that must be given its due.

Einstein's realism comes out most clearly in his realist language. That language, I urge, must not be taken at face value. It does not mark a set of beliefs about "reality." It is, rather, the dues that Einstein felt worth paying for his passionate commitment to science, and for the meaning that scientific work gave to his life. Einstein's realism, then, is motivational. It is not adequately expressed by any special set of beliefs about the world, nor even by the injunction to pursue realist theories. Motivational realism is really not a doctrine but a way of being, the incorporation of a realist imago and its expression in the activities of one's daily, scientific life. That this incorporation and way of life actually produces confirmed theories, and hence "knowledge," was—appropriately—considered by Einstein to be a "miracle," concerning which he wrote to Solovine (March 30, 1952): "The curious thing is that we must be content with circumscribing the "miracle" without having any legitimate way to approach it" (Solovine 1956, p. 115).

We should be wary, therefore, of any attempt to "legitimate" Einstein's realism by construing it as a set of realist doctrines (or beliefs). For Einstein, realism was motivational, and the language of realism was just his way of "circumscribing the 'miracle.' "

42. Letter to J. Pirone, November 6, 1953.

The Natural Ontological Attitude

Let us fix our attention out of ourselves as much as possible; let us chace our imagination to the heavens, or to the utmost limits of the universe; we never really advance a step beyond ourselves, nor can conceive any kind of existence, but those perceptions, which have appear'd in that narrow compass. This is the universe of the imagination, nor have we any idea but what is there produced.

Hume, *Treatise*, book 1, part II, section VI

Realism is dead. Its death was announced by the neopositivists who realized that they could accept all the results of science, including all the members of the scientific zoo, and still declare that the questions raised by the existence claims of realism were mere pseudo-questions. Its death was hastened by the debates over the interpretation of quantum theory, where Bohr's nonrealist philosophy was seen to win out over Einstein's passionate realism. Its death was certified, finally, as the last two generations of physical scientists turned their backs on realism and have managed, nevertheless, to do science successfully without it. To be sure, some recent philosophical literature has appeared to pump up the ghostly shell and to give it new life. I think these efforts will eventually be seen and understood as the first stage in the process of mourning, the stage of denial. But I think we shall pass through this first stage and into that of acceptance, for realism is well and truly dead, and we have work to get on with, in identifying a suitable successor. To aid that

My thanks to Charles Chastain, Gerald Dworkin, and Paul Teller for useful preliminary conversations about realism and its rivals, but especially to Charles— for only he, then, (mostly) agreed with me, and surely that deserves special mention. This paper was written by me, but cothought by Micky Forbes. I don't know any longer whose ideas are whose. That means that the responsibility for errors and confusions is at least half Micky's (and she is two-thirds responsible for "NOA"). Finally, I am grateful to the many people who offered comments and criticisms at the conference on realism sponsored by the Department of Philosophy, University of North Carolina at Greensboro in March 1982, where an earlier version of this chapter was first presented under the title "Pluralism and Scientific Progress." I am also grateful to the National Science Foundation for a grant in support of this research.

work I want to do three things in this essay. First, I want to show that the arguments in favor of realism are not sound, and that they provide no rational support for belief in realism. Then, I want to recount the essential role of nonrealist attitudes for the development of science in this century, and thereby (I hope) to loosen the grip of the idea that only realism provides a progressive philosophy of science. Finally, I want to sketch out what seems to me a viable nonrealist position, one that is slowly gathering support and that seems a decent philosophy for postrealist times.[1]

1. Arguments for Realism

Recent philosophical argument in support of realism tries to move from the success of the scientific enterprise to the necessity for a realist account of its practice. As I see it, the arguments here fall on two distinct levels. On the ground level, as it were, one attends to particular successes; such as novel, confirmed predictions, striking unifications of disparate-seeming phenomena (or fields), successful piggybacking from one theoretical model to another, and the like. Then, we are challenged to account for such success, and told that the best and, it is slyly suggested, perhaps, the *only* way of doing so is on a realist basis. I do not find the details of these ground-level arguments at all convincing. Neither does Larry Laudan (1984) and, fortunately, he has provided a forceful and detailed analysis which shows that not even with a lot of handwaving (to shield the gaps in the argument) and charity (to excuse them) can realism itself be used to explain the very successes to which it invites our attention. But there is a second level of realist argument, the methodological level, that derives from Popper's (1972) attack on instrumentalism, which he attacks as being inadequate to account for the details of his own, falsificationist methodology. Arguments on this methodological level have been skillfully developed by Richard Boyd (1981, 1984), and by one of the earlier Hilary Putnams (1975). These arguments focus on the methods embedded in scientific practice, methods teased out in ways that seem to me accurate and perceptive about ongoing science. We are then challenged to account for why these methods lead to scientific success and told

1. In the final section, I call this postrealism "NOA." Among recent views that relate to NOA, I would include Hilary Putnam's "internal realism," Richard Rorty's "epistemological behaviorism," the "semantic realism" espoused by Paul Horwich, parts of the "Mother Nature" story told by William Lycan, and the defense of common sense worked out by Joseph Pitt (as a way of reconciling W. Sellars's manifest and scientific images). For references, see Putnam (1981a), Rorty (1979), Horwich (1982), Lycan (1982), and Pitt (1981).

that the best and, (again) perhaps, the only truly adequate way of explaining the matter is on the basis of realism.

I want to examine some of these methodological arguments in detail to display the flaws that seem to be inherent in them. But first I want to point out a deep and, I think, insurmountable problem with this entire strategy of defending realism, as I have laid it out above. To set up the problem, let me review the debates in the early part of this century over the foundations of mathematics, the debates that followed Cantor's introduction of set theory. There were two central worries here, one over the meaningfulness of Cantor's hierarchy of sets insofar as it outstripped the number-theoretic content required by Kronecker (and others); the second worry, certainly deriving in good part from the first, was for the consistency (or not) of the whole business. In this context, Hilbert devised a quite brilliant program to try to show the consistency of a mathematical theory by using only the most stringent and secure means. In particular, if one were concerned over the consistency of set theory, then clearly a set-theoretic proof of consistency would be of no avail. For if set theory were inconsistent, then such a consistency proof would be both possible and of no significance. Thus, Hilbert suggested that finite constructivist means, satisfactory even to Kronecker (or Brouwer) ought to be employed in meta-mathematics. Of course, Hilbert's program was brought to an end in 1931, when Gödel showed the impossibility of such a stringent consistency proof. But Hilbert's idea was, I think, correct even though it proved to be unworkable. Metatheoretic arguments must satisfy more stringent requirements than those placed on the arguments used by the theory in question, for otherwise the significance of reasoning about the theory is simply moot. I think this maxim applies with particular force to the discussion of realism.

Those suspicious of realism, from Osiander to Poincaré and Duhem to the "constructive empiricism" of van Fraassen,[2] have been worried about the significance of the explanatory apparatus in scientific investigations. While they appreciate the systematization and coherence brought about by scientific explanation, they question whether acceptable explanations need to be true and, hence, whether the entities mentioned in explanatory principles need to exist.[3] Suppose they are right. Suppose, that is, that the usual explanation-inferring devices in scientific practice do not lead

---

2. Van Fraassen (1980). See especially pp. 97–101 for a discussion of the truth of explanatory theories. To see that the recent discussion of realism is joined right here, one should contrast van Fraassen with Newton-Smith (1981), especially chap. 8.
3. Cartwright (1983) includes some marvelous essays on these issues.

to principles that are reliably true (or nearly so), nor to entities whose existence (or near existence) is reliable. In that case, the usual abductive methods that lead us to good explanations (even to "the best explanation") cannot be counted on to yield results even approximately true. But the strategy that leads to realism, as I have indicated, is just such an ordinary sort of abductive inference. Hence, if the nonrealist were correct in his doubts, then such an inference to realism as the best explanation (or the like), while possible, would be of no significance—exactly as in the case of a consistency proof using the methods of an inconsistent system. It seems, then, that Hilbert's maxim applies to the debate over realism: to argue for realism one must employ methods more stringent than those in ordinary scientific practice. In particular, one must not beg the question as to the significance of explanatory hypotheses by assuming that they carry truth as well as explanatory efficacy.

There is a second way of seeing the same result. Notice that the issue over realism is precisely the issue of whether we should believe in the reality of those individuals, properties, relations, processes, and so forth, used in well-supported explanatory hypotheses. Now what *is* the hypothesis of realism, as it arises as an explanation of scientific practice? It is just the hypothesis that our accepted scientific theories are approximately true, where "being approximately true" is taken to denote an extratheoretical relation between theories and the world. Thus, to address doubts over the reality of relations posited by explanatory hypotheses, the realist proceeds to introduce a further explanatory hypothesis (realism), itself positing such a relation (approximate truth). Surely anyone serious about the issue of realism, and with an open mind about it, would have to behave inconsistently if he were to accept the realist move as satisfactory.

Thus, both at the ground level and at the level of methodology, no support accrues to realism by showing that realism is a good hypothesis for explaining scientific practice. If we are open-minded about realism to begin with, then such a demonstration (even if successful) merely begs the question that we have left open ("need we take good explanatory hypotheses as true?"). Thus, Hilbert's maxim applies, and we must employ patterns of argument more stringent than the usual abductive ones. What might they be? Well, the obvious candidates are patterns of induction leading to empirical generalizations. But, to frame empirical generalizations, we must first have some observable connections between observables. For realism, this must connect theories with the world by way of approximate truth. But no such connections are observable and, hence, suitable as the basis for an inductive inference. I do not want to labor the points at issue here. They amount to the well-known idea that realism commits one to an unverifiable correspondence with the world. So far as I am aware, no recent defender of realism has tried to make a case based on a Hilbert strategy of using suitably stringent grounds and, given the problems over correspondence, it is probably just as well.

The strategy of arguments for realism as a good explanatory hypothesis, then, *cannot* (logically speaking) be effective for an open-minded nonbeliever. But what of the believer? Might he not, at least, show a kind of internal coherence about realism as an overriding philosophy of science, and should that not be of some solace, at least for the realist?[4] Recall, however, the analogue with

4. Some realists may look for genuine support, and not just solace, in such a coherentist line. They may see in their realism a basis for general epistemology, philosophy of language, and so forth (as does Boyd 1981, 1984). If they find in all this a coherent and comprehensive worldview, then they might want to argue for their philosophy as Wilhelm Wien argued (in 1909) for special relativity, "What speaks for it most of all is the inner consistency which makes it possible to lay a foundation having no self-contradictions, one that applies to the totality of physical appearances." (Quoted by Gerald Holton, "Einstein's Scientific Program: Formative Years," in H. Woolf (1980), p. 58.) Insofar as the realist moves away from the abductive defense of realism to seek support, instead, from the merits of a comprehensive philosophical system with a realist core, he marks as a failure the bulk of recent defenses of realism. Even so, he will not avoid the critique pursued in the text. For although my argument above has been directed, in particular, against the abductive strategy, it is itself based on a more general maxim; namely, that the form of argument used to support realism must be more stringent than the form of argument embedded in the very scientific practice that realism itself is supposed to ground—on pain of begging the question. Just as the abductive strategy fails because it violates this maxim, so too would the coherentist strategy, should the realist turn from one to the other. For, as we see from the words of Wien, the same coherentist line that the realist would appropriate for his own support is part of ordinary scientific practice in framing judgments about competing theories. It is, therefore, not a line of defense available to the realist. Moreover, just as the truth-bearing status of abduction is an issue dividing realists from various nonrealists, so too is the status of coherence-based inference. Turning from abduction to coherence, therefore, still leaves the realist begging the question. Thus, when we bring out into the open the character of arguments *for* realism, we see quite plainly that they do not work. See Fine (1986) for a more detailed discussion.

In support of realism there seem to be only those "reasons of the heart" which, as Pascal says, reason does not know. Indeed, I have long felt that belief in realism involves a profound leap of faith, not at all dissimilar from the faith that animates deep religious convictions. I would welcome engagement with realists on this understanding, just as I enjoy conversation on a similar basis with my religious friends. The dialogue will proceed more fruitfully, I think, when the realists finally stop pretending to a rational support for their faith, which they do not have. Then we can all enjoy their intricate and sometimes beautiful philosophical constructions (of, e.g., knowledge, or reference, etc.), even though to us, as nonbelievers, they may seem only wonder-full castles in the air.

consistency proofs for inconsistent systems. That sort of harmony should be of no solace to anyone. But for realism, I fear, the verdict is even harsher. For, so far as I can see, the arguments in question just do not work, and the reason for that has to do with the same question-begging procedures that I have already identified. Let me look closely at some methodological arguments in order to display the problems.

A typical realist argument on the methodological level deals with what I shall call the problem of the "small handful." It goes like this. At any time, in a given scientific area, only a small handful of alternative theories (or hypotheses) are in the field. Only such a small handful are seriously considered as competitors, or as possible successors to some theory requiring revision. Moreover, in general, this handful displays a sort of family resemblance in that none of these live options will be too far from the previously accepted theories in the field, each preserving the well-confirmed features of the earlier theories and deviating only in those aspects less confirmed. Why? Why does this narrowing down of our choices to such a small handful of cousins of our previously accepted theories work to produce good successor theories?

The realist answers this as follows. Suppose that the already existing theories are themselves approximately true descriptions of the domain under consideration. Then surely it is reasonable to restrict one's search for successor theories to those whose ontologies and laws resemble what we already have, especially where what we already have is well confirmed. And if these earlier theories were approximately true, then so will be such conservative successors. Hence, such successors will be good predictive instruments; that is, they will be successful in their own right.

The small-handful problem raises three distinct questions: (1) why only a small handful out of the (theoretically) infinite number of possibilities? (2) why the conservative family resemblance between members of the handful? and (3) why does the strategy of narrowing the choices in this way work so well? The realist response does not seem to address the first issue at all, for even if we restrict ourselves just to successor theories resembling their progenitors, as suggested, there would still, theoretically, always be more than a small handful of these. To answer the second question, as to why conserve the well-confirmed features of ontology and laws, the realist must suppose that such confirmation is a mark of an approximately correct ontology and approximately true laws. But how could the realist possibly justify such an assumption? Surely, there is no valid inference of the form, "T is well-confirmed; therefore, there exist objects pretty much of the sort required by T and satisfying laws approximating those of T." Any of the dramatic shifts of ontology in science show the invalidity of this schema. For example, the loss of the ether from the turn-of-the-century electrodynamic theories demonstrates this at the level of ontology, and the dynamics of the Rutherford-Bohr atom vis-à-vis the classical energy principles for rotating systems demonstrates it at the level of laws. Of course, the realist might respond that there is no question of a strict inference between being well confirmed and being approximately true (in the relevant respects), but there is a probable inference of some sort. But of what sort? Certainly there is no probability relation that rests on inductive evidence here. For there is no independent evidence for the relation of approximate truth itself; at least, the realist has yet to produce any evidence that is independent of the argument under examination. But if the probabilities are not grounded inductively, then how else? Here, I think the realist may well try to fall back on his original strategy and suggest that being approximately true provides the best explanation for being well confirmed. This move throws us back to the ground-level realist argument, the argument from specific success to an approximately true description of reality, which Lauden (1984) has criticized. I should point out, before looking at the third question, that if this last move is the one the realist wants to make, then his success at the methodological level can be no better than his success at the ground level. If he fails there, he fails across the board.

The third question, and the one I think the realist puts most weight on, is why does the small-handful strategy work so well. The instrumentalist, for example, is thought to have no answer here. He must just note that it does work well and be content with that. The realist, however, can explain why it works by citing the transfer of approximate truth from predecessor theories to the successor theories. But what does this explain? At best, it explains why the successor theories cover the same ground as well as their predecessors, for the conservative strategy under consideration assures that. But note that here the instrumentalist can offer the same account: if we insist on preserving the well-confirmed components of earlier theories in later theories, then, of course, the later ones will do well over the well-confirmed ground. The difficulty, however, is not here at all but rather in how to account for the successes of the later theories in new ground, or with respect to novel predictions, or in overcoming the anomalies of the earlier theories. And what can the realist possibly say in this area except that the theorist, in proposing a new theory, has happened to make a good guess? For nothing in the approximate truth of the old theory can guarantee (or even make it likely) that modifying the theory in its less-confirmed parts will produce a progressive shift. The history of science shows well enough how such tinkering succeeds only now and again, and fails for the most part. This history of failures can scarcely be adduced to explain the occasional success. The idea that by extending what is approximately true one is likely to bring new approximate truth is a chimera. It finds support neither in the logic of approximate truth nor in the history of science. The problem for the realist is how to explain the *occasional success* of a strategy that *usually fails*.[5] I think he has no special resources with which to do this. In particular, his usual fallback onto approximate truth provides nothing more than a gentle pillow. He may rest on it comfortably, but it does not really help to move his cause forward.

The problem of the small handful raises three challenges: why small? why narrowly related? and why does it work? The realist has no answer for the first of these, begs the question as to the truth of explanatory hypotheses on the second, and has no resources for addressing the third. For comparison, it may be useful to see how well his archenemy, the instrumentalist, fares on the same turf. The instrumentalist, I think, has a substantial basis for addressing the questions of smallness and narrowness, for he can point out that it is extremely difficult to come up with alternative theories that satisfy the many empirical constraints posed by the instrumental success of theories already in the field. Often it is hard enough to come up with even one such alternative. Moreover, the common apprenticeship of scientists working in the same area certainly has the effect of narrowing down the range of options by channeling thought into the commonly accepted categories. If we add to this the instrumentally justified rule, "If it has worked well in the past, try it again," then we get a rather good account, I think, of why there is usually only a small and narrow handful. As to why this strategy works to produce instrumentally successful science,

---

5. I hope all readers of this essay will take this idea to heart. For in formulating the question as to how to explain why the methods of science lead to instrumental success, the realist has seriously misstated the explanandum. Overwhelmingly, the results of the conscientious pursuit of scientific inquiry are failures: failed theories, failed hypotheses, failed conjectures, inaccurate measurements, incorrect estimations of parameters, fallacious causal inferences, and so forth. If explanations are appropriate here, then what requires explaining is why the very same methods produce an overwhelming background of failures and, occasionally, also a pattern of successes. The realist literature has not yet begun to address this question, much less to offer even a hint of how to answer it.

we have already noted that for the most part it does not. Most of what this strategy produces are failures. It is a quirk of scientific memory that this fact gets obscured, much as do the memories of bad times during a holiday vacation when we recount all our "wonderful" vacation adventures to a friend. Those instrumentalists who incline to a general account of knowledge as a social construction can go further at this juncture and lean on the sociology of science to explain how the scientific community "creates" its knowledge. I am content just to back off here and note that over the problem of the small handful, the instrumentalist scores at least two out of three, whereas the realist, left to his own devices, has struck out.[6]

I think the source of the realist's failure here is endemic to the methodological level, infecting all of his arguments in this domain. It resides, in the first instance, in his repeating the question-begging move from explanatory efficacy to the truth of the explanatory hypothesis. And in the second instance, it resides in his twofold mishandling of the concept of approximate truth: first, in his trying to project from some body of assumed approximate truths *to* some further and novel such truths, and second, in his needing genuine access to the relation of correspondence. There are no general connections of this first sort, however, sanctioned by the logic of approximate truth, nor secondly, any such warranted access. However, the realist must pretend that there are in order to claim explanatory power for his realism. We have seen those two agents infecting the realist way with the problem of the small handful. Let me show them at work in another methodological favorite of the realist, the "problem of conjunctions."

The problem of conjunctions is this. If T and T' are independently well-confirmed, explanatory theories, and if no shared term is ambiguous between the two, then we expect the conjunction of T and T' to be a reliable predictive instrument (provided, of course, that the theories are not mutually inconsistent). Why? challenges the realist, and he answers as follows. If we make the realist assumption that T and T', being well confirmed, are approximately true of the entities (etc.) to which they refer, and if the unambiguity requirement is taken realistically as requiring a domain of common reference, then the conjunction of the two theories will also be approximately true and, hence, it will produce reliable observational predictions. Q.E.D.

6. Of course, the realist can appropriate the devices and answers of the instrumentalist, but that would be cheating, and anyway, it would not provide the desired support of realism per se.

But notice our agents at work. First, the realist makes the question-begging move from explanations to their approximate truth, and then he mistreats approximate truth. For nothing in the logic of approximate truth sanctions the inference from "T is approximately true" and "T' is approximately true" to the conclusion that the conjunction "$T \cdot T'$" is approximately true. Rather, in general, the tightness of an approximation dissipates as we pile on further approximations. If T is within ϵ, in its estimation of some parameter, and T' is also within ϵ, then the only general thing we can say is that the conjunction will be within 2ϵ of the parameter. Thus, the logic of approximate truth should lead us to the opposite conclusion here; that is, that the conjunction of two theories is, in general, *less* reliable than either (over their common domain). But this is neither what we expect nor what we find. Thus, it seems quite implausible that our actual expectations about the reliability of conjunctions rest on the realist's stock of approximate truths.

Of course, the realist could try to retrench here and pose an additional requirement of some sort of uniformity on the character of the approximations, as between T and T'.[7] It is difficult to see how the realist could do this successfully without making reference to the distance between the approximations and "the truth." For what kind of internalist requirement could possibly insure the narrowing of this distance? But the realist is in no position to impose such requirements, since neither he nor anyone else has the requisite access to "the truth." Thus, whatever uniformity-of-approximation condition the realist might impose, we could still demand to be shown that this leads closer to the truth, not farther away. The realist will have no demonstration, except to point out to us that it all works (sometimes!). But that was the original puzzle.[8] Actually, I think the puzzle is not very difficult. For surely, if we do not entangle ourselves with issues over approximation, there is no deep mystery as to why two compatible and successful theories lead us to expect their conjunction to be successful. For in forming the conjunction, we just add the reliable predictions of one onto the reliable predictions of the other, having antecedently ruled out the possibility of conflict.

7. Paul Teller has made this suggestion to me in conversation.

8. Niiniluoto (1982) contains interesting formal constructions for "degree of truthlikeness," and related versimilia. As conjectured above, they rely on an unspecified correspondence relation to the truth and on measures of the "distance" from the truth. Moreover, they fail to sanction that projection, from some approximate truths to other, novel truths, which lies at the core of realist rationalizations.

There is more to be said about this topic. In particular, we need to address the question of why we expect the logical gears of the two theories to mesh. However, I think that a discussion of the realist position here would only bring up the same methodological and logical problems that we have already uncovered at the center of the realist argument.

Indeed, this schema of knots in the realist argument applies across the board and vitiates every single argument at the methodological level. Thus my conclusion here is harsh, indeed. The methodological arguments for realism fail, even though, were they successful, they would still not support the case. For the general strategy they are supposed to implement is just not stringent enough to provide rational support for realism. In the next two sections, I will try to show that this situation is just as well, for realism has not always been a progressive factor in the development of science and, anyway, there is a position other than realism that is more attractive.

2. Realism and Progress

If we examine the two twentieth-century giants among physical theories, relativity and the quantum theory, we find a living refutation of the realist's claim that only his view of science explains its progress, and we find some curious twists and contrasts over realism as well. The theories of relativity are almost single-handedly the work of Albert Einstein. Einstein's early positivism and his methodological debt to Mach (and Hume) leap right out of the pages of the 1905 paper on special relativity.[9] The same positivist strain is evident in the 1916 general relativity paper as well, where Einstein (in section 3 of that paper) tries to justify his requirement of general covariance by means of a suspicious-looking verificationist argument which, he says, "takes away from space and time the last remnants of physical objectivity" (Einstein et al. 1952, p. 117). A study of his tortured path to general relativity[10] shows the repeated use of this Machist line, always used to deny that some concept has a real referent. Whatever other, competing strains there were in Einstein's philosophical orientation (and there certainly were others), it would be hard to deny the importance of this instrumentalist/

9. See Gerald Holton, "Mach, Einstein, and the Search for Reality," in Holton (1973), pp. 219–59. I have tried to work out the precise role of this positivist methodology in chapter 2. See also Fine (1981a).

10. Earman and Glymour (1978). The tortuous path detailed by Earman is sketched by B. Hoffmann (1972), pp. 116–28. A nontechnical and illuminating account is given by John Stachel (1979).

positivist attitude in liberating Einstein from various realist commitments. Indeed, on another occasion, I would argue in detail
that without the "freedom from reality" provided by his early
reverence for Mach, a central tumbler necessary to unlock the secret
of special relativity would never have fallen into place.[11] A few
years after his work on general relativity, however, roughly around
1920, Einstein underwent a philosophical conversion, turning away
from his positivist youth (he was forty-one in 1920) and becoming
deeply committed to realism (see chapter 6). In particular, following
his conversion, Einstein wanted to claim genuine reality for the
central theoretical entities of the general theory, the four-
dimensional space-time manifold and associated tensor fields. This
is a serious business, for if we grant his claim, then not only do
space and time cease to be real but so do virtually all of the usual
dynamical quantities.[12] Thus motion, as we understand it, itself
ceases to be real. The current generation of philosophers of space
and time (led by Howard Stein and John Earman) have followed
Einstein's lead here. But, interestingly, not only do these ideas boggle the mind of the average man in the street (like you and me),
they boggle most contemporary scientific minds as well.[13] That is,
I believe the majority opinion among working, knowledgeable scientists is that general relativity provides a magnificent organizing
tool for treating certain gravitational problems in astrophysics and
cosmology. But few, I believe, give credence to the kind of realist
existence and nonexistence claims that I have been mentioning.
For relativistic physics, then, it appears that a nonrealist attitude
was important in its development, that the founder nevertheless
espoused a realist attitude to the finished product, but that most
who actually use it think of the theory as a powerful instrument,
rather than as expressing a "big truth."

With quantum theory, this sequence gets a twist. Heisenberg's
seminal paper of 1925 is prefaced by the following abstract, an-
nouncing, in effect, his philosophical stance: "In this paper an
attempt will be made to obtain bases for a quantum-theoretical
mechanics based exclusively on relations between quantities observable in principle" (Heisenberg 1925, p. 879). In the body of

11. I have in mind the role played by the analysis of simultaneity in Einstein's
path to special relativity. Despite the important study by Arthur Miller (1981) and
an imaginative pioneering work by John Earman et al. (1983), I think the role of
positivist analysis in the 1905 paper has yet to be properly understood.

12. Roger Jones in "Realism about What?" (in draft) explains very nicely some
of the difficulties here.

13. I think the ordinary, deflationist attitude of working scientists is much like
that of Steven Weinberg (1972).

the paper, Heisenberg not only rejects any reference to unobservables, he also moves away from the very idea that one should try
to form any picture of a reality underlying his mechanics. To be
sure, Schrödinger, the second father of quantum theory, seems
originally to have had a vague picture of an underlying wavelike
reality for his own equation. But he was quick to see the difficulties
here and, just as quickly, although reluctantly, abandoned the attempt to interpolate any reference to reality.[14] These instrumentalist moves away from a realist construal of the emerging quantum
theory were given particular force by Bohr's so-called philosophy
of complementarity. This nonrealist position was consolidated at
the time of the famous Solvay Conference, in October 1927, and
is firmly in place today. Such quantum nonrealism is part of what
every graduate physicist learns and practices. It is the conceptual
backdrop to all the brilliant successes in atomic, nuclear, and particle
physics over the past fifty years. Physicists have learned to think
about their theory in a highly nonrealist way, and doing just that
has brought about the most marvelous predictive success in the
history of science.

The war between Einstein, the realist, and Bohr, the nonrealist,
over the interpretation of quantum theory was not, I believe, just
a sideshow in physics, nor an idle intellectual exercise. It was an
important endeavor undertaken by Bohr on behalf of the enterprise of physics as a progressive science. For Bohr believed (and
this fear was shared by Heisenberg, Sommerfeld, Pauli, and Born—
and all the big guys) that Einstein's realism, if taken seriously, would
block the consolidation and articulation of the new physics and,
thereby, stop the progress of science. They were afraid, in particular, that Einstein's realism would lead the next generation of the
brightest and best students into scientific dead ends. Alfred Landé,
for example, as a graduate student, was interested in spending some
time in Berlin to sound out Einstein's ideas. His supervisor was
Sommerfeld, and recalling this period, Landé (1974, p. 460) writes,
"The more pragmatic Sommerfeld . . . warned his students, one of
them this writer, not to spend too much time on the hopeless task
of "explaining" the quantum but rather to accept it as fundamental
and help work out its consequences."

The task of "explaining" the quantum, of course, is the realist
program for identifying a reality underlying the formulas of the
theory and thereby explaining the predictive success of the formulas as approximately true descriptions of this reality. It is this

14. See Wessels (1979), and chapter 5.

program that I have criticized in the first part of this chapter, and this same program that the builders of quantum theory saw as a scientific dead end. Einstein knew perfectly well that the issue was joined right here. In the summer of 1935, he wrote to Schrödinger, "The real problem is that physics is a kind of metaphysics; physics describes 'reality.' But we do not know what 'reality' is. We know it only through physical description. . . . But the Talmudic philosopher sniffs at 'reality,' as at a frightening creature of the naive mind."[15]

By avoiding the bogey of an underlying reality, the "Talmudic" originators of quantum theory seem to have set subsequent generations on precisely the right path. Those inspired by realist ambitions have produced no predictively successful physics. Neither Einstein's conception of a unified field, nor the ideas of the de Broglie group about pilot waves, nor the Bohm-inspired interest in hidden variables has made for scientific progress. To be sure, several philosophers of physics, including another Hilary Putnam and myself, have fought a battle over the last decade to show that the quantum theory is at least consistent with some kind of underlying reality. I believe that Hilary has abandoned the cause, perhaps in part on account of the recent Bell-inequality problem over correlation experiments, a problem that van Fraassen (1982) calls "the Charybdis of realism." My own recent work in the area suggests that we may still be able to keep realism afloat in this whirlpool.[16] But the possibility (as I still see it) for a realist account of the quantum domain should not lead us away from appreciating the historical facts of the matter.

One can hardly doubt the importance of a nonrealist attitude for the development and practically infinite success of the quantum theory. Historical counterfactuals are always tricky, but the sterility of actual realist programs in this area at least suggests that Bohr and company were right in believing that the road to scientific progress here would have been blocked by realism. The founders of quantum theory never turned on the nonrealist attitude that served them so well. Perhaps that is because the central underlying theoretical device of quantum theory, the densities of a complex-valued and infinite-dimensional wave function, are even harder to take seriously than is the four-dimensional manifold of relativity. But now there comes a most curious twist. For just as the practitioners of relativity, I have suggested, ignore the *realist* interpre-

---

15. Letter to Schrödinger, June 19, 1935.
16. See my (1982d) for part of the discussion and also Chapter Nine.

tation in favor of a more pragmatic attitude toward the space/time structure, the quantum physicists would appear to make a similar reversal and to forget their nonrealist history and allegiance when it comes time to talk about new discoveries.

Thus, anyone in the business will tell you about the exciting period, in the fall of 1974, when the particle group at Brookhaven, led by Samuel Ting, discovered the J particle, just as a Stanford team at the Stanford Linear Accelerator Center, under Burton Richter, independently found a new particle they called ψ. These turned out to be one and the same, the so-called ψ/J particle (Mass 3,098 MeV, Spin 1, Resonance 67 keV, Strangeness 0). To explain this new entity, the theoreticians were led to introduce a new kind of quark, the so-called charmed quark. The ψ/J particle is then thought to be made up out of a charmed quark and an anticharmed quark, with their respective spins aligned. But if this is correct, then there ought to be other such pairs antialigned, or with variable spin alignments, and these ought to make up quite new observable particles. Such predictions from the charmed-quark model have turned out to be confirmed in various experiments.

I have gone on a bit in this story in order to convey the realist feel to the way scientists speak in this area. For I want to ask whether this is a return to realism or whether, instead, it can somehow be reconciled with a fundamentally nonrealist attitude.[17] I believe that the nonrealist option is correct.

3. Nonrealism

Even if the realist happens to be a talented philosopher, I do not believe that, in his heart, he relies for his realism on the rather sophisticated form of abductive argument that I have examined and rejected in the first section of this chapter, and which the history of twentieth-century physics shows to be fallacious. Rather, if his heart is like mine, then I suggest that a more simple and homely sort of argument is what grips him. It is this, and I will put it in the first person. I certainly trust the evidence of my senses, on the whole, with regard to the existence and features of everyday objects. And I have similar confidence in the system of "check, double-check, check, triple-check" of scientific investiga-

17. The nonrealism that I attribute to students and practitioners of the quantum theory requires more discussion and distinguishing of cases and kinds than I have room for here. It is certainly not the all-or-nothing affair I make it appear in the text. I carry out some of the required discussion in chapter 9. My thanks to Paul Teller and James Cushing, each of whom saw the need for more discussion.

tion, as well as the other safeguards built into the institutions of science. So, if the scientists tell me that there really are molecules, and atoms, and ψ/J particles, and, who knows, maybe even quarks, then so be it. I trust them and, thus, must accept that there really are such things with their attendant properties and relations. Moreover, if the instrumentalist (or some other member of the species "nonrealistica") comes along to say that these entities and their attendants are just fictions (or the like), then I see no more reason to believe him than to believe that *he is* a fiction, made up (somehow) to do a job on me; which I do not believe. It seems, then, that I had better be a realist. One can summarize this homely and compelling line as follows: it is possible to accept the evidence of one's senses and to accept, *in the same way*, the confirmed results of science only for a realist; hence, I should be one (and so should you!).

What is it to accept the evidence of one's senses and, *in the same way*, to accept confirmed scientific theories? It is to take them into one's life as true, with all that implies concerning adjusting one's behavior, practical and theoretical, to accommodate these truths. Now, of course, there are truths, and truths. Some are more central to us and our lives, some less so. I might be mistaken about anything, but were I mistaken about where I am right now, that might affect me more than would my perhaps mistaken belief in charmed quarks. Thus, it is compatible with the homely line of argument that some of the scientific beliefs that I hold are less central than some, for example, perceptual beliefs. Of course, were I deeply in the charmed-quark business, giving up that belief might be more difficult than giving up some at the perceptual level. (Thus we get the phenomenon of "seeing what you believe," well known to all thoughtful people.) When the homely line asks us, then, to accept the scientific results "in the same way" in which we accept the evidence of our senses, I take it that we are to accept them both as true. I take it that we are being asked not to distinguish between kinds of truth or modes of existence or the like, but only among truths themselves in terms of centrality, degrees of belief, or such.

Let us suppose this understood. Now, do you think that Bohr, the archenemy of realism, could toe the homely line? Could Bohr, fighting for the sake of science (against Einstein's realism) have felt compelled either to give up the results of science, or else to assign its "truths" to some category different from the truths of everyday life? It seems unlikely. And thus, unless we uncharitably think Bohr inconsistent on this basic issue, we might well come to question whether there is any necessary connection moving us from accepting the results of science as true to being a realist.[18]

Let me use the term "antirealist" to refer to any of the many different specific enemies of realism: the idealist, the instrumentalist, the phenomenalist, the empiricist (constructive or not), the conventionalist, the constructivist, the pragmatist, and so forth. Then, it seems to me that both the realist and the antirealist must toe what I have been calling "the homely line." That is, they must both accept the certified results of science as on par with more homely and familiarly supported claims. That is not to say that one party (or the other) cannot distinguish more from less well-confirmed claims at home or in science; nor that one cannot single out some particular mode of inference (such as inference to the best explanation) and worry over its reliability, both at home and away. It is just that one must maintain parity. Let us say, then, that both realist and antirealist accept the results of scientific investigations as "true," on par with more homely truths. (I realize that some antirealists would rather use a different word, but no matter.) And call this acceptance of scientific truths the "core position."[19] What distinguishes realists from antirealists, then, is what they add onto this core position.

The antirealist may add onto the core position a particular analysis of the concept of truth, as in the pragmatic and instrumentalist

18. I should be a little more careful about the historical Bohr than I am in the text. For Bohr himself would seem to have wanted to truncate the homely line somewhere between the domain of chairs and tables and atoms, whose existence he plainly accepted, and that of electrons, where he seems to have thought the question of existence (and of realism, more generally) was no longer well defined. An illuminating and provocative discussion of Bohr's attitude toward realism is given by Paul Teller (1981). Thanks, again, to Paul for helping to keep me honest.

19. In this context, for example, van Fraassen's "constructive empiricism" would prefer the concept of empirical adequacy, reserving "truth" for an (unspecified) literal interpretation and believing in that truth only among observables. I might mention here that in this classification Putnam's internal realism comes out as antirealist. For Putnam accepts the core position, but he would add to it a Peircean construal of truth as ideal rational acceptance. This is a mistake, which I expect that Putnam will realize and correct in future writings. He is criticized for it by Horwich (1982) whose own "semantic realism" turns out, in my classification, to be neither realist nor antirealist. Indeed, Horwich's views are quite similar to what is called "NOA" below, and could easily be read as sketching a philosophy of language compatible with NOA. Finally, the "epistemological behaviorism" espoused by Rorty (1979) is a form of antirealism that seems to me very similar to Putnam's position, but achieving the core parity between science and common sense by means of an acceptance that is neither ideal nor especially rational, at least in the normative sense. (I beg the reader's indulgence over this summary treatment of complex and important positions. I have been responding to Nancy Cartwright's request to differentiate these recent views from NOA.) See chapter 8 for a discussion of these antirealisms.

and conventionalist conceptions of truth. Or the antirealist may
add on a special analysis of concepts, as in idealism, constructivism,
phenomenalism, and in some varieties of empiricism. These addenda will then issue in a special meaning, say, for existence statements. Or the antirealist may add on certain methodological stric-
tures, pointing a wary finger at some particular inferential tool, or
constructing his own account for some particular aspects of science
(e.g., explanations or laws). Typically, the antirealist will make several such additions to the core.

What then of the realist, what does he add to his core acceptance
of the results of science as really true? My colleague, Charles Chastain, suggested what I think is the most graphic way of stating the
answer—namely, that what the realist adds on is a desk-thumping,
foot-stamping shout of "Really!" So, when the realist and antirealist
agree, say, that there really are electrons and that they really carry
a unit negative charge and really do have a small mass (of about
9.1×10^{-28} grams), what the realist wants to add is the emphasis
that all this is really so. "There really are electrons, really!" This
typical realist emphasis serves both a negative and a positive function. Negatively, it is meant to deny the additions that the antirealist
would make to that core acceptance which both parties share. The
realist wants to deny, for example, the phenomenalistic reduction
of concepts or the pragmatic conception of truth. The realist thinks
that these addenda take away from the substantiality of the accepted
claims to truth or existence. "No," says he, "they *really* exist, and
not in just your diminished antirealist sense." Positively, the realist
wants to explain the robust sense in which *he* takes these claims to
truth or existence; namely, as claims about reality—what is really,
really the case. The full-blown version of this involves the conception of truth as correspondence with the world, and the surrogate
use of approximate truth as near-correspondence. We have already
seen how these ideas of correspondence and approximate truth
are supposed to explain what *makes* the truth *true* whereas, in fact,
they function as mere trappings, that is, as superficial decorations
that may well attract our attention but do not compel rational belief.
Like the extra "really," they are an arresting foot thump and, logically speaking, of no more force.

It seems to me that when we contrast the realist and the antirealist
in terms of what they each want to add to the core position, a third
alternative emerges—and an attractive one at that. It is the core
position itself, *and all by itself*. If I am correct in thinking that, at
heart, the grip of realism only extends to the homely connection
of everyday truths with scientific truths, and that good sense dictates

our acceptance of the one on the same basis as our acceptance of the other, then the homely line makes the core position, all by itself, a compelling one, one that we ought to take to heart. Let us try to do so and see whether it constitutes a philosophy, and an attitude toward science, that we can live by.

The core position is neither realist nor antirealist; it mediates between the two. It would be nice to have a name for this position, but it would be a shame to appropriate another "ism" on its behalf, for then it would appear to be just one of the many contenders for ontological allegiance. I think it is not just one of that crowd but rather, as the homely line behind it suggests, it is for commonsense epistemology—the natural ontological attitude. Thus, let me introduce the acronym *NOA* (pronounced as in "Noah"), for *natural ontological attitude*, and, henceforth, refer to the core position under that designation.

To begin showing how NOA makes for an adequate philosophical stance toward science, let us see what it has to say about ontology. When NOA counsels us to accept the results of science as true, I take it that we are to treat truth in the usual referential way, so that a sentence (or statement) is true just in case the entities referred to stand in the referred-to relations. Thus, NOA sanctions ordinary referential semantics and commits us, via truth, to the existence of the individuals, properties, relations, processes, and so forth referred to by the scientific statements that we accept as true. Our belief in their existence will be just as strong (or weak) as our belief in the truth of the bit of science involved, and degrees of belief here, presumably, will be tutored by ordinary relations of confirmation and evidential support, subject to the usual scientific canons. In taking this referential stance, NOA is not committed to the progressivism that seems inherent in realism. For the realist, as an article of faith, sees scientific success, over the long run, as bringing us closer to the truth. His whole explanatory enterprise, using approximate truth, forces his hand in this way. But, a "NOAer" (pronounced as "knower") is not so committed. As a scientist, say, within the context of the tradition in which he works, the NOAer, of course, will believe in the existence of those entities to which his theories refer. But should the tradition change, say, in the manner of the conceptual revolutions that Kuhn dubs "paradigm shifts," then nothing in NOA dictates that the change be assimilated as being progressive, that is, as a change where we learn more accurately about *the same things*. NOA is perfectly consistent with the Kuhnian alternative, which counts such changes as wholesale changes of reference. Unlike the realist, adherents to NOA are free to examine the facts in cases of paradigm shift, and to see whether or not a convincing case for stability of reference across paradigms can be made without superimposing on these facts a realist-progressivist superstructure. I have argued elsewhere (Fine 1975) that if one makes oneself free, as NOA enables one to do, then the facts of the matter will not usually settle the case; and that this is a good reason for thinking that cases of so-called incommensurability are, in fact, genuine cases where the question of stability of reference is indeterminate. NOA, I think, is the right philosophical position for such conclusions. It sanctions reference and existence claims, but it does not force the history of science into prefit molds.

So far I have managed to avoid what, for the realist, is the essential point: what of the "external world"? How can I talk of reference and of existence claims unless I am talking about referring to things right out there in the world? And here, of course, the realist, again, wants to stamp his feet.[20] I think the problem that makes the realist want to stamp his feet, shouting "Really!" (and invoking the external world) has to do with the stance the realist tries to take vis-à-vis the game of science. The realist, as it were, tries to stand outside the arena watching the ongoing game and then tries to judge (from this external point of view) what the point is. It is, he says, *about* some area external to the game. The realist, I think, is fooling himself. For he cannot (really!) stand outside the arena, nor can he survey some area off the playing field and mark it out as what the game is about.

Let me try to address these two points. How are we to arrive at the judgment that, in addition to, say, having a rather small mass, electrons are objects "out there in the external world"? Certainly, we can stand off from the electron game and survey its claims, methods, predictive success, and so forth. But what stance could we take that would enable us to judge what the theory of electrons is *about*, other than agreeing that it is about electrons? It is not like matching a blueprint to a house being built, or a map route to a country road. For we are *in* the world, both physically and conceptually.[21] That is, *we* are among the objects of science, and the concepts and procedures that we use to make judgments of subject

20. In his remarks at the Greensboro conference, my commentator, John King, suggested a compelling reason to prefer NOA over realism; namely, because NOA is less percussive! My thanks to John for this nifty idea, as well as for other comments.

21. "There is, I think, no theory-independent way to reconstruct phrases like 'really there'; the notion of a match between the ontology of a theory and its 'real' counterpart in nature now seems to me illusive in principle." T. S. Kuhn (1970), p. 206. The same passage is cited for rebuttal by Newton-Smith (1981). But the "rebuttal" sketched there in chapter 8, sections 4 and 5, not only runs afoul of the

matter and correct application are themselves part of that same scientific world. Epistemologically, the situation is very much like the situation with regard to the justification of induction. For the problem of the external world (so-called) is how to satisfy the realist's demand that we justify the existence claims sanctioned by science (and, therefore, by NOA) as claims to the existence of entities "out there." In the case of induction, it is clear that only an inductive justification will do, and it is equally clear that no inductive justification will do at all. So too with the external world, for only ordinary scientific inferences to existence will do, and yet none of them satisfies the demand for showing that the existent is really "out there." I think we ought to follow Hume's prescription on induction with regard to the external world. There is no possibility for justifying the kind of externality that realism requires, yet it may well be that, in fact, we cannot help yearning for just such a comforting grip on reality.

If I am right, then the realist is chasing a phantom, and we cannot actually do more, with regard to existence claims, than follow scientific practice, just as NOA suggests. What then of the other challenges raised by realism? Can we find in NOA the resources for understanding scientific practice? In particular (since it was the topic of the first part of this chapter), does NOA help us to understand the scientific method, say, the problems of the small handful or of conjunctions? The sticking point with the small handful was to account for why the few and narrow alternatives that we can come up with, result in successful novel predictions, and the like. The background was to keep in mind that most such narrow alternatives are not successful. I think that NOA has only this to say. If you believe that guessing based on some truths is more likely to succeed than guessing pure and simple, then if our earlier theories were in large part true and if our refinements of them conserve the true parts, then guessing on this basis has some relative likelihood of success. I think this is a weak account, but then I think the phenomenon here does not allow for anything much stronger since, for the most part, such guesswork fails. In the same way, NOA can help with the problem of conjunctions (and, more generally, with problems of logical combinations). For if two consistent theories in fact have overlapping domains (a fact, as I have just

---

objections stated here in my first section, it also fails to provide for the required theory-independence. For Newton-Smith's explication of verisimilitude (p. 204) makes explicit reference to some unspecified background theory. (He offers either current science or the Peircean limit as candidates.) But this is not to rebut Kuhn's challenge (and mine); it is to concede its force.

suggested, that is not so often decidable), and if the theories also have true things to say about members in the overlap, then conjoining the theories just adds to the truths of each and, thus, *may*, in conjunction, yield new truths. Where one finds other successful methodological rules, I think we will find NOA's grip on the truth sufficient to account for the utility of the rules.

Unlike the realist, however, I would not tout NOA's success at making science fairly intelligible as an argument in its favor, vis-à-vis realism or various antirealisms. For NOA's accounts are available to the realist and the antirealist, too, provided what they add to NOA does not negate its appeal to the truth, as does a verificationist account of truth or the realist's longing for approximate truth. Moreover, as I made plain enough in the first section of this chapter, I am sensitive to the possibility that explanatory efficacy can be achieved without the explanatory hypothesis being true. NOA may well make science seem fairly intelligible and even rational, but NOA could be quite the wrong view of science for all that. If we posit as a constraint on philosophizing about science that the scientific enterprise should come out in our philosophy as not too unintelligible or irrational, then, perhaps, we can say that NOA passes a minimal standard for a philosophy of science.

Indeed, perhaps the greatest virtue of NOA is to call attention to just how minimal an adequate philosophy of science can be. (In this respect, NOA might be compared to the minimalist movement in art.) For example, NOA helps us to see that realism differs from various antirealisms in this way: realism adds an outer direction to NOA, that is, the external world and the correspondence relation of approximate truth; antirealisms (typically) add an inner direction, that is, human-oriented reductions of truth, or concepts, or explanations (as in my opening citation from Hume). NOA suggests that the legitimate features of these additions are already contained in the presumed equal status of everyday truths with scientific ones, and in our accepting them both as *truths*. No other additions are legitimate, and none are required.

It will be apparent by now that a distinctive feature of NOA, one that separates it from similar views currently in the air, is NOA's stubborn refusal to amplify the concept of truth by providing a theory or analysis (or even a metaphorical picture). Rather, NOA recognizes in "truth" a concept already in use and agrees to abide by the standard rules of usage. These rules involve a Davidsonian-Tarskian referential semantics, and they support a thoroughly classical logic of inference. Thus NOA respects the customary "grammar" of "truth" (and its cognates). Likewise, NOA respects the customary epistemology, which grounds judgments of truth in perceptual judgments and various confirmation relations. As with the use of other concepts, disagreements are bound to arise over what is true (for instance, as to whether inference to the best explanation is always truth-conferring). NOA pretends to no resources for settling these disputes, for NOA takes to heart the great lesson of twentieth-century analytic and continental philosophy, namely, that there *are* no general methodological or philosophical resources for deciding such things. The mistake common to realism and all the antirealisms alike is their commitment to the existence of such nonexistent resources. If pressed to answer the question of what, then, does it *mean* to say that something is true (or to what does the truth of so-and-so commit one), NOA will reply by pointing out the logical relations engendered by the specific claim and by focusing, then, on the concrete historical circumstances that ground that particular judgment of truth. For, after all, there *is* nothing more to say.[22]

Because of its parsimony, I think the minimalist stance represented by NOA marks a revolutionary approach to understanding science. It is, I would suggest, as profound in its own way as was the revolution in our conception of morality, when we came to see that founding morality on God and his order was *also* neither legitimate nor necessary. Just as the typical theological moralist of the eighteenth century would feel bereft to read, say, the pages of *Ethics*, so I think the realist must feel similarly when NOA removes that "correspondence to the external world" for which he so longs. I too have regret for that lost paradise, and too often slip into the realist fantasy. I use my understanding of twentieth-century physics to help me firm up my convictions about NOA, and I recall some words of Mach, which I offer as a comfort and as a closing. With reference to realism, Mach writes,

It has arisen in the process of immeasurable time without the intentional assistance of man. It is a product of nature, and preserved by nature. Everything that philosophy has accomplished . . . is, as compared with it, but an insignificant and ephemeral product of art. The fact is,

22. No doubt I am optimistic, for one can always think of more to say. In particular, one could try to fashion a general, descriptive framework for codifying and classifying such answers. Perhaps there would be something to be learned from such a descriptive, semantical framework. But what I am afraid of is that this enterprise, once launched, would lead to a proliferation of frameworks not so carefully descriptive. These would take on a life of their own, each pretending to ways (better than its rivals) to settle disputes over truth claims, or their import. What we need, however, is less bad philosophy, not more. So here, I believe, silence is indeed golden.

every thinker, every philosopher, the moment he is forced to abandon
his one-sided intellectual occupation . . . , immediately returns [to
realism].

Nor is it the purpose of these "introductory remarks" to discredit the
standpoint [of realism]. The task which we have set ourselves is simply
to show why and for what purpose we hold that standpoint during most
of our lives, and why and for what purpose we are . . . obliged to abandon it.

These lines are taken from Mach's *The Analysis of Sensations* (sec.
14). I recommend that book as effective realism-therapy, a therapy
that works best (as Mach suggests) when accompanied by histori-
cophysical investigations (real versions of the breakneck history of
my second section). For a better philosophy, however, I recommend
NOA.

And Not Antirealism Either

1. *Realism*: "Out yonder there was this huge world, which exists independently of us human beings. . . . The mental grasp of this extra-personal world hovered before me as the highest goal."

Albert Einstein, "Autobiographical Notes"

2. *Anti-Realism*: "to get at something absolute without going out of your own skin!"

William James, letter to Tom Ward, October 9, 1868

1. Introduction

As my title suggests, this paper is another episode in a continuing story. In the last chapter the body of realism was examined, the causes of its death identified, and then the project of constructing a suitable successor for these postrealist times was begun. I called that successor the "natural ontological attitude" or NOA, for short, and I shall return to it below. In today's episode, however, the subject of criticism becomes antirealism, and this is a live and, therefore, a shiftier target. For the death of realism has revived interest in several antirealist positions and, appropriately enough, recent philosophical work has explored modifications of these anti-realisms to see whether they can be refurbished in order to take over, from realism, as the philosophy-of-science "of choice." My first object here will be to show that just as realism will not do for this choice position, neither will antirealism. That job accomplished, I shall then sing some more in praise of NOA.

To understand antirealism we first have to backtrack a bit and reexamine realism. Given the diverse array of philosophical positions that have sought the "realist" label, it is probably not possible to give a sketch of realism that will encompass them all. Indeed, it may be hopeless to try, even, to capture the essential features of realism. Yet, that is indeed what I hope to do in identifying the core of realism with the following ideas. First, realism holds that

This paper was written during the tenure of a Guggenheim Fellowship. I want to thank the foundation for their support. Thanks, too, to Micky Forbes for struggling with me through the ideas, and their expression.

there exists a definite world; that is, a world containing entities with relations and properties that are to a large extent independent of human acts and agents (or the possibilities therefore). Second, according to realism, it is possible to obtain a substantial amount of reliable and relatively observer-independent information concerning this world and its features, information not restricted, for example, to just observable features. I shall refer to these components of realism as (1) belief in a definite world structure and (2) belief in the possibility of substantial epistemic access to that structure. This realism becomes "scientific" when we add to it a third component; namely, (3) the belief that science aims at (and, to some extent, achieves) all the epistemic access to the definite world structure that realism holds to be possible.

This sketch of realism highlights the ontological features that seem to me characteristic of it. But there is a semantical aspect as well. For in order to see science as working toward the achievement of the realist goal of substantial access to features of the definite world structure, the theories and principles of science must be understood to be *about* that world structure. Thus the *truth* of scientific assertions gets a specifically realist interpretation; namely, as a *correspondence* with features of the definite world structure.

I can put it very succinctly this way. The realist adopts a standard, model-theoretic, correspondence theory of truth; where the model is just the definite world structure posited by realism and where correspondence is understood as a relation that reaches right out to touch the world.

The "antirealisms" that I want to examine and reject here all oppose the three tenets of realism understood as above (in spirit, if not always in words). They also reject the characteristically realist picture of truth as external-world correspondence. They divide among themselves over the question of whether or not that realist picture of truth ought to be replaced by some other picture. But they agree (again in spirit, if not in words) that although the realist has the aim of science wrong, in his third tenet above, it is important for us to understand what the correct aim of science is. This agreement is the mark of what I shall call "scientific" antirealism. And the disagreement over offering truth pictures, then, divides the scientific antirealists into those who are truthmongers, and those who are not.

2. Truthmongers

The history of philosophy has witnessed a rather considerable trade in truth; including wholesale accounts like correspondence and coherence theories, or consensus and pragmatic theories, or indexical and relativist theories. There have also been special reductions available including phenomenalisms and idealisms. Among scientific antirealists the wholesalers, recently, have tried to promote some kind of consensus-cum-pragmatic picture. I will try to give this picture a canonical representation so that we can identify the features that these particular antirealisms have in common. So represented, it portrays the truth of a statement P as amounting to the fact that a certain class of subjects would accept P under a certain set of circumstances. If we let the subjects be "perfectly rational" agents and the circumstances be "ideal" ones for the purposes of the knowledge trade (perhaps those marking the Peircean limit?), then we get the picture of truth as ideal rational acceptance, and this is the picture that Hilary Putnam (1981a) paints for his "internal realism."[1] If the subjects are not perfectly rational and yet conscientious and well intentioned about things, and we let the circumstances be those marking a serious dialogue of the kind that makes for consensus, where consensus is attainable, then we get the Wittgensteinian position that Richard Rorty (1979) calls "epistemological behaviorism."[2] Finally, if our subjects are immersed in the matrix of some paradigm and the circumstances are those encompassed by the values and rules of the paradigm, then we get the specifically paradigm-relative concept of truth (and of reference) that is characteristic of Thomas Kuhn's (1970) antirealism. With these three applications in mind, I want to examine the merits—which is to say, to point out the demerits—of this sort of acceptance theory of truth.

Let us first be clear that these acceptance pictures of truth make for an antirealist attitude toward science. That is a somewhat subtle issue, for the old Machian debates over the reality of molecules and atoms might suggest that realism turns on the putative truth (or not) of certain existence claims, especially claims about the existence of "unobservables." Since acceptance theories of truth, of the sort outlined above, might very well issue in the truth of such existence claims, one might be tempted to suggest, as well, that holders of

1. Putnam (1981a) is an extended discussion, usefully supplemented by Putnam (1982a, b). Originally, rational acceptability was merely offered as a "picture" of truth. But later it emerged as a "characterization," and as providing "the only sense in which we have a vital and working notion of it" (Putnam 1982b, p. 5).
2. In his symposium talk for the March 1983 Pacific Division, American Philosophical Association meetings (in Berkeley), Rorty announced a new position that he called "revisionary pragmatism." This new stance pulls back from various of Rorty's earlier commitments, including some of his ideas about truth. I have not been able to figure out, however, just what it rejects or what it retains. See Rorty (1982), introduction.

acceptance theories could be realists. While there is no doubt a distinction to be drawn between those who do and those who do not believe in the existence, let us say, of magnetic monopoles, I think it would be a mistake to take that as distinguishing the realists from the others.[3] For it is not the *form* of a claim held true that marks off realism, it is rather the significance or content of the claim. The realist, say, wants to know whether there *really* are magnetic monopoles. He understands that in the way explained above, so that a positive answer here would signify a sort of reaching *out* from electrodynamic discourse *to* the very stuff of the world. The fact that scientific practice involves serious monopole talk, including what is described as manipulating monopoles and intervening in their behavior, does not even begin to address the issue of realism. For what realism is after is a very particular interpretation of that practice. This is exactly the interpretation that the picture of truth-as-acceptance turns us away from.

The special sort of correspondence that is built into the realist conception of truth orients us to face "*out* on the world," striving in our science to grab hold of significant chunks of its definite structure. The idea of truth as acceptance, however, turns us right around again to look back at our own collective selves, and at the interpersonal features that constitute the practice of the truth game. (Compare the two epigraphs that introduce this chapter.) This turnabout makes for a sort of Ptolemaic counterrevolution. We are invited to focus on the mundane roots of truth-talk and its various mundane purposes and procedures. Concepts having to do with acceptance provide a rich setting for all these mundane happenings. If we then take truth just to *be* the right sort of acceptance, we reap a bonus for, when we bring truth down to earth in this way, we obtain insurance against the inherent, metaphysical aspects of realism.

I can well understand how the sight of realism unveiled might bring on disturbing, metaphysical shudders. And it is understandable, I think, that we should seek the seeming security provided

---

3. Cartwright (1983) and Hacking (1983, 1984) adopt this way of distinguishing a significant form of realism. See chapters 7 and 9 for a critique. The only background that seems to me to support the idea that the truth of certain existence claims makes for realism is an account of truth as external-world correspondence. I do not believe that Hacking adopts such a view. I do not know about Cartwright. I might mention here that Putnam's tactic of calling his position a kind of realism (an "internal" kind), while also seeing in it a "transcendental idealism" (Putnam 1981b, n.6), seems founded on nothing more than the amusing idea that whatever is not solipsism is, ipso facto, a realism. See Putnam (1982a), p. 162, and (1982b), p. 13.

by sheltering for awhile in a nest of interpersonal relations. But it would be a mistake to think that we will find truth there. For the antirealism expressed in the idea of truth-as-acceptance is just as metaphysical and idle as the realism expressed by a correspondence theory.

I have not been able to locate a significant line of argument in the recent literature that moves to supply the warrant for an acceptance theory of truth. Rather, as I have noted, these antirealists seem to have taken shelter in that corner mainly in reaction to realism. For when one sees that the realist conception of truth creates a gap that keeps the epistemic access one wants always just beyond reach, it may be tempting to try to refashion the idea of truth in epistemic terms in order, literally, to make the truth accessible. What allows the truthmongers to think that this is feasible, so far as I can tell, is a common turning toward behaviorism. In one way or another, these antirealists seem sympathetic to the behaviorist idea that the working practices of conceptual exchange exhaust the meaning of that exchange, giving it its significance and providing it with its content. Thus we come to the idea that if the working practices of the truth exchange are the practices of acceptance, then acceptance is what truth is all about, and nothing but acceptance.

I do not have any new critique to offer concerning the flaws in behaviorism. Just about everyone recognizes that various special applications of behaviorism are wrong; for example, operationalism, or Watson-Skinnerism. So too, just about everyone has a sense of the basic error; namely, that behaviorism makes out everything it touches to be less than it is, fixing limits where none exist. Such, indeed, is the way of these antirealisms: they fix the concept of truth, pinning it down to acceptance. One certainly has no more warrant for imposing this constraint on the basic concept of truth, however, than the operationalist has for imposing his constraints on more derivative concepts (like length or mass).

In fact, I think the warrant for behaviorism with regard to truth is considerably more suspicious than anything the operationalist ever had in mind. For whatever might possibly warrant the behaviorist conception of truth-as-acceptance should at least make that a conception we can take in and understand. Even if, as some maintain, truth is merely a regulative ideal, it must still be an ideal we can understand, strive for, believe in, glimpse—and so forth. But if, as behaviorism holds, judgments of truth are judgments of what certain people would accept under certain circumstances, what are the ground rules for arriving at those judgments and working with them as required? Naively, it looks like what we are called upon to do is to extrapolate from what *is* the case with regard to actual acceptance behavior to what *would be* the case under the right conditions. But how are we ever to establish what *is* the case, in order to get this extrapolation going, when that determination itself calls for a prior, successful round of extrapolation? It appears that acceptance locks us into a repeating pattern that involves an endless regress. Moreover, if we attend to the counterfactuality built into the "would accept" in the truth-as-acceptance formula, then I think we encounter a similar difficulty. To understand this conception of truth we must get a sense of how things would be were they different in certain respects from what they are now. Whatever your line about counterfactuals, this understanding involves at least either the idea of truth in altered circumstances, or the idea of truth in these actual circumstances. But each alternative here folds in upon itself, requiring in turn further truths. I believe there is no grounding for this process unless we turn away from the acceptance picture at some point.

It seems to me that the acceptance idea never *can* get off the ground, and that we cannot actually understand the picture of truth that it purports to offer. If we think otherwise, that is probably because we are inclined to read into the truthmongers' project some truths (or ideas of truth) not having to do with acceptance at all—perhaps, even, some truths via correspondence! Thus, with respect to warrant and intelligibility, the acceptance picture emerges as quite on par with the correspondence picture.[4]

There is, as I have noted, a very close connection between these two conceptions. It is a typical dialectic that binds the metaphysics of realism to the metaphysics of behaviorism. Realism reaches out for *more* than can be had. Behaviorism reacts by pulling back to the "secure" ground of human behavior. In terms of that it tries to impose a limit, short of what realism has been reaching for. The limit imposed by behaviorism, however, is simply *less* than what we

---

4. Other ways of displaying the gap between "truth" and the favored version of acceptance would be to ask whether the acceptance formula is true, or what "accept as true" comes to under the formula, or what now would guarantee the idempotency of "is true." Pursuing such lines of inquiry, along with the ones in the text, will show that the sense and grammar of truth is not that of acceptance. But, of course, it does not follow that truth is not acceptance (really!). Nor could such lines of inquiry really subvert the program of replacing "truth" by acceptance, if one were determined to carry on with the program. One can always dodge the arguments and, where that fails, bite the argumentative bullets. In philosophy, as in other areas of rational discourse, inquiry must end in judgments. One can try to inform and tutor good judgment, but it cannot be compelled—not even by good-looking reasons.

require. So realism reacts by positing something more, and then reaches out for it again. What we can learn from this cycle is just what makes it run, and how to stop it.

Both the scientific realist and the scientific antirealist of the acceptance sort share an attitude toward the concept of truth. They think it is appropriate to give a theory, or account, or perhaps just a "picture" of truth. As Hilary Putnam (1982b, pp. 20–21) pleads,

> But if all notions of rightness, both epistemic and (metaphysically) realist are eliminated, then what are our statements but noisemakings? What are our thoughts but *mere* subvocalizations? . . . Let us recognize that one of our fundamental self-conceptualizations, in Rorty's phrase, is that we are *thinkers*, and that *as* thinkers we are committed to there being *some* kind of truth, some kind of correctness which is substantial and not merely "disquotational."

Of course we are all committed to there being some kind of truth. But need we take that to be something like a "natural" kind? This essentialist idea is what makes the cycle run, and we can stop it if we stop conceiving of truth as a substantial something—something for which theories, accounts, or even pictures are appropriate. To be sure, the antirealist is quite correct in his diagnosis of the disease of realism, and in his therapeutic recommendation to pay attention to how human beings actually operate with the family of truth concepts. Where he goes wrong is in trying to fashion out of these practices a completed concept of truth as a substantial something, one that will then act as a limit for legitimate human aspirations. If we do not join him in this undertaking and if we are also careful not to replace this antirealist limit on truth by something else that goes beyond practice, then we shall have managed to avoid both realism and these truthmongering antirealisms as well.

3. Empiricism

But there are other antirealisms to contend with. One well-known brand is empiricism, and this had made some notable progress in the sophisticated version that Bas van Fraassen (1980) calls "constructive empiricism." This account avoids the reductive and foundationalist tendency of earlier empiricisms that sought to ground all truths in a sense-data or phenomenalist base. It also avoids the modification of this idea that ensnared logical empiricism: the conception of a theory as a deductively closed logical system on the vocabulary of which there is imposed an epistemologically significant distinction between observables and unobservables. Instead constructive empiricism takes a semantical view of a scientific theory; it views it as a family of models. And it lets science itself dictate what is or is not observable, where the "able" part refers to us and our limitations according to science. As for truth, it does not engage in trade but plumps for a literal construal.[5] The important concept for this brand of empiricism is the idea of empirical adequacy. This idea applies to theories conceived of as above. Such a theory is empirically adequate just in case it has some model in which all truths about observables are represented. If truths about observables are called "phenomena," then a theory is empirically adequate just in case it saves the phenomena, *all* the phenomena. The distinctively antirealist thesis of constructive empiricism in twofold: (1) that science aims only to provide theories that are empirically adequate and (2) that acceptance of a theory involves as belief only that it *is* empirically adequate. The intended contrast is with a realism that posits true theories as the goal of science and that takes acceptance of a theory to be belief in the truth of the theory. Since truth here is to be taken literally, the realist could well be committed to believing in the existence of unobservable entities literally, but never the constructive empiricist.

Indeed this brand of empiricism, along with its ancestors, involves a strong limitation on what it is legitimate for us to believe (in the sense of believe to be true). Where science is taken as the legitimating basis, we are allowed to believe that the scientific story about observables is true, and no more than that. It seems to me that there are two obvious testing points to probe with regard to any stance that seeks to impose limits on our epistemic attitudes. The first is to see whether the boundary can be marked off in a way that does not involve suspicious or obnoxious assumptions.

---

5. Although van Fraassen (1980, especially pp. 9–11) is quite explicit about taking truth literally, he also seems tempted by the interpretative metaphor of realist-style correspondence. "A statement is true exactly if the actual world accords with the statement" (1980, p. 90). "I would still identify the truth of a theory with the condition that there is an exact correspondence between reality and one of its models" (1980, p. 197). If van Fraassen is taken literally in these passages, then for him truth *is,* literally, real-world correspondence. If this were correct, then van Fraassen's empiricism would appear to be a restricted version of realism, a version where the epistemic access is restricted to observables. This makes his "antirealism" seem considerably less radical than one might have thought. I, at any rate, had thought his idea of literal truth included the notion that "truth" was not to be further interpreted. On this understanding I thought that if he were persuaded out of his attachment to observables, then his ideas would fit right in with NOA. But now I think that may be wrong. If we were to make constructive empiricism lose its attachment to observables, we would (it seems) merely have regained realism, full blown.

The second is to see what the rationale is for putting the boundary just there, and to what extent that placement is arbitrary. Let me take these in order.

A difficulty of the first sort begins to show up as soon as we ask why an attitude of belief is appropriate for the scientific judgment that something is observable. After all, that is supposed to be just another bit of science, and so our empiricism says that it is a candidate for affirmative belief (as opposed to agnostic reserve) just in case it is itself a judgment entirely within the realm of observables (according to science). What does that mean? Well, one might suppose that since the judgment that something is observable has a simple subject/predicate form, then both the subject of the judgment and the predicate must refer to what science holds to be observable. So, for example, the judgment that carrots are mobile would be a candidate for belief if, as we suppose, science classifies both carrots and mobility as observables. What then of the judgment that carrots are observable? In order for *it* to be a candidate for belief, we must suppose that science classifies both carrots and observability as observables. But now I think we ought to come to a full stop.

For if we accept the moves made so far, then we see that the combination of, first, limiting belief to the observable and, second, letting science determine what counts as observable, has a terribly odd consequence. Namely, in order to believe in any scientific judgment concerning what is observable, we must take as a presupposition that the "property" or "characteristic" (or whatever) of "being observable" is itself an observable, *according to science*. Thus when we go down the list of entities, supposedly using our science to determine which ones are observable and which are not, the property of "being observable" must be classified as well, and indeed it must come out as observable. But this is surely something forced on us a priori by this empiricist philosophical stance. If there actually were such a property as "being observable," and science did actually classify it, who is to say how it must come out—or even whether it must come out at all as observable or not. *Science* is supposed to speak here, not philosophy. Thus if we accept the moves in the argument, this empiricism is suspiciously near to an inconsistency: it forces the hand of science exactly where it is supposed to follow it.

What then if we try to reject some move in the argument? What shall we question? Surely the requirement that we respect grammar and ask separately of subject and predicate whether it refers to an observable is not a necessary one. After all, to speak somewhat realistically, who can tell how a judgment confronts the world? Let us then give up the grammatical requirement and think again how to deal with the judgment that something is an observable; that is, how to understand it as a judgment entirely within the realm of observables. If I judge, scientifically, that carrots are observable, then I suppose I would have to identify some properties or features of carrots and show that these would induce the right sort of effects in an interaction, one party to which is a human being, qua observing instrument. To back up the counterfactual here (what effects would be induced), certainly several laws would enter the argument, very likely connecting entities that may themselves not be observable. Now, according to the empiricism at issue, I do not have to believe this whole theoretical story, only its observational part. *That* I do have to believe if it is to warrant my belief in the observability of carrots. But since the question here was precisely how to identify the observational part of a simple judgment (that carrots are observable), I think I am stuck. I do not know what to believe in my scientific story that issues in the observability of carrots, unless I can pick out its observational parts. And I cannot identify a part of the story as observational unless I can support that identification by means of beliefs based on observational parts of still other covering stories. I really think that we cannot break out of this cycle—or rather break in to get it going—without some external stipulations, or the like, as to what to believe to be observable. Thus an a priori resolution of the philosophical squabble over what to take as observable seems required by this empiricism, just as it was by the older ones.

There is, however, a deft maneuver that could get things going again. It is simply not to raise the question of observability where what is at stake is itself a judgment of observability. Thus we could exempt those special judgments from the test of observability and allow ourselves to believe them in just the way that we would if they had actually passed the test. Indeed, if we allow this exception for judgments of observability, then no difficulties seem to arise by way of beliefs being sanctioned that are not really warrranted. But if we try to avoid obnoxious assumptions concerning what is observable by granting exemptions from the general empiricist rule in certain special cases, then why—we must ask—should that rule be necessary for the others? This brings us to the second testing point for a philosophy that seeks to impose limits on one's epistemic attitudes; namely, to examine the rationale for the limit—especially to see how arbitrary it is.

We can push this question hard if we recognize that there is a loosely graded vocabulary concerning observability. We do, after all, draw a distinction between what is *observable,* which is rather strict, and what is *detectable,* which is somewhat looser. To get a feel for the distinction, we might, for instance, picture the difference here as between what we would "observe," in the right circumstances, with our sense organs as they are, and what we would "detect" in those same circumstances were our eyes, for example, replaced by electron microscopes. In this grading system, then, atoms would count as detectable but not (strictly) observable. It seems to me that distinctions of this sort are, in fact, at work in the vocabulary of observation, and van Fraassen (1980, pp. 16–17) certainly recognizes some such. With this in mind, then, I think we can make the question of observability, as a warrant for belief, very acute by asking, why restrict the realm of belief to what is observable, as opposed, say, to what is detectable?

I think the question is acute, because I cannot imagine any answer that would be compelling. Are we supposed to refrain from believing in atoms, and various truths about them, because we are concerned over the possibility that what the electron microscope reveals is merely an artifact of the machine? If this is our concern, then we can address it by applying the cautious and thorough procedures and analyses involved in the use and construction of that machine, as well as the cross-checks from other detecting devices, to evaluate the artifactuality (or not) of the atomic phenomena. If we can do this satisfactorily according to tough standards, are we then still not supposed to frame beliefs about atoms, and why not now? Surely the end product of such inquiries, when each one pursues a specific area of uncertainty or possible error, can only be a very compelling scientific documentation of the grounds for believing that we are, actually, detecting atoms.[6] Faced with such substantial reasons for believing that we are detecting atoms, what, except purely a priori and arbitrary conventions, could possibly dictate the empiricist conclusion that, nevertheless, we are unwarranted actually to engage in *belief* about atoms? What holds for detectability holds as well for the other information-bearing

6. The themes just touched on, especially the insistence on the specificity of scientific doubt and on following the scientific rationale that informs the vocabulary of observation, are forcefully elaborated by Shapere (1982). Part B ("intervening") of Hacking (1983) is also required reading here.

modalities, ones that may be even more remotely connected with strict observability. The general lesson is that, in the context of science, adopting an attitude of belief has as warrant precisely that which science itself grants, nothing more but certainly nothing less.[7]

The stance of empiricism, like that of the truthmongers, is (in part) a moral stance. They both regard metaphysics, and in particular the metaphysics of realism, as a sin. They both move in the direction of their antirealism in order to avoid that sin. But the behaviorism to which the truthmongers turn, as we have seen, locks them into a comic dance with realism, a *pas de deux* as wickedly metaphysical as ever there was. The empiricist, I think, carries a comparable taint. For when he sidesteps science and moves into his courtroom, there to pronounce his judgments of where to believe and where to withhold, he avoids metaphysics only by committing, instead, the sin of epistemology. We ought not to follow him in this practice. Indeed, I think courtesy requires, at this point, a discreet withdrawal.

4. NOA: The Natural Ontological Attitude

The "isms" of this paper each derive from a philosophical program in the context of which they seek to place science. The idea seems to be that when science is put in that context its significance, rationality, and purpose, as it were, just click into place. Consequently, the defense of these "isms," when a defense is offered, usually takes the form of arguing that the favorite one is better than its rivals because it makes better sense of science than its rivals do.[8]

What are we to conclude from this business of placing science in a context, supplying it with an aim, attempting to make better sense of it, and so forth? Surely, it is that realism and antirealism alike view science as susceptible to being set in context, provided with a goal, and being made sense of. And what manner of object, after all, could show such susceptibilities other than something that could not or did not do these very things for itself? What binds

7. See Hellman (1983), especially pp. 247–48, for some cosmological "unobservables" in which we might have good scientific grounds for belief. But don't forget more familiar sorts of objects either, like unconscious (or "subliminal") causal factors in our behavior or, even, the nightly activity we call "dreaming"!

8. "However, there is also a positive argument for constructive empiricism—it makes better sense of science, and of scientific activity, than realism does and does so without inflationary metaphysics" (van Fraassen 1980, p. 73). I think van Fraassen speaks here for all the antirealists. While I cannot recommend this as a defense of antirealism, I think van Fraassen's own critique of the explanationist defenses of realism is very incisive, especially if complemented with the attack of Laudan (1984). Recall that the preceding chapter contains a metatheorem showing why such explanationist (or coherentist) defenses of realism are bound to fail.

realism and antirealism together is this. They see science as a set of practices in need of an interpretation, and they see themselves as providing just the right interpretation.

But science is not needy in this way. Its history and current practice constitute a rich and meaningful setting. In that setting questions of goals or aims or purposes occur spontaneously and *locally*. For what purpose is a particular instrument being used, or why use a tungsten filament here rather than a copper one? What significant goals would be accomplished by building accelerators capable of generating energy levels in excess in 10^4 GeV? Why can we ignore gravitational effects in the analysis of Compton scattering? Etc. These sorts of questions have a teleological cast and, most likely, could be given appropriate answers in terms of ends, or goals, or the like. But when we are asked what is the aim of science itself, I think we find ourselves in a quandary, just as we do when asked "What is the purpose of life?" or indeed the corresponding sort of question for any sufficiently rich and varied practice or institution. As we grow up, I think we learn that such questions really do not require an answer, but rather they call for an empathetic analysis to get at the cognitive (and temperamental) sources of the question, and then a program of therapy to help change all that.

Let me try to collect my thoughts by means of a metaphor (or is it an allegory?). The realisms and antirealisms seem to treat science as a sort of grand performance, a play or opera, whose production requires interpretation and direction. They argue among themselves as to whose "reading" is best.[9] I have been trying to suggest that if science is a performance, then it is one where the audience and crew play as well. Directions for interpretation are also part of the act. If there are questions and conjectures about the meaning of this or that, or its purpose, then there is room for those in the production too. The script, moreover, is never finished, and no past dialogue can fix future action. Such a performance is not susceptible to a reading or interpretation in any global sense, and it picks out its own interpretations, locally, as it goes along.

9. This way of putting it suggests that the philosophies of realism and antirealism are much closer to the hermeneutical tradition than (most of) their proponents would find comfortable. Similarly, I think the view of science that has emerged from these "isms" is just as contrived as the shallow, mainline view of the hermeneuts (science as control and manipulation, involving only dehumanized and purely imaginery models of the world). In opposition to this, I do not suggest that science is hermeneutic-proof, but rather that in science, as elsewhere, hermeneutical understanding has to be gained *from the inside*. It should not be prefabricated to meet external, philosophical specifications. There is, then, no legitimate hermeneutical *account* of science, but only an hermeneutical activity that is a lively part of science itself.

To allow for such an open conception of science, the attitude one adopts must be neither realist nor antirealist. It is the attitude of NOA, the natural ontological attitude. The quickest way to get a feel for NOA is to understand it as undoing the idea of interpretation and the correlative idea of invariance (or essence).

The attitude that marks NOA is just this: try to take science on its own terms, and try not to read things into science. If one adopts this attitude, then the global interpretations, the "isms" of scientific philosophies, appear as idle overlays to science: not necessary, not warranted, and in the end, probably not even intelligible. It is fundamental to NOA that science has a history, rooted indeed in everyday thinking. But there need not be any aspects invariant throughout that history, and hence, contrary to the isms, no necessary uniformity in the overall development of science (including projections for the future). NOA is, therefore, basically at odds with the temperament that looks for definite boundaries demarcating science from pseudoscience, or that is inclined to award the title "scientific" like a blue ribbon on a prize goat. Indeed, the antiessentialist aspect of NOA is intended to be very comprehensive, applying to all the concepts used in science, even the concept of truth.

Thus NOA is inclined to reject *all* interpretations, theories, construals, pictures, etc., of truth, just as it rejects the special correspondence theory of realism and the acceptance pictures of the truthmongering antirealisms. For the concept of truth is the fundamental semantical concept. Its uses, history, logic, and grammar are sufficiently definite to be partially catalogued, at least for a time. But it cannot be "explained" or given an "account of" without circularity. Nor does it require anything of the sort. The concept of truth is open-ended, growing with the growth of science. Particular questions (Is this true? What reason do we have to believe in the truth of that? Can we find out whether it is true? Etc.) are addressed in well-known ways. The significance of the answers to those questions is rooted in the practices and logic of truth judging (which practices, incidentally, are by no means confined to acceptance or the like), but that significance branches out beyond current practice along with the growing concept of truth. For present knowledge not only redistributes truth-values among past judgments, present knowledge also reevaluates the whole character of past practice. There is no saying, in advance, how this will go. Thus there is no projectable sketch now of what truth signifies, nor of what areas of science (e.g., "fundamental laws") truth is exempt from—nor will there ever be. Some questions, of course, are not settled by the current practices of truth judging. Perhaps some never will be settled.

NOA is fundamentally a heuristic attitude, one that is compatible with quite different assessments of particular scientific investigations, say, investigations concerning whether or not there are magnetic monopoles. At the time of this writing the scientific community is divided on this issue. There is a long history of experimental failure to detect monopoles, and one recent success—maybe. I believe that there are a number of new experiments under way, and considerable theoretical work that might narrow down the detectable properties of monopoles.[10] In this context various ways of putting together the elements that enter into a judgment about monopoles will issue in various attitudes toward them, ranging from complete agnosticism to strong belief. NOA is happy with any of these attitudes. All that NOA insists is that one's ontological attitude toward monopoles, and everything else that might be collected in the scientific zoo (whether observable or not), be governed by the very same standards of evidence and inference that are employed by science itself. This attitude tolerates all the differences of opinion and all the varieties of doubt and skepticism that science tolerates. It does not, however, tolerate the prescriptions of empiricism or of other doctrines that externally limit the commitments of science. Nor does it overlay the judgment, say, that monopoles do exist, with the special readings of realism or of the truthmongering antirealisms. NOA tries to let science speak for itself, and it trusts in our native ability to get the message without having to rely on metaphysical or epistemological hearing aids.

I promised to conclude these reflections by singing in praise of NOA. The refrain I had in mind is an adaptation of a sentiment that Einstein once expressed concerning Mozart. Einstein said that the music of Mozart (read "NOA") seems so natural that, by contrast, the music of other composers (read "realism" or "antirealism") sounds artificial and contrived.

10. See Trower and Cabrera (1983).

Is Scientific Realism Compatible with Quantum Physics?

9

The "new" quantum theory that developed in the decade following 1925 was buffeted by two conflicting influences. On the one hand, it inherited the legacy of the old quantum theory, whose machinery was used so skillfully (e.g., by Einstein and Planck) to support the reality of a microworld made up of molecules and atoms. On the other hand, the new quantum theory also grew up alongside the new positivism, a movement that was itself struggling to come to terms with the older "there-are-no-atoms" positivism of Ostwald, Stallo, and Mach. The upshot of these contradictory influences and companions on the quantum theory is a kind of schizophrenia that the theory seems to exhibit over the issue of realism. For the quantum theory of today is reputed to support realism with respect to a variety of entities, including molecules and atoms and electrons and photons, a whole zoo of elementary particles, quarks maybe—and perhaps some even more unlikely things like magnetic monopoles. Yet that very same quantum theory is also reputed to be incompatible with realism, an incompatability suspected by Born as long ago as 1926[1] and recently brought out with clarity and force in the investigations of John Bell and others over hidden variables.

My purpose in this chapter is to examine this schizophrenia over realism. In the best therapeutic tradition, I will try to show that the quantum theory has an integrity of its own which conforms to neither of these opposing images; that is, that quantum theory neither supports that realism of atoms and molecules, etc., to which the old positivism was opposed, nor does it deny it. Thus I will urge the forgotten moral of the new positivism; namely, that realism is a metaphysical doctrine that finds neither support nor refutation in scientific theories or investigations. I would not, however, go on

An earlier version of this chapter was presented at a symposium to the Pacific Division of the American Philosophical Association in March 1983. I would like to thank my cosymposiast there, Linda Wessels, for helpful suggestions. I also want to thank a referee for *Nous*, and Hector Castenada, the editor, who accepted the earlier version for publication but who kindly allowed me to withdraw it for revision and publication here.

1. See the concluding paragraph of Born (1926).

to endorse the principle that Carnap generalized from Karl Menger's discussions in the philosophy of mathematics,[2] the principle that one should be tolerant concerning "external questions," like that of realism. For I believe that where ideas can be graded into "better" and "worse" one should always choose the better. And certainly NOA provides a much better framework for science than the metaphysics of so-called scientific realism.

As I emphasized in the preceding chapters, realism involves a special interpretive stance toward science. It sees science as providing reliable information about the features of a definite world structure, and thus it construes the truth of scientific statements as involving some sort of articulated external-world correspondence. When we come to existence claims, say, the claim that there are quarks, the realist picture is that the truth of the claim corresponds to a certain feature of the world structure (presumably a quarklike part). Obviously, the mere truth of the claim, say, that there are quarks, has nothing specifically to do with realism. That is, we could certainly agree with the physicists that there are quarks without necessarily imposing on that conclusion the special interpretive stance of realism. (We might, for instance, adopt the stance of some antirealist truthmonger or, better still, follow NOA's recommendation and not adopt any special stance at all.) Granting this, the realist might, nevertheless, hope to carry his argument forward by suggesting that there are in fact good grounds for imposing a realist construal. In particular, with respect to existence claims the realist might well suggest that the details of the scientific practice that grounds such claims provides the rationale for his special interpretive stance. The idea is that if we look carefully at the procedures that lead to the general, scientific endorsement of existence claims, then we will discern a practice of assessment, a critical aspect of which involves precisely the interpretive stance of realism.

I am afraid that only immersion in the details of quite lengthy case studies can give one a feel for the texture of decision making over existence claims in a highly structured science like quantum physics. For that procedure involves a truly exquisite balance between experimental and theoretical work. On the experimental side, one has the varied and skillful generation of effects in the laboratory, effects whose very recognition requires intricate data analysis and reduction on a sometimes massive scale, and whose significance is often, at best, only marginal, even at the statistical

2. Menger (1974), p. 111, contains references to his papers from 1928 to 1933 relating to this point.

level. On the theoretical side, there is the calculation of the likelihood of such effects by means of a network of approximations that are only loosely derived from complex and varied theoretical considerations.[3] The most important feature of the whole process, and the one it is most difficult to get a feeling for in the abstract, is that every stage of the experimental design and analysis, as well as every stage of the theoretical reconciliation, involves significant matters of judgment. These are matters not closed by experiment or theory or by any of the modalities that the realist might want to subsume under the rubric of "contact with reality."[4] These judgments express norms, and often transient ones, for pursuing the scientific craft. Thus the decision to accept as true a particular existence claim is the decision to accept the complex network of judgments that ground it. That network itself constitutes an open-ended array of partially overlapping theories and norms. It is precisely the setting of the existence claim within this array that constitutes the scientific practice of truth judging for the claim. The existence claim will be accepted as true just to the extent that the relevant scientific community goes along with the network of normative judgments and the concomitant ranges of theories.[5]

But if this is a fair summary of what goes on when an existence claim is examined and judged to be correct, then the realist ambition to discern in that practice the special interpretive stance of realism is bound to be frustrated. For all that the process displays is how particular judgments of truth are anchored in a network of much more general judgments and normative practices. Hence, when we view this activity without prejudice we do not discern realism; that is, the working through of the realist project for external-world correspondence (or the like). Rather, what we see at work is the critical elaboration of tentative truth claims arising out of locally constrained practical reason and judgment. Thus the realist ambition here is frustrated, for what we see at work in the validation of existence claims is not realism at all but rather NOA.[6]

3. Galison (1985) gives one a good sense for the complexities on the experimental side, and Cartwright (1983), essay 6 especially, does the same on the side of theory.

4. For the particular case of the existence of quarks this is compellingly documented in a fascinating narrative by Pickering (1984).

5. Simplifying the conclusion of a complex story, Galison writes, "The discovery of the muon was inseparably bound to the resurrection of quantum electrodynamics" (Galison 1983, p. 308).

6. Overlapping considerations lead Hacking (1983) to the same conclusion, in his "experimental argument" for "realism." For insofar as Hacking seems to lean toward a Davidsonian "no-theory" theory of truth, what Hacking (and perhaps Davidson as well) calls "realism" seems rather a version of NOA. See Rorty (1986a, b) for the suggestion of connecting Davidson with NOA.

So far I have been trying to address the following line of thought. When we look at the things that exist, according to quantum physics, we find a large and fascinating variety of objects; in particular, various particles and fields with their attendant properties and relations. A naive inference from this might be that at least with respect to *these* objects, the ones that are supposed to exist, the physics is realist. In order to show that, in fact, no such inference is warranted I have tried to emphasize that realism requires substantially more than just the truth of certain claims. What it requires is that this truth (or these claims) have a certain, special aura—so to speak—an aura that reaches out to reality itself. Since this realist emanation is not to be found in the mere fact of the truth of these existence claims, I have asked whether it might be found to be attached to those claims by the scientific practices that ground their truth. But although those practices are somewhat elusive, they are still definite enough to be seen not to involve the subtle emanations of realism. I conclude that when the realist attaches the aura of his realism to science, he goes well beyond what is warranted either by the truth of specific scientific claims or by the features of scientific practice that ground those claims. In short, realism is unwarranted, even if we restrict it only to the existence claims of quantum physics.

So far, despite some mention of quantum physics and its objects, I have been trying to set out a line of thought that is perfectly general. It is that in the context of any reasonably developed science the realist attempt to ground his special requirements either in the existence claims made by the science or in the practices that certify the correctness of those claims seems bound to fail. The "externality," the reaching out to definite features of a definite world structure, is not found in science itself. It is a kind of overlay to the text of science, an overlay that the realist seems to need in order to direct and focus his own reading of the text. While I am sure the realist would be happy if we were to accept the naive inference from particular existence claims (or even claims of a more general sort) to his realism, I also believe that, in his heart, the realist knows full well that such an inference is fallacious. That is why, in recent years, the patterns of argument for realism have been rather more sophisticated. These recent arguments are the explanationist and coherentist ones for which the "metatheorem" of chapter 7 provides a powerful rebuttal. But this too is a general consideration and makes no use of special features of the quantum theory that are relevant to the possibility of realism there.

A particular feature of relevance is the prima facie difficulty in reconciling quantum physics with the definiteness that realism requires. For the entities, properties, and relations that enter into the realist world structure are supposed to be observer-independent (or largely so). But the probability-laden formulas of quantum theory all seem to make at least tacit reference to an observer. For the probabilities of the theory are generally understood as probabilities for various measurement outcomes and, so understood, suppose a prearranged apparatus for measurement—and hence a measurer-observer of some sort. Then, too, well-known and densely packed difficulties over the evolution (and collapse) of the state function also appear to involve observer-driven interaction in an essential way. The problem here of whether it is possible to construct a definite world picture on the basis of quantum theory used to be referred to, barbarously, as the problem of "unobjectifiability."[7] I think the consensus of investigators is that "objectifiability" (i.e., the possibility of there being a definite world picture that accords with the detailed predictions of quantum theory), if not actually ruled out, has, at any rate, dim prospects in quantum physics. I must confess, however, that apart from certain recent investigations, including those generated by the work of John Bell, I have never found the various lines of argument for this pessimistic conclusion at all compelling.[8] I will begin to examine the implications of Bell's work for realism in a moment, but first I just want to state the conclusion on realism so far. It is that even without attending to features of observation in quantum theory, realism finds no support there. If it should turn out, in addition, that the role of the observer in the theory actually excludes the possibility for there being a definite world structure compatible with the physics, then so much the worse for realism.

But is realism actually incompatible with quantum physics? That is the conclusion, with one qualification or another, that several investigators have wanted to draw on the basis of Bell's work. The qualifications will turn out to be of central importance. In order to highlight this, let me begin the evaluation of the impact of the Bell literature on realism by sketching a very general argument to show that no theory can actually be incompatible with realism per se, unless the theory is itself inconsistent. The argument is, simply, that—in the logician's sense—every consistent theory has a model.

7. This is the terminology of von Weizsäcker (1952), who adopts it from Pauli (1933).

8. Fine (1973a) expresses some of my reservations concerning the older literature. Perhaps I inherited this attitude from my teacher in this subject, Henry Mehlberg. See Mehlberg (1960, 1980) who tries to make realism ride piggyback on the idea of treating quantum probabilities as transition probabilities, an idea that had lost its way until Cartwright (1983) found it anew.

The model automatically provides for referents, via correspondence to the terms in the vocabulary of the theory, and the conditions for truth-in-the-model embody the realist requirements for a correspondence theory of truth. Hence, if we add to the model the realist injunction that the model structure is the real, definite world structure, we get out precisely the desired compatibility of realism with the theory in question.

Now, bracketing off the difficult and interesting logical constructions involved in proving that every consistent theory has a model, one might well think that the argument I have just sketched is really too general, indeed too trivial, to be of much interest in the debate over realism. While I do not want to place *too* much emphasis on this line of argument, I do think it has some genuine interest. In the first place, I think the argument does show that there is no possibility to *refute* realism using some science or scientific practice as a basis. If one combines this conclusion with the one I have been urging up to this point (namely, that there is no way to *support* realism using some science or scientific practice), then the picture of realism that emerges is very much like the one drawn by the neopositivists. Realism emerges as a metaphysical doctrine that transcends human experience and rational support, in a manner similar to that, say, of a religious doctrine. Thus at this level of generality, the only way to support a genuine incompatibility between science and realism would be to attend to a scientific domain whose theory or practice is inconsistent. What comes to mind is a protoscience containing several partially overlapping but irreconcilable-looking theories. For such a domain the possibility of a realist interpretation would not be guaranteed by my model-theoretic argument. Curiously, modern physics may itself be just such a protoscience with quantum physics and general relativistic physics the irreconcilable pairs.[9] Of course, since several lively and different contemporary research programs are moving toward a unified physics,[10] this toehold for antirealism will probably not support it for long.

Related model-theoretic considerations are involved in Hilary Putnam's recent attack on realism (he calls his target "metaphysical realism," as though there were some other, more physical kind).[11] For Putnam wants to attack the idea that realism could actually establish correspondence relations that would pin down the real

9. Joseph (1980) is a nice discussion of this antirealist idea. For those who adopt the semantic approach to theories, a theory *is* a family of models. Q.E.D. Joseph's puzzle may be an interesting challenge, or growing point, for this semantic approach.

10. See, for example, Fayet and Ferrara (1977) and Levy and Deser (1979).

11. See Putnam (1981a) and references there to his earlier work.

referents. To this end he uses the observation that a model is only defined up to isomorphism,[12] so that the actual elements in the domain of the definite world structure—considered as a model of some theory—would always elude us, even if we supplement the theory with reference-fixing addenda. It seems to me that Putnam's argument is good enough to make the realist reexamine his vague requirement of substantial epistemic access to features of the world structure. For in the light of Putnam's challenge to the possibility of specifying reference, the realist may want to relativize epistemic access to certain reference-fixing conventions that are not themselves to be considered part of science, and hence not to be thrown into the model at all. Or, the realist may want to reduce the extent of the epistemic access to merely structural features of the world. It is an open question to what extent the consequent conventionalism or the structuralism, which are both familiar moves in the history of epistemology, would support a lively realism. I believe, therefore, that Putnam's argument shows something important about the metaphysical character of realism, insofar as it demonstrates inherent limitations on the specificity of realist correspondence relations. For just this reason, however, Putnam's argument is actually useful to the realist as a means of defense from the "unobjectifiability" that has been urged against realism on behalf of the quantum theory. For those who see difficulties in providing an observer-independent world picture for quantum physics generally agree that if we do bring the observer into the picture then we can indeed find a consistent interpretive scheme. The "Copenhagen interpretation" (in some definite form), for example, might do. But if this were granted, then we could deploy Putnam's strategy to construct out of an observer-laden ontology an observer-independent one isomorphic to the original. Thus if we grant the viability of a Copenhagen-like interpretation for the quantum theory, we can use Putnam's observation to insure the viability of a realist, observer-independent interpretation. This idea, I think, closes what some may have perceived as a gap in my model-theoretic argument for the compatibility of realism with any consistent theory. For how, one might have asked, can we be sure that there is a model that is definite in the sense required by realism? The answer, given above, is this: The realist can always putnamize.

Finally, lest one still think that such general model-theoretic considerations are simply too far-fetched and, perhaps, too easy to attract the interest of genuine realists, I should point out that one

---

12. Actually, Putnam cites versions of the Löwenheim-Skolem theorem, which do not seem essential to his point.

realist program for quantum mechanics seems to me to have been derived from precisely such considerations. I have in mind the program of quantum logic in its realist version. In the case of nonrelativistic quantum theory, at any rate, one can construct a model in something much like the logician's sense from the geometry of Hilbert space. Now I do not suppose it would occur to very many people to try to use this fact to declare that reality (i.e., the definite world structure posited by realism) *is* a Hilbert space. But it has certainly occurred to some to contend that the "possibility structure" (or the logical structure) of reality is that of the lattice of closed subspaces of a Hilbert space. (The technical idea is to use that lattice to provide a model for a "quantum logic" of propositions in just the way that the two-element Boolean algebra is used to provide a model for the classical logic of propositions. There are other quantum logical programs that employ somewhat different structures, e.g., the category of partial Boolean algebras. For present purposes I will not distinguish between them.) This is a merely structural realism of the sort one might retreat to in the face of Putnam's argument about reference. It does not attempt to specify what the real possibilities, whose structure is given by the Hilbert space lattice, are really possibilities for. Indeed, one of the persistent anomalies of this quantum logical program has been over the idea of a property and what "having a property" amounts to if the structure is quantum logical. These days the program seems to be a degenerating one, like the program of realism itself. The reasons for that are much like the reasons rehearsed above in connection with realism; namely, that interpreting the application of quantum mechanics as the working out of inferences via a new logic goes well beyond the ordinary practice of the physics, including practices for judging truth. Moreover, as a device for explaining puzzling features of the physics, or puzzling features of experiments (like the tangled statistics of some correlation experiments), quantum logic is clearly sterile for it already assumes that reality contains structural features corresponding to the puzzling explananda. (The technical side is that the probabilistic relations of the theory are already fixed by the lattice structure.) Thus the form of a typical "explanation" proffered by quantum logic is that so-and-so is strange because reality is strange. And that, I think, is the sort of explanation that we usually dismiss as being no explanation at all.[13] If, however, realist quantum logic—like realism more generally—fails

13. Stairs (1983) is an excellent statement of realist quantum logical ambitions, emphasizing especially how the very rationale for the program is that it is supposed to offer explanatory insight. (The point is that it does not.)

to obtain any support from quantum physics, still it remains compatible with the physics; a testament, if you like, to quantum logic's metaphysical status.

Insofar as this discussion of the general compatibility of realism with quantum physics has been persuasive, it will have made as plain as can be that if there actually were a difficulty in reconciling realism with the Bell theorem, that difficulty would be generated by very special assumptions. It should be equally plain that one can indeed make trouble for realism if one does make strong enough background assumptions. For example, suppose we require that our realism be monistic, so that all the things that exist will be of exactly one kind. Suppose, further, that we require the correspondence relations to respect identity. That is, if A and B are distinct according to our science, then the real referent of A must be distinct from the real referent of B. Clearly, if our monism allows for only certain individuating properties and our theory entails sufficient diversity, we may not be able to model the truths of the theory by our monism in a way that respects identity. Of course it would be misleading to advertise this failure as a defeat of realism, or even of monism. For the constraints on correspondence would have played an essential role here. More generally, if our realism is eliminatively reductive, then there will be strong restrictions on the correspondence relations, restrictions that effect the reduction of the "theoretical entities" (to speak picturesquely) to aggregates, or whatever, of the "real stuff." From the difficulties involved in various attempted microreductions of just this sort (for instance, nation-states to aggregates of individuals, genes to DNA structures, or heat to molecules in motion), we have come to expect a mismatch between the reductive base and the original theory-to-be-reduced. Of course the significance of the mismatch is not clear. (Do we conclude that nation-states exist over and above the individuals that they comprise, or that political theory is simply a mistake, or just that our reductive correspondence rules are flawed?) What is clear, I hope, is that an eliminative or reductive realism can be incompatible with a specific theory, and that when this occurs its significance requires careful assessment.

I want to show, now, how the application of the Bell results involves such an eliminatively reductive realism. To see just how eliminative the required reduction is, I want to contrast this reductive realism with a nonreductive sort. Let me begin then by introducing a realist scheme for the quantum theory, a scheme that I shall call *minimal realism*, because it posits a structure that must be reproduced, at least approximately, by any realist construal of the theory.[14] When we contrast Bell's reductive realism with this minimal one, we will be able to pinpoint the reductive constraints, and this will assist us in assessing the significance of the mismatch between quantum theory and the posited reductively realist structure.

Any realist approach to quantum theory will have to specify what (in the real world) corresponds to the systems, observables, states, and probabilities that make up the theoretical apparatus. The nature of the systems is an old and intractable issue. Are they waves or particles or what? Let us not try to decide this issue (keeping in mind, for example, that we could always putnamize from one ontological category to another anyway). Instead let us just say that, according to minimal realism, quantum systems correspond to real objects. The observables of the theory (spin, position, momentum, etc.) will each correspond to some generic feature of the real objects, a feature that can take on any one of several particular forms. We will assume as part of our minimal realism that each real object has (or "possesses") some particular form (or other) of every generic feature. One can think of these particular forms as definite properties of the object. The states, then, will correspond to the various ways of attributing the particular forms of generic features to the real objects. (Formally, a state is a function from real objects to the particular forms of generic features, a function that assigns to each object exactly one form of each generic feature.) Then a system S has a state ψ (or "is in" the state ψ) just in case the real object corresponding to S has the array of particular forms of the generic features that ψ attributes to that object. We must now make some further assumptions about the forms of these features. Suppose A is an observable. Then there will be a number of classical (i.e., Lebesgue) probability measures on the real line that are concentrated on the possible values of A (i.e., on its spectrum). I want to suppose that each particular form of the generic feature that corresponds to A is associated with one such measure on the possible values of A. (You could think of this association as a property of the form; i.e., as a second-order property of the object.) Finally, we can specify the realist truth conditions for the probabilistic assertions of the theory as follows. If system S is in state ψ and A is

14. The "at least approximately" here is intended to hedge minimal realism by leaving open the possibility of variations in the realist structure; e.g., replacing properties of the real objects by relations, or allowing states to be only partial functions (or even multiple-place functions) on the real objects, and so on. Aficionados will recognize these perennial variations on the realist theme. The openness of these possibilities is significant. I suggest why at the conclusion of the chapter.

an observable of S, then ψ attributes to the real object corresponding to S a particular form of the generic feature that corresponds to A. If and only if that particular form is associated with the probability distribution that quantum mechanics assigns for finding values of A, will we say that these various probabilistic assertions are true for system S in state ψ. Roughly speaking, various probabilistic assertions hold just in case the object has the right forms of the features; that is, the right properties.

This minimal realism is, of course, merely a structural realism, a skeleton that could be fleshed out in different ways. In various publications I have suggested some ways to try. One of them is to take each generic feature to be what I call a "statistical variable"; that is, a real-valued function with a probability measure defined on the Borel subsets of its range. This is a concept well known in empirical statistics (to be distinguished from the different concept of a random variable), and which seems just to fit the quantum mechanical uses of probability.[15] Then the particular forms of a statistical variable would just be pairings of the function with a particular measure on its range, which automatically yields the association to probabilities. Another suggestion is to consider the observables as extended entities with variably concentrated extensions.[16] Thus the generic features become functions, associating with each object a set with a probability density over that set (i.e., statistical variable-valued functions). Their particular forms are their "values"; i.e., their variably concentrated extensions (or "spreads"), and this variable concentration is the associated probability measure. Finally, I might mention that quantum logic also fits into the framework of minimal realism—although not necessarily with an interpretation as "logic." For it is sufficient for doing quantum physics to restrict the observables to just those taking 0 or 1 as values. These are called "questions" and correspond to the projec-

15. See Fine (1968) for the background to this idea, and Fine (1973a, 1976, 1982b) for its development.

16. See Fine (1971, 1973b). Teller (1979, 1984) makes up some pretty, motivating stories for this idea, especially for continuous magnitudes, promoting it as an "inexact values interpretation"; and Stairs (1983), focusing on the discrete case, makes it the core of his "M-quantum logic" ("M" for "modest") under the guise of "disjunctive facts." In the articles cited, I had anticipated these interpretive moves and criticized them without then realizing, as emphasized in chapter 5, that the interpretive dead end here was already precisely the point of the Schrödinger cat paradox. Recall Einstein's "exploding gunpowder" letter to Schrödinger (August 8, 1935) where he puts the difficulty as plainly as can be, "Through no art of interpretation can this psi-function be turned into an adequate description of a real state of affairs; for in reality there is just no intermediary between exploded and not-exploded." Exit my extended entities; a.k.a. "spreads," "disjunctive facts," and "inexact values"!

tion operators (or closed subspaces). Then quantum logic would have the generic features that correspond to these questions understood as "real possibilities." The various probabilities for realizing these possibilities are, then, the particular forms.

Let me now apply this minimal realist framework to the correlation experiments treated in the Bell literature. These involve a system S in a fixed state ψ. The system is composed of two subsystems, which we can refer to as particles—particle (1) and particle (2). On each of the particles we have in mind to perform one of several mutually incompatible measurements, (each of which is maximal on the subsystem); say $A_1, A_2, \ldots$ on particle (1) and $B_1, B_2, \ldots$ on particle (2). Further, we will suppose that the particles are spatially separated, and that the measurements on the pair are made simultaneously. (If you prefer, say that each pair of measurement events is spacelike separated.) In typical arrangements, quantum mechanics assigns a probability for each individual measurement outcome. It also assigns probabilities for the various pairs of outcomes. That is, quantum theory determines a single distribution for the outcomes of each measurement separately, and a joint distribution for the simultaneous outcomes of each AB pair. However, quantum mechanics assigns no joint probability to *any* pair of A's nor to *any* pair of B's. Indeed the joint outcomes of, say, B_1 and B_2 are generally held not to be well defined. They certainly do not enter into the probabilistic formulas of the theory.

From the perspective of minimal realism we can treat the system S as one real object with two parts, the "particles." In state ψ the generic features of the object take particular forms. Let us say that corresponding to the A measurement on particle (1) (technically the observable $A \otimes I$) the object has the form α of the feature corresponding to A. Similarly, the B measurement on particle (2) (the $I \otimes B$ observable) corresponds to the form β. And corresponding to the joint measurements of A on particle (1) and B on particle (2) (the observable $A \otimes B$) let the object have the form $\alpha\beta$, according to ψ. Thus when the system is in state ψ the object already has certain properties (the various α, β, and $\alpha\beta$), and these properties ground the probabilities for the various measurement outcomes. For we have that α is already associated with some definite probability distribution on the outcomes of the A measurement, β with a distribution on the B outcomes, and $\alpha\beta$ with a distribution on the joint AB outcomes. The quantum mechanical description of the system (i.e., single probabilities and joint AB pairs as specified) will be correct just in case it matches these distributions that correspond to the properties of the object. Thus in typical realist fashion we can say that the quantum theory for such a correlated system is correct just to the extent that it matches aspects of the definite world structure. More especially, the probabilities of the theory are correct to the extent to which they actually *are* the probabilities associated with properties of the real object.

There are at least three respects in which this minimal framework may be considered too minimal. First, we have made no provision in the model for the actual outcomes of measurements, only for the likelihood of such. Second, we have made probabilities in the theory correspond to special properties in the model (or in the real world, if you like), and thus taken probability as fundamental. Third, we have not built into the association of the probability measures with properties, the relation of the outcome of the joint measurement to the outcomes of the individual ones.

One could rectify all these omissions, it may seem, if one adopted a standard, eliminative strategy over the probabilities. For one might be motivated to alter the correspondence rules for probability in such a way as to reduce, or eliminate, the correspondents of probabilities as part of the inventory of the world. The standard procedure here is to treat the probabilities as mere averages over a single well-determined ensemble, and to support that treatment as what is forced on us (or, at any rate, reasonable to do) in the face of ignorance of the finer details of things. The probabilistic assertions, then, would signify merely a restriction on the epistemic accessibility of the world. This eliminative strategy could be seen as expressing a deterministic attitude, and in the Bell literature especially it is commonly so labeled.[17] But determinism alone cannot be at the root of the strategy, for the minimal realist framework is already determinist in its regular attribution of a definite array of particular forms of the features in every state. Moreover, one could even sharpen the determinism by enhancing the minimal realism in such a way as to make every outcome of a measurement correspond to some additional property already determined prior to the measurement. This is a feature of the prism models discussed in chapter 4, which are deterministic, as above, even over mea-

17. I have in mind the common terminology of "deterministic hidden variables." Recent commentators have noted that the determinism here does not relate to the time evolution of the system but rather to the definiteness of the values of observables at a single time. To make this distinction, Wessels (1986) introduces the useful terminology of "evolutionary determinism" versus "vertical determinism." In her language, the determinism mentioned in my text is vertical not evolutionary. In chapter 1 the term used for this was "determinateness."

surement outcomes.[18] Indeed, one point of the models was to show that, in addition to determinism, the Bell results require further constraints. What they in fact require, beyond determinism, is the eliminative strategy for probabilities—or something equivalent to it. More precisely, one can give rigorous content to the following theorem. *The Bell inequalities hold if, and only if, it is possible to reduce the probabilities (for the observables mentioned in the inequalities) to averages over a single ensemble.*

Let me use the term *reductive realism* for that type of realism whose concern over the reality of probabilities leads it to adopt the eliminative strategy suggested above.[19] In the context of the quantum theory, reductive realism amounts to requiring, first, that the measures of minimal realism all be dispersion free, and then to changing the correspondence rule for the states to treat them the way statistical mechanics treats macrostates. These modifications result in the probabilistic construct of an ensemble representation which then provides the definite world structure of reductive realism.[20] It follows from this structure that if B and B' are *any* two observables, then not only do they both have values for each real object but there is always, in the real world, a well-defined joint probability for their values, relative to any ensemble that corresponds to a quantum state. But if B and B' are incompatible, according to quantum theory, then they are not both assigned values in *any* state, nor do they have a joint distribution. Thus reductive realism necessarily involves features of the world not touched on by the quantum theory. In particular, the way it treats probability has a uniformity to it that one does not find in quantum theory itself. The price of reduction, then, seems to be to make out of the quantum theory an account of the world that is doubly incomplete. It is incomplete descriptively, because it fails to describe the values of incompatible observables. It is incomplete probabilistically, because it fails to specify the well-defined joint distributions for incompatible observables.

I call attention to the way in which the joint probabilities of reductive realism necessarily outstrip those of quantum theory because this particular feature, which is deeply at variance with quantum mechanics, turns out to characterize this special brand of re-

18. Fine (1982a) also introduces other models for the correlation experiments—synchronization models—with this same deterministic feature.

19. I do not want to suggest by this terminology that concern over the reality of probabilities is a reductive disease to which only quantum realists are susceptible, for that sort of reductionism can infect quantum antirealists as well; witness Leeds (1984).

20. Recall the discussion of ensemble representations in chapter 4.

alism *all by itself*. That is, any framework that allows for well-defined joint distributions for the incompatible observables can be given an ensemble representation. Let me restate this more carefully for the correlation experiments.

Recall that in this case we have a single state ψ and, say, observables $A_1 \ldots A_n; B_1 \ldots B_m$, where each pair A_i, B_j has a quantum mechanical distribution in state ψ, and no pair A_i, A_j or B_i, B_j has a quantum mechanical distribution. I will say that *there is a well-defined distribution for* $B_1, \ldots B_m$ (relative to the A's) in case (1) for each i, there is a joint distribution for $A_i, B_1, \ldots, B_m$ that returns (as marginals) the quantum mechanical distributions for A_i, B_j ($j = 1, 2, \ldots m$) and (2) each of these distributions just mentioned returns one and the same joint distribution for $B_1 \ldots, B_m$. Then, regardless of the cardinality of the spectra of the observables, of their number, or of their single distributions (i.e., not necessarily all ½), the following theorem holds: *there exists an ensemble representation for* $A_1, \ldots, A_n; B_1, \ldots, B_m$ *if and only if there is a well-defined distribution for* $B_1, \ldots, B_m$ *(relative to the A's).*[21]

The Bell literature generally refers to what I have been calling an "ensemble representation" as a local (or "factorizable") hidden variables theory—more especially, a deterministic one. (The literature also treats a stochastic variety. But it turns out that there is a stochastic, factorizable theory iff there is a deterministic one.[22] So where all that is at stake is the possibility of hidden variables, we can stick with the deterministic kind.) Several special cases of the general situation of the preceding theorem have been studied in some detail. For these cases, quantum mechanical systems have been found whose probabilities cannot be given an ensemble representation. These results can be referred to, collectively, as the *Bell theorem*. (They usually proceed by showing that the quantum probabilities violate some relation necessary for an ensemble representation, a relation like the inequality originally derived by Bell.)

The Bell theorem, then, shows that reductive realism cannot ground the truth of all the probabilistic assertions of quantum theory. This is just the sort of mismatch between a theory and a special sort of realism that, as I suggested earlier, one might well expect in general. In particular, since reductive realism for correlated systems turns out to be fully *equivalent* to the existence of a well-defined distribution for the incompatible observables of each

---

21. This is a consequence of Theorem 1 of Fine (1982b) and the equivalence of deterministic hidden variables with a suitable joint probability function, demonstrated there on p. 1308.

22. This is shown in Fine (1982c).

subsystem, quantum mechanics would be seen as incomplete over the most essential features of the world if it *could* be given a realist reduction. That reductive program, it has always seemed to me, is so widely at variance with the theory as to make it a very implausible candidate for shaping a realist worldview for quantum theory. From this perspective, then, the Bell theorem is a welcome result, for it shows that an implausible form of realism for quantum theory is actually numerically inconsistent with the theory.

But there are other perspectives. As we saw in chapter 4, a common one in the scientific community is to focus on the so-called locality involved in reductive realism and to see the variance between it and quantum theory as a demonstration that a realist construal of quantum theory will have to countenance certain peculiar and suspect nonlocal effects. Recall that the "locality" condition (or as I prefer to call it, "factorizability") is already built into the idea of an ensemble representation. It is the requirement that the quantum correlation for joint measurement outcomes on each pair of particles (i.e., the joint probability for each *A, B* pair) arises by averaging over the product of the probability for the outcomes on each particle separately. It is easy to show that this requirement is actually equivalent to the implausible condition already discussed; namely, that all the incompatible observables for one subsystem have a well-defined joint distribution (relative to the observables of the other subsystem). This equivalence certainly ought to make us wonder about the physical grounds for "locality." Indeed, although the required factorizability is related to a condition of stochastic independence, there is no reason to suppose that violations of the independence condition must involve real, nonlocal effects—something like genuine action-at-a-distance.[23]

Nevertheless, the issue of "locality" seems especially hard to deal with, and I think this is because there are deep background beliefs at work. These beliefs, whatever their propositional content, issue in an attitude that makes correlations between spatially separated systems appear puzzling in themselves, and that then restricts the possible ways of explaining the correlations to just two: either they are due to a common background cause that operated when the systems were interacting, or they arise by an exchange of infor-

23. Perhaps the most important contribution of the Bell literature is just this: it has made us recognize a general problem in connecting the fact of suitably independent causal histories for stochastic processes with the requirement of stochastic independence of their outcomes. This problem is the Achilles' heel of the quantum nonlocality interpretation of the Bell theorem. See Jarrett (1984) and Wessels (1986) for excellent analyses of the options here; Earman (forthcoming) for the many difficulties involved in the requisite concept of "locality"; and Fine (1981b) for several demonstrations of the problem.

mation that occurs after the systems are already separated. The first route here, the common cause idea, is simply equivalent to the existence of an ensemble representation for the correlations.[24] The second route, when we rule out by experimental design all but instantaneous exchanges, is precisely the imputed nonlocality. If one approaches Bell's theorem with the attitude sketched above, then of course, one is going to see it as entailing nonlocality for the correlated systems of quantum mechanics to which the theorem applies. Faced with this attitude, I think there are only two ways to go. One is to try to undermine the suspicion that attaches to distant correlations, to try to see them as an ordinary part of the natural world—a feature to be catalogued rather than explained. Here one might take certain simple varieties of distant correlations as natural paradigms (Toulmin's "ideals of natural order" or Sellars's "unexplained explainers") and try to build the others up from these.[25] A second way of dealing with the suspicion of nonlocality would be to suggest that there are ways of explaining distant correlations other than via common background causes or exchanges of information. Here the realist can point to the explanation embedded in minimal realism. In general, the realist can explain why certain probabilities are found by showing how they are grounded in the particular forms taken by generic features of the real objects. In the case of correlated systems, the real object with the two particles as parts already has, in the fixed state ψ, for any A measurement on one particle and B on the other, a particular form $\alpha\beta$ for the generic feature corresponding to the joint measurement. The correlation between the distant measurement outcomes is due, according to minimal realism, to the presence *in* the real object of this particular property. Not only does minimal realism offer this *explanation* for correlated statistics, an explanation that is free of nonlocal effects, minimal realism could not possibly be convicted of harboring any such effects. For the world of minimal realism includes only objects and particular forms of their features (with associated probabilities). In the world of minimal realism there are no actions at all, certainly none propagating instantaneously across space (or the like).

Of course those suspicious about distant correlations will probably not be satisfied by this minimalist explanation. They may well respond, as I did earlier over quantum logic, that it only explains

24. This follows from results in Suppes and Zannotti (1981) and Fine (1982c).

25. Toulmin (1961) and Sellars (1961). In Fine (1981b) I introduced the idea of "random devices in harmony" as an illustrative paradigm of this sort. Although I was unaware of it at the time, it turns out that a similar concept, called "stochastic coupling," is used in simulation studies. See Fishman (1973).

puzzling features of the theory (or of our observations) by invoking mysterious features of the world. I have considerable sympathy with that response, the general drift of which is to point to the sterility of realism as such. Nevertheless, if the suspicious attitude toward distant correlations makes them stand out as requiring explanation and yet will not accept explanations for them in terms of such structural features of the world, then I think that these particular suspicions could only be addressed by an account of how the correlations are generated in time from uncorrelated, individual outcomes. Since such an explanation would be tantamount to an ensemble representation, Bell's theorem rules it out. The upshot is that one cannot lay the suspicions to rest. Thus there is no help for those who are trapped in this circle; they must struggle, I think, to undo their suspicious nature. But they could, still, be clear enough in their own thinking to see that the difficulties they experience cannot be blamed on realism, but only on their own reductive worldview.

So far I have taken for granted that the incompatibility brought out by Bell's theorem between quantum theory and reductive realism is to be dealt with by abandoning that brand of realism. I am inclined to this attitude because, as I see it, reductive realism should never have been offered in the first place as a plausible candidate for the quantum worldview. But one could be more cautious for, as I pointed out earlier, when one finds a reductive mismatch one ought to be open to asking which side of the reduction should we give up; and not only this, for one can also ask whether the correspondence rules linking the sides may not be at fault. Thus one can certainly wonder, concerning just those areas where reductive realism clashes with the quantum theory, which one will stand the test of experiment. A number of correlation experiments have been run to try to settle this question.[26] On one analysis of experimental error these experiments can be taken as confirming the predictions of quantum theory, and they are generally so regarded. It is, however, also possible to factor in the experimental errors differently to see the experimental results as entirely consistent with reductive realism. Indeed, from the fact that for the range of experiments to date the inequalities of Clauser and Horne (1974) are sufficient (as well as necessary) for an ensemble representation, one can prove that such a representation is always possible for a simple spin-$\frac{1}{2}$ experiment whenever the single-detector efficiency in the experi-

---

26. For important, recent ones see Aspect (1982a, b) which also contain references to the literature.

ment is less than, roughly, 90%.[27] Since no experiment so far even comes close to this level of efficiency, it follows that there is not yet any really crucial test between quantum mechanics and reductive realism. As of today, then, one could still hope to see quantum theory as a merely approximate account of a reductively realist world structure, an account doubly incomplete and just wrong at certain points. As technology develops, however, highly efficient correlation experiments may remove that way of reconciling the difference.

There would, nevertheless, still be the option of reexamining the reductive correspondence rules. This is precisely the issue treated at length in my essay on Einstein and Bell in chapter 4. The argument there was that Einstein's "statistical interpretation" need not be understood as the technical construct of an ensemble representation, but rather it could be understood even better as involving the machinery of prism models. Since Einstein's attitude toward probabilities was certainly reductive, that argument is relevant here, for it shows, constructively, how the elimination of probabilities as fundamental (or "real") need not necessarily lead to an ensemble representation (or, equivalently, to a deterministic hidden variables model). That reductive program could instead, for example, be satisfied by an interpretation based on prism models. Such a shift in the reductive program would certainly avoid the obstacle posed by the Bell theorem. The question of efficiency, however, is also relevant to the survival of the prism models, and it remains to be seen whether the flexible resources of these models will stand up to highly efficient tests.[28]

To sum things up, we can conclude that there is no incompatibility possible between quantum physics and realism as such. We've yet to see whether the possible incompatibility brought out by Bell's theorem between the quantum theory and reductive realism will even go against that peculiar and implausible brand of realism. But the realist should draw no solace from this, because there is no support for realism to be found in quantum physics either. The existence claims of the physics do not support realism, nor does physical practice support the semantics of realism. If my general argument in the first part of this chapter did not persuade you of

27. See Fine (1982c) and Garg (1983).
28. This issue is discussed in Fine (1981b, 1982d), but general methods for calculating error bounds using the prism idea have yet to be developed. Certainly all extant correlation experiments can be prismed, including the Aspect (1982a, b) experiments, whose symmetries with regard to error rates exactly match the simplest of the prism models.

the extent to which realism transcends the physics, then perhaps my later working out of the structure of minimal realism will have done the job. For what reason do we have to believe that "right out here in the world" there are real objects having particular forms of certain generic features which are associated with special probability measures? Indeed, what sense can we make of this idea?

In formulating such a realism I have pursued the standard procedure for playing the quantum realism game. It consists, to begin with, in taking the salient quantum theoretical apparatus, wholesale, as one big truth. Then it follows up by asking what the world must be like *in order* for the quantum theory to be true. We have seen in chapter 7 that the first step here, the move from successful applications and extensions (what I call local judgments of truth) to the truth of the whole theoretical covering story, is already a controversial one, and one for which there seems to be no general or overriding warrant. But even if we part company with instrumentalism on this score and make this move to truth (perhaps out of special warrant or, maybe, just out of charity), how then do we proceed with the game? Even if we accept the truth of the quantum theory, what now constrains what the world *must* be like? Must it be like minimal realism (with "spreads," or "inexact values," or "disjunctive facts"?), or instead like some viable reductive realism (which one?)? Should the fundamental formulas be read interactively, so that the observables and states are construed as relations (in which particular way?)? Should superpositions be taken as describing nonintersecting branches of many actual worlds, of which we are just one among the many? Or should we take that, perhaps, as just a picturesque way of speaking about an interpretation where the state function never collapses? Now I've said it, *interpretation;* so now, perhaps, we can see what it is. After we have agreed to hold the theory true, or approximately so, the realist still needs to ask, given that, what the world is like. The answer is an "interpretation of the quantum theory"; that is, a model structure plus rules of correspondence (or "satisfaction") according to which the theory comes out to be true, or approximately so. Since these constraints on interpretation are nowhere near specific enough to entail categoricity, there will be nonisomorphic models, as many of them as one likes. Among them the realist, having satisfied the truth constraints, can now only pick and choose according to his needs, desires, or tastes. In the end game, then, we find that the quantum realist, ironically, joins hands with his idealist and constructivist enemies. For just like them, in fashioning his "interpretation of the quantum theory," he is simply constructing his own "real" world according to personal (or social) constraints. As we saw, even Einstein's cautiously hedged and empirically grounded realism was motivational in the end, ultimately universalizing his own felt needs as a scientific investigator. In charging the instrumentalist Copenhagen theorists with playing a shaky game with reality, Einstein was certainly correct. But it would be an error of judgment on our part to suppose that when the realist moves beyond the truth of the quantum theory to constuct its interpretation, he is doing anything other than playing a game himself, and one rather *too* shaky because, granted truth, the rules of this realist game have now been cut loose from any ongoing scientific practice.

To be sure we do have reason to believe that there are molecules and atoms, as well as reason to believe that there are in fact no joint probabilities for incompatible observables (which fact it is reasonable to take as supporting the general validity of the Heisenberg uncertainty formulas). There is growing reason to believe in variously accomplished and decked out quarks, and in the soundness of programs that ground particle properties in the irreducible representations of symmetry transformations of field theories. There is even some reason to believe that certain correlation experiments produce tangled statistics, ones that cannot be modeled by an ensemble representation of the experiment. The reasons here are embedded in the various overlapping and ever-open practices that constitute the judgment of those claims by the community of concerned scientists. They are good reasons, in some cases the best we are likely to find in support of *any* belief. Of course to see such grounds as sufficient for belief in the truth of the claims is a far cry from realism. It has none of realism's splendor, none of that special joy and comfort that realism finds in constructing from the actual scientific endeavor a reaching out to the hidden details of an exquisite and elaborate world structure. Still, although more modest and homely, the attitude that seeks to ground scientific belief in reasonable practice—and to understand that belief in those terms—seems itself a reasonable stance to adopt. I do so, and urge you to do likewise. That is, exactly, NOA—the natural ontological attitude.

Bibliography

Aspect, A., et al. 1982a. Experimental realization of Einstein-Podolsky-Rosen-Bohm *Gedankenexperiment*: A new violation of Bell's inequalities. *Physical Review Letters* 49:91–94.

———. 1982b. Experimental test of Bell's inequalities using time-varying analyzers. *Physical Review Letters* 49:1804–7.

Asquith, P., and R. Giere, eds. 1981. *PSA: 1980*. Vol. 2. East Lansing, Mich.: Philosophy of Science Association.

Bach, A. 1982. Quantum-mechanical aspects of the theorem of Gleason, Kahane, Zelazko. *Lettere al Nuovo Cimento* 35:377–80.

Ballentine, L. 1972. Einstein's interpretation of quantum mechanics. *American Journal of Physics* 40:1763–71.

———. 1974. Comment on Stapp's "Copenhagen Interpretation" and the significance of Bell's theorem. *American Journal of Physics* 42:81–82.

Barker, P. 1981. Einstein's later philosophy of science. In *After Einstein*, edited by P. Barker and C. G. Shugart, 133–45. Memphis: Memphis State University Press.

Bell, J. S. 1981. Bertlmann's socks and the nature of reality. *Journal de Physique* 42, *Colloque* C2, 41–61.

———. 1982. On the impossible pilot wave. *Foundations of Physics* 12:989–1000.

Bohm, D. 1951. *Quantum theory*. Englewood Cliffs, N.J.: Prentice-Hall.

———. 1952. A suggested interpretation of the quantum theory in terms of hidden variables. *Physical Review* 85:166–93.

Bohr, N. 1935. Can quantum mechanical description of physical reality be considered complete? *Physical Review* 48:696–702.

———. 1949. Discussion with Einstein on epistemological problems in atomic physics. In *Albert Einstein: Philosopher scientist*, 199–241. See Schilpp 1949.

———. 1961. *Atomic theory and the description of nature*. Cambridge: Cambridge University Press.

Borges, J. L. 1976. *Chronicles of Bustos Domecq*. Translated by N. T. Di Giovanni. New York: Dutton.

Born, M. 1926. Zur Quantenmechanik der Stossvorgänge. *Zeitschrift für Physik* 37:863–67.

———. 1971. *The Born-Einstein letters*. New York: Walter and Co.

Boyd, R. 1981. Scientific realism and naturalistic epistemology. In *PSA: 1980*, 613–62. See Asquith and Giere 1981.

———. 1984. The current status of scientific realism. In *Scientific realism*, 41–82. See Leplin 1984.

Brush, S. 1980. The chimerical cat: Philosophy of quantum mechanics in historical perspective. *Social Studies of Science* 10:393–447.

Cartwright, N. 1983. *How the laws of physics lie.* New York: Clarendon Press.

Clauser, J. F., and M. A. Horne. 1974. Experimental consequences of objective local theories. *Physical Review D* 10:526–35.

Dirac, P. 1925. The fundamental equations of quantum mechanics. *Proceedings of the Royal Society of London A* 109:642–53.

Dukas, H., and B. Hoffman, eds. 1979. *Albert Einstein: The human side.* Princeton: Princeton University Press.

Earman, J. Forthcoming. Locality, non-locality, and action-at-a-distance: A skeptical review of some philosophical dogmas. In *Theoretical Physics in the 100 years since Kelvin's "Baltimore Lectures,"* edited by P. Achinstein, et al. Cambridge: MIT-Bradford Press.

Earman, J., and C. Glymour. 1978. Lost in the tensors. *Studies in History and Philosophy of Science* 9:251–78.

Earman, J., et al. 1983. On writing the history of special relativity. In *PSA: 1982,* vol. 2, edited by P. Asquith and T. Nichols, 403–16. East Lansing, Mich.: Philosophy of Science Association.

Einstein, A. 1918. Principles of research. In *Ideas and opinions,* 224–27. See Einstein 1954.

———. 1921. Geometry and experience. In *Ideas and opinions,* 232–46. See Einstein 1954.

———. 1927. The mechanics of Newton and their influence on the development of theoretical physics. In *Ideas and opinions,* 253–61. See Einstein 1954.

———. 1928. Fundamental concepts of physics and their most recent changes. *St. Louis Post-Dispatch,* Supplement, December 9, p. 7, Cols. 1–4.

———. 1929. On scientific truth. In *Ideas and opinions,* 261–62. See Einstein 1954.

———. 1931. Maxwell's influence on the evolution of the idea of physical reality. In *Ideas and opinions,* 266–70. See Einstein 1954.

———. 1933. On the method of theoretical physics. In *Ideas and opinions,* 270–76. See Einstein 1954.

———. 1934. *Essays in science.* New York: Philosophical Library.

———. 1936. Physik und Realität. *Journal of the Franklin Institute* 221:313–47. Translated as "Physics and Reality," 221:349–82. Reprinted in *Ideas and opinions,* 290–323. See Einstein 1954.

———. 1940. Considerations concerning the fundaments of theoretical physics. *Science* 91:487–92. Reprinted in *Ideas and opinions,* 323–35. See Einstein 1954.

———. 1948. Quanten-Mechanik und Wirklichkeit. *Dialectica* 2:320–24. Translated as "Quantum Mechanics and Reality" in *The Born-Einstein letters,* 168–73. See Born 1971.

———. 1950a. *Out of my later years.* New York: Philosophical Library.

———. 1950b. Physics, philosophy and scientific progress. *Journal of the International College of Surgeons* 14:755–58.

———. 1953a. Einleitende Bemerkugen über Grundbegriffe. In *Louis de Broglie: Physicien et penseur,* edited by A. George, 5–15. Paris: Editions Albin Michel.

———. 1953b. Elementare Überlegungen zur Interpretation der Grundlagen der Quanten-Mechanik. In *Scientific papers presented to Max Born,* 33–40. Edinburgh: Oliver & Boyd.

———. 1954. *Ideas and opinions.* New York: Crown Publishing Co.

Einstein, A., and L. Infeld. 1938. *The evolution of physics.* New York: Simon and Schuster.

Einstein, A., B. Podolsky, and N. Rosen. 1935. Can quantum mechanical description of physical reality be considered complete? *Physical Review* 47:777–80 (EPR).

Einstein, A., R. C. Tolman, and B. Podolsky. 1931. Knowledge of past and future in quantum mechanics. *Physical Review* 37:780–81.

Einstein, A., et al. 1952. *The principle of relativity.* Translated by W. Perrett and G. B. Jeffrey. New York: Dover.

Fayet, P., and S. Ferrara. 1977. Supersymmetry. *Physics Reports* 32(5):249–334.

Fine, A. 1968. Logic, probability and quantum theory. *Philosophy of Science* 35:101–11.

———. 1971. Probability in quantum mechanics and in other statistical theories. In *Problems in the Foundations of Physics,* edited by M. Bunge, 79–92. New York: Springer-Verlag.

———. 1973a. Probability and the interpretation of quantum mechanics. *British Journal for the Philosophy of Science* 24:1–37.

———. 1973b. The two problems of quantum measurement. In *Logic, methodology and philosophy of science,* vol. 4, edited by P. Suppes, 567–81. Amsterdam: North-Holland.

———. 1974. On the completeness of quantum theory. *Synthese* 29:257–89.

———. 1975. How to compare theories: Reference and change. *Nous* 9:17–32.

———. 1976. On the completeness of quantum theory. In *Logic and probability in quantum mechanics,* edited by P. Suppes, 249–81. Dordrecht: Reidel.

———. 1981a. Conceptual change in mathematics and science: Lakatos' stretching refined. In *PSA: 1978, vol. 2,* edited by P. Asquith and I. Hacking, 328–41. East Lansing, Mich.: Philosophy of Science Association.

———. 1981b. Correlations and physical locality. In *PSA: 1980,* 535–62. See Asquith and Giere 1981.

———. 1982a. Some local models for correlation experiments. *Synthese* 50:279–94.

———. 1982b. Joint distributions, quantum correlations, and commuting observables. *Journal of Mathematical Physics* 23:1306–10.

————. 1982c. Hidden variables, joint probability and the Bell inequalities. *Physical Review Letters* 48:291–95.

————. 1982d. Antinomies of entanglement: The puzzling case of the tangled statistics. *Journal of philosophy* 79:733–47.

————. 1986. Unnatural attitudes: Realist and instrumentalist attachments to science. *Mind,* forthcoming.

Fishman, G. S. 1973. *Concepts and methods in discrete event simulation.* New York: Wiley.

Galison, P. 1983. The discovery of the muon and the failed revolution against quantum electrodynamics. *Centaurus* 26:262–316.

————. 1985. Bubble chambers and the experimental workplace. In *Experiment and observation in modern science,* edited by P. Achinstein and O. Hannaway. Cambridge: MIT-Bradford Press.

Garg, A. 1983. Detector error and Einstein-Podolsky-Rosen correlations. *Physical Review D* 28:785–90.

Hacking, I. 1979. Imre Lakatos's philosophy of science. *British Journal for the Philosophy of Science* 27:329–62.

————. 1983. *Representing and intervening.* Cambridge: Cambridge University Press.

————. 1984. Experimentation and scientific realism. In *Scientific realism,* 154–72. See Leplin 1984.

Heisenberg, W. 1925. Über quantentheoretische Umdeutung kinematischer und mechanischer Beziehungen. *Zeitschrift für Physik* 33:879–93.

————. 1927. Über den anschaulichen Inhalt der quantentheoretischen Kinematik und Mechanik. *Zeitschrift für Physik* 43:172–98.

Hellman, G. 1982. Stochastic Einstein-locality and the Bell theorems. *Synthese* 53:461–504.

————. 1983. Realist principles. *Philosophy of Science* 50:227–49.

Hermann, A., ed. 1968. *Albert Einstein/Arnold Sommerfeld Briefwechsel.* Stuttgart: Schwabe & Co-Verlag.

————. 1971. *The genesis of quantum theory.* Cambridge: MIT Press.

Hoffmann, B. 1972. *Albert Einstein, creator and rebel.* New York: Viking Press.

Holton, G. 1973. *Thematic origins of scientific thought.* Cambridge: Harvard University Press.

Hooker, C. 1972. The nature of quantum mechanical reality. In *Paradigms and paradoxes,* edited by R. G. Colodny, 267–302. Pittsburgh: University of Pittsburgh Press.

Horwich, P. 1982. Three forms of realism. *Synthese* 51:181–201.

Howard, D. 1983. Critique: What kind of realist was Einstein? Preprint.

Jammer, M. 1974. *The philosophy of quantum mechanics.* New York: Wiley.

————. 1982. Einstein and quantum physics. In *Albert Einstein: Historical and cultural perspectives,* edited by G. Holton and Y. Elkana, 59–79. Princeton: Princeton University Press.

Jarrett, J. 1984. On the physical significance of the locality conditions in the Bell arguments. *Nous* 12:569–89.

Joseph, G. 1980. The many sciences and the one world. *Journal of Philosophy* 77:773–91.

Kirsten, C., and H. Treder, eds. 1979. *Albert Einstein in Berlin, 1913–1933*. Vol. 1. Berlin: Akademie-Verlag.

Klein, M. 1971. Einstein, Albert. In *Dictionary of scientific biography*, edited by C. C. Gillespie, 4:312–19. New York: Scribner.

Kuhn, T. S. 1970. *The structure of scientific revolutions*. 2d ed. Chicago: University of Chicago Press.

Landé, A. 1974. Albert Einstein and the quantum riddle. *American Journal of Physics* 42:459–64.

Laudan, L. 1984. A confutation of convergent realism. In *Scientific realism*, 218–49. See Leplin 1984.

Leeds, S. 1984. Chance, realism, quantum mechanics. *Journal of Philosophy* 81:567–78.

Leplin, J., ed. 1984. *Scientific realism*. Berkeley: University of California Press.

Levy, M., and S. Deser. 1979. *Recent developments in gravitation*. New York: Plenum Press.

Lo, T. K., and A. Shimony. 1981. Proposed molecular test of local hidden-variables theories. *Physical Review A* 23:3003–12.

Lycan, W. 1982. Epistemic value. Preprint.

McMullin, E. 1976. The fertility of theory and the unit for appraisal in science. In *Boston studies in the philosophy of science*, vol. 39, edited by R. S. Cohen, et al., 395–432. Dordrecht: Reidel.

Mehlberg, H. 1960. The observational problem in quantum theory. *Proceedings XII International Philosophical Congress* 5:385–91. Florence: Sansoni.

———. 1980. Philosophical interpretations of quantum physics. In *Time, causality and the quantum theory*, vol. 2, 3–74. Dordrecht: Reidel.

Menger, K. 1974. *Morality, decision and social organization*. Dordrecht: Reidel.

Miller, A. 1981. *Albert Einstein's special theory of relativity*. Reading, Mass: Addison-Wesley.

Newton-Smith, W. H. 1981. *The rationality of science*. London: Routledge and Kegan Paul.

Niiniluoto, I. 1982. What shall we do with verisimilitude? *Philosophy of Science* 49:181–97.

Pais, A. 1982. *Subtle is the Lord*. New York: Oxford University Press.

Pauli, W. 1933. Der allgemeinen Prinzipien der Wellenmechanik. In *Handbuch der Physik*, vol. 24, part 1, 83–272. Berlin: Springer-Verlag.

Pickering, A. 1984. *Constructing quarks*. Chicago: University of Chicago Press.

Pitt, J. 1981. *Pictures, images and conceptual change*. Dordrecht: Reidel.

Popper, K. 1972. *Conjectures and refutations*. London: Routledge and Kegan Paul.

Przibam, K., ed. 1967. *Letters on wave mechanics*. New York: The Philosophical Library.

Putnam, H. 1975. The meaning of "Meaning." In *Language, mind and knowledge,* edited by K. Gunderson, 131–93. Minneapolis: University of Minnesota Press.

————. 1981a. *Reason, truth and history.* Cambridge: Cambridge University Press.

————. 1981b. Quantum mechanics and the observer. *Erkenntnis* 16:193–220.

————. 1982a. Why there isn't a ready-made world. *Synthese* 51:141–67.

————. 1982b. Why reason can't be naturalized. *Synthese* 52:3–23.

Rorty, R. 1979. *Philosophy and the mirror of nature.* Princeton: Princeton University Press.

————. 1982. *Consequences of pragmatism.* Minneapolis: University of Minnesota Press.

————. 1986a. Pragmatism, Davidson and truth. In *The philosophy of Donald Davidson: A perspective on inquiry into truth and interpretation,* edited by E. LePore. Oxford: Basil Blackwell.

————. 1986b. Beyond realism and anti-realism. In *Wiener Riehe: Themen der Philosophie,* vol. 1., edited by H. Nagl-Docekal et al.

Rozental, S. 1967. *Niels Bohr.* Amsterdam: North-Holland.

Schaffner, K. 1974. Einstein versus Lorentz: Research programmes and the logic of comparative theory evaluation. *British Journal for the Philosophy of Science* 25:45–78.

Schilpp, P. A., ed. 1949. *Albert Einstein: Philosopher scientist.* La Salle, Ill.: Open Court.

Schrödinger, E. 1926. Quantisierung als Eigenwertproblem. *Annalen der Physik* 79:361–76.

————. 1935a. Discussion of probability relations between separated systems. *Proceedings of the Cambridge Philosophical Society* 31:555–63 (*PCPS*).

————. 1935b. Die gegenwärtige Situation in der Quantenmechanik. *Die Naturwissenschaften* 23:807–12, 824–28, 844–49 (*NW*).

————. 1936. Probability relations between separated systems. *Proceedings of the Cambridge Philosophical Society* 32:446–52.

————. 1956. *"What is life?" and other scientific essays.* Garden City, N.Y.: Doubleday Anchor Books.

Seelig, C. 1956. *Albert Einstein, A documentary biography.* London: Staples Press.

Sellars, W. 1961. The Language of Theories. In *Current issues in the philosophy of science,* edited by H. Feigl and G. Maxwell, 57–77. New York: Holt, Rinehart and Winston.

Shapere, D. 1982. The concept of observation in science and philosophy. *Philosophy of Science* 49:485–525.

Shimony, A. 1981. "Critique of the papers of Fine and Suppes." In *PSA: 1980,* vol. 2, 572–80. See Asquith and Giere 1981.

————. 1984. Contextual hidden variables and Bell's inequalities. *British Journal for the Philosophy of Science* 35:25–45.

Solovine, M., ed. 1956. *Albert Einstein: Lettres à Maurice Solovine.* Paris: Gauthier-Villars.

Speziali, P., ed. and trans. 1972. *Albert Einstein-Michele Besso correspondence, 1903–1955.* Paris: Hermann.

Stachel, J. 1979. The genesis of general relativity. In *Einstein symposium Berlin,* edited by H. Nelkowski, 428–42. Berlin: Springer-Verlag.

———. 1983. Einstein and the quantum. In *From quarks to quasars,* edited by R. Colodny. Pittsburgh: University of Pittsburgh Press.

Stairs, A. 1983. Quantum logic, realism, and value definiteness. *Philosophy of Science* 50:578–602.

Suppes, P. 1961. Probability concepts in quantum mechanics. *Philosophy of Science* 28:278–89.

Suppes, P., and M. Zannotti. 1981. When are probabilistic explanations possible? *Synthese* 48:191–98.

Teller, P. 1979. Quantum mechanics and the nature of continuous physical quantities. *Journal of Philosophy* 76:345–61.

———. 1981. The projection postulate and Bohr's interpretation of quantum mechanics. In *PSA: 1980,* pp. 201–23. See Asquith and Giere 1981.

———. 1984. The projection postulate: A new perspective. *Philosophy of Science* 51:369–95.

Toulmin, S. 1961. *Foresight and understanding.* New York: Harper and Row.

Trimmer, J. 1980. The present situation in quantum mechanics: A translation of Schrödinger's "Cat Paradox" paper. *Proceedings of the American Philosophical Society* 124:323–38.

Trower, W. P., and B. Cabrera. 1983. Magnetic monopoles: Evidence since the Dirac conjecture. *Foundations of Physics* 13:195–216.

van Fraassen, B. 1980. *The scientific image.* Oxford: Clarendon Press.

———. 1982. The Charybdis of realism: Epistemological implications of Bell's inequality. *Synthese* 52:25–38.

von Neumann, J. 1932. *Mathematische Grundlagen der Quantenmechanik.* Berlin: Springer-Verlag. Translated by E. Beyer, *Mathematical foundations of quantum mechanics.* Princeton: Princeton University Press, 1955.

von Weizsäcker, C. F. 1952. *The worldview of physics.* Translated by M. Grene. Chicago: University of Chicago Press. Originally, *Zum Weltbild der Physik.* Leipzig: S. Hirzel, 1945.

Weinberg, S. 1972. *Gravitation and cosmology: Principles and applications of the general theory of relativity.* New York: Wiley.

Wessels, L. 1979. Schrödinger's route to wave mechanics. *Studies in History and Philosophy of Science* 10:311–40.

———. 1986. Locality, factorability and the Bell inequalities. *Nous,* forthcoming.

Wigner, E. P. 1932. On the quantum correction for thermodynamic equilibrium. *Physical Review* 40:749–59.

Wilson, R. 1979, 1980, 1981. *Schrödinger's cat. Vols. 1–3.* New York: Simon and Schuster.

Woolf, H., ed. 1980. *Some strangeness in the proportion.* Reading: Addison-Wesley.

Worrall, J., and G. Currie, eds. 1978. *The methodology of scientific research programmes.* Cambridge, Cambridge University Press.

Index